QUEENS OF THE WILD

Ronald Hutton is Professor of History at the University of Bristol and a leading authority on the British Isles in the sixteenth and seventeenth centuries, on ancient and medieval paganism and magic, and on the global context of witchcraft beliefs. He is the author of seventeen books.

Further praise for *Queens of the Wild*:

'Rather than being a pedant seeking to disenchant the world, Hutton treats mistakes and inventions as parts of the biographies of his super-human subjects . . . Authoritative yet open-minded, scholarly without being needlessly combative.'

George Morris, *Literary Review*

'A rich historical account of four Goddess-like figures who defy easy categorisation.'

James Sewry, *Aspects of History*

'Hutton's blend of skepticism with humility renders him a uniquely refreshing guide to his field.'

Barbara Newman, *Medieval Review*

'Rich and fascinating, full of myriad products of human creativity, which grow and change so quickly and thoroughly that, in the end, they cannot with certainty be traced.'

Tallis Harrill, *Greenmantle*

'Clear, objective, rigorous . . . Ronald Hutton's is a wise voice indeed but also a hugely entertaining one.'

Eva Humphrey-Lahti, *Druid Network*

'A wonderful book, deeply thoughtful and engaging, packed with great research and thought-provoking ideas.'

Marion Gibson, author of *Witchcraft: The Basics*

'This splendid book greatly expands our knowledge of how apparently pagan divine figures of European tradition evolved.'

Mark Williams, author of *The Celtic Myths That Shape the Way We Think*

'England's favourite historian has done it again . . . Shows us the vitality of human creativity and its shaping of tradition.'

Sabina Magliocco, author of *Witching Culture*

QUEENS OF
THE WILD

PAGAN GODDESSES
IN CHRISTIAN EUROPE:
AN INVESTIGATION

RONALD HUTTON

YALE UNIVERSITY PRESS
NEW HAVEN AND LONDON

For information about this and other Yale University Press publications, please contact:
U.S. Office: sales.press@yale.edu   yalebooks.com
Europe Office: sales@yaleup.co.uk   yalebooks.co.uk

Set in Adobe Garamond Pro by IDSUK (DataConnection) Ltd
Printed in Great Britain by Clays Ltd, Elcograf S.p.A

Library of Congress Control Number: 2023938319

ISBN 978-0-300-26101-1 (hbk)
ISBN 978-0-300-27334-2 (pbk)

A catalogue record for this book is available from the British Library.

10 9 8 7 6 5 4 3 2

CONTENTS

List of Plates vi
Preface and Acknowledgements viii

1. What is a Pagan Survival? 1
2. Mother Earth 41
3. The Fairy Queen 75
4. The Lady of the Night 110
5. The Cailleach 143
Epilogue: The Green Man 159
Conclusion 193

Notes 198
Index 227

LIST OF PLATES

1. Cerne Abbas Giant, Cerne Abbas in Dorset, UK. Jack Sullivan / Alamy Stock Photo.
2. Frontispiece to *Utriusque cosmi maioris scilicet et minoris metaphysica, physica atque technica historia . . . [Tractatus secundus de naturae simia seu technica macrocosmi historia]* by Robert Fludd, seventeenth century. Wellcome Collection.
3. *Wildeman op een eenhoorn*, by Meester van het Amsterdamse Kabinet, 1473–77. Rijksmuseum, RP-P-OB-915.
4. Green Man carving in Winchester Cathedral. Michael Foley / Alamy Stock Photo.
5. *Wildemans-vrouw met kinderen op een hert*, by Meester van het Amsterdamse Kabinet, 1473–77. Rijksmuseum, RP-P-OB-914.
6. Sir Gawain beheading the Green Knight. Manuscript illumination from *Gawain and the Green Knight*, English, c.1400. Held in British Library, Cotton Nero MS A x. Granger Historical Picture Archive / Alamy Stock Photo.
7. Illustration from *'Le Livre de messire Lancelot du Lac', la Quête du Saint Graal, la Mort d'Arthus* by 'Gautier Map'. BNF f.109r. Bibliothèque nationale de France. Département des Manuscrits. Français 111.

LIST OF PLATES

8. *Merlin and the Fairy Queen*, by John Duncan, nineteenth century. Paisley / Artepics / Alamy Stock Photo.

9. *Edmund Spenser*, by James Thomson (Thompson), early nineteenth century. © National Portrait Gallery, London.

10. *Prince Arthur and the Fairy Queen*, by Johann Heinrich Fuseli, c.1788. Alamy, Kunstmuseum Basel.

11. *Oberon, Titania, and Puck with Fairies Dancing*, by William Blake. classicpaintings / Alamy Stock Photo.

12. *Queen Mab*, after Alfred Edward Chalon, print made by William Say, published by John Dickinson, 1827. © Trustees of the British Museum.

13. Illustration from *Freiherr: Das festliche Jahr* by Otto von Reinsberg-Düringsfeld, Leipzig: Spamer, 1863. Bayerische StaatsBibliothek / CC NC 1.0.

14. Illustration from *Household Stories* from the collection of the Brothers Grimm, Lucy Crane [translator]; Walter Crane [illustrator], original printing 1882.

15. *Beira*, by John Duncan, from *Wonder tales from Scottish Myth & Legend* by Alexander MacKenzie, 1917. New York Public Library, archive.org.

16. *Riders of the Sidhe*, by John Duncan, 1911. Artepics / Alamy Stock Photo.

17. *Jane Ellen Harrison*, by Theo van Rysselberghe, 1925. © National Portrait Gallery, London.

18. *Sir James George Frazer*, by Walter Stoneman, 1924. © National Portrait Gallery, London.

19. *Julia Somerset (née Hamilton), Lady Raglan*, by Bassano Ltd, 5 April 1923. © National Portrait Gallery, London.

20. *May Day or Jack in the Green*, after Isaac Cruikshank, 1795. SiGarb / CC BY-SA 3.0.

21. *The Wicker Man* film poster, 1973. British Lion Film Corporation / Ronald Grant Archive / Mary Evans.

PREFACE AND
ACKNOWLEDGEMENTS

L ike a great many publications sent to press at the end of 2020, this was one, to use the old expression, 'written in time of pestilence'. I was therefore fortunate to be working on this book during the period of Covid-related restrictions; it required relatively little additional research as I had amassed most of the material for it over the previous thirty years – although I now wished to ask new questions of it and put it to fresh uses. There was still some work to be done, however, and for this I had to await the reopening of libraries and negotiate the precautions taken by each to limit the spread of infection. In this context I would especially like to express my gratitude to Alan Brown of the Bodleian Library, for reserving a seat there for me when the online booking system broke down for the day. In the end, all the additional reading that I needed for the book was completed, save for one or two German works which could not be obtained in the circumstances of the epidemic other than by a very long wait and which were marginal to the work as a whole.

In more general terms, I remain grateful to all the staff of libraries and archives who assisted me beyond the normal call of duty in the long period of preceding decades in which I was accumulating the material. In the short term, I thank the two sets of readers employed by Yale University

PREFACE AND ACKNOWLEDGEMENTS

Press to scrutinize first the proposal and then the manuscript, and – as always now at this point – Heather McCallum, its managing director, who is responsible for my lengthy loyalty to her press. Mark Williams read my fifth chapter in draft and made invaluable suggestions. Synopses of the arguments in the book were presented and tested as an address to a conference at Leuven in 2018 and in my Stenton Lecture at Reading in 2019, and the former paper published in the proceedings of the event, edited by Joseph Verheyden and Daniela Müller and entitled *Imaging Paganism in the Middle Ages*, from Peeters in 2020.

The greatest point of difficulty in getting the book into publication was the question of the title, over which weeks were spent in a tug of war between the press's natural desire for one as colourful and alluring as possible and my pedantic anxiety to settle on one that most accurately reflected the contents of the book. The result was the press's suggestion that I liked best: it does not quite deal with the problem of whether the subjects of the book were either pagan or goddesses, strictly speaking, but it is certainly charismatic, and the clause 'an investigation' may suggest that the problem spoken of may exist.

CHAPTER 1

WHAT IS A PAGAN SURVIVAL?

The Twentieth-Century Model

For most of the late nineteenth and twentieth centuries, the expression 'pagan survival' would have had an obvious and uncontentious meaning for both most professional scholars and the general public interested in history. It was linked to a widely held belief that the ancient pre-Christian religions of Europe, generally known by the umbrella term of 'paganism', had in some form and by some definition survived beyond the introduction of Christianity as the official faith. Moreover, it was as commonly believed that they did so for some considerable time, extending through the Middle Ages and far into the early modern period. This was thought to be true to some extent of the entire continent, but considerations of space and expertise mean that it will be examined in depth now with respect to Britain and publications in the English language.

The belief concerned was often asserted in general terms. In 1892 a leader of the newly formed British Folk-Lore Society informed his colleagues that English commoners had barely been Christianized even as late as the seventeenth century, and as such had preserved a pagan culture barely recognizable to the social elite.[1] Thirty years later, a leading expert on the institutions of the medieval English Church, in the few lines that he devoted to the beliefs of ordinary villagers, declared confidently that they had been 'cheerful semi-pagans'. He continued, more lyrically, to assert that 'the old idols remained under the old Christian veneer' and that 'in church, the women crowded around Mary, yet they paid homage to the old deities by their nightly fireside, or at the time-honoured haunts, grove or stone or spring'.[2] In 1952 an American historian of art, discussing medieval folk belief, suggested that paganism had not merely persisted into the Middle Ages but gained renewed strength at times. He spoke of 'a new thrust of pagan forces instilling virulence into customs which otherwise would have been slowly neutralized', though he added that the 'history of this second pagan movement, which must have been naturalized in Western Europe by the . . . twelfth century, is known only fragmentarily and opinions of it amongst scholars vary widely'.[3]

All of these were highly respected authorities, although none of them knew much about medieval popular religion. They could make these statements with such confidence because they were based on a mass of apparent evidence of different kinds which had been interpreted in ways which tended towards the general conclusions just cited. One striking example of this in the British context was the Cerne Abbas Giant, the outline of a man 180 feet tall carved from the chalk rock on a hillside in Dorset, brandishing a 120-foot club. Two aspects of the figure are especially meaningful in this context. One is his virility, for he has pronounced genitals, including a 30-foot erect phallus. The other is that the valley below him had been occupied by one of England's most important and long-lived medieval abbeys, which seemed to present the inescapable conclusion that if the giant were ancient – as his primeval appearance would seem to suggest – then the Christian monks had at least connived in his preservation for six centuries. A very popular and erudite guide to the ancient monuments of England and Wales published in the 1950s summed up the prevalent opinion concerning the figure. It stated that the giant was probably Romano-British, and that it must have been kept in being by the common people, overruling not only their parish priests but also the monks their neighbours in a 'frank assertion' of a symbol of 'unabashed paganism'.[4]

Famous legends as well as famous monuments could inspire similar suggestions. Another of the early luminaries of the Folk-Lore Society opined that the story of Lady Godiva's nude ride through the city of Coventry to save her people from heavy taxation actually testified to the late survival of pagan belief and worship in the city. He believed that the latter had been centred on the cult of a horse-riding goddess.[5] British folklorists, however, found much more luxuriant evidence for a persisting paganism in the contemporary beliefs and customs which they collected in such abundance from rural people in particular in the decades around 1900. They followed the ideas of preceding German scholars in concluding that these ideas and activities represented living fossils of ancient religion, rites now kept up from tradition and for amusement which had once been sacred ceremonies intended to ensure the welfare of local communities and the fertility of their farms.[6] Three popular nineteenth-century midwinter customs, the southern English mummers' play, the North Country sword dance and the East Midland plough play, all featured a mock combat leading to the death and then the resurrection of one combatant. Between 1890 and 1935, folklorists achieved a consensus that they therefore all derived from the same prehistoric rite, concerned with the renewal of life at the winter solstice. In the words of one of the most influential, the climax of this came when 'skin-clad worshippers, accompanied by a traditional Woman, capered about the slain figure of a man who had been King of the feast'.[7] Over the same period they came to believe that the leaping folk dance called the morris, performed by teams of men at midwinter or in early summer, had been another ancient ritual, to ensure the fertility of the land.[8] Customs carried on in the nineteenth century involving the disguising of a person as a horse, ram or bull, and the parading or dancing of that person house to house or through the streets – mostly at midwinter but also sometimes on May Day – were interpreted confidently as remnants of prehistoric animal cults.[9]

Unique and extraordinary customs, carried on in particular places, were subjected to the same treatment. The Haxey Hood Game is an annual contest held each Twelfth Day between two Lincolnshire villages in which each team tries to get a coil of rope inside a leather tube to a pub in their own settlement. The struggle is presided over by eleven red-garbed people called 'boggins', a Lord and a Fool, who is wreathed in smoke from a fire as he explains the rules beforehand. In 1896 another of the leading members of the Folk-Lore Society decided that it was a rite of ancient solar worship and human sacrifice, and this became the accepted reading.[10] The Abbots Bromley Horn Dance, now performed in September but formerly in midwinter, consists of six men carrying reindeer antlers, plus a hobby horse and a man dressed as a woman. Unsurprisingly, in 1933 another prominent folklorist declared that it was an archetypal relic of an ancient pagan custom involving ritual animal disguise, and that became the orthodoxy.[11] By that decade, such interpretations were being made at a feverish pace, so that, in a single presidential address to the Folk-Lore Society in 1937, it could be suggested that pancake tossing on Shrove Tuesday had been a magical rite to make crops grow, team sports on that day had begun as ritual struggles representing the forces of winter dark and spring light, and Mother's Day was a remnant of the worship of the prehistoric Corn Mother.[12] By now, some theorists were intervening in seasonal local customs and attempting to 'correct' them if aspects of the current performance did not fit the particular interpretation which the experts concerned were making of them as survivals of prehistoric religion.[13]

During the 1940s, 1950s and 1960s these interpretations were continued, elaborated and reinforced, and – whereas until now they had been published mainly in specialist journals and monographs – embodied in popular survey books which carried them to a large general public.[14] These often extended the earlier ideas in yet more vivid flights of imagination. One in 1962 declared that the sword dance had united a Neolithic ritual to awaken the earth from winter sleep with a Bronze Age one that conferred manhood.[15] The same author, in a different work, showed a momentary uneasy consciousness that the historical record actually seemed remarkably bare after about the year 1000 of persistent pagan rites of this sort, until the seasonal customs which were supposed to embody them were recorded from the nineteenth century. She smothered it by declaring that 'as the Church grew stronger it tried more and more to ignore what it did not care to remember'.[16] Confident restatements of the belief that folk customs recorded as traditional between 1800 and 1914 were remnants of pagan religion continued into the 1970s in popular British works of folklore.[17]

If accessibly written books on folk customs reached a large audience, exciting works of pure fiction reached an even larger one, and it is not surprising, in view of these scholarly developments, that a particular genre of British fantasy novels and essays appeared in parallel during the same period. It featured an outsider – through whose eyes the storyline develops and whose Christian or rationalist viewpoint is presumed to reflect that of the reader – coming to live in a rural British community. This protagonist then slowly discovers that it is inhabited by natives secretly practising a surviving pagan religion; and this is always an unpleasant one, thoroughly transgressive of current social norms, with which the heroine or hero comes into conflict. The message is that paganism is essentially a malign force which makes the people who continue it do bad things. Clearly, this trope was one which spun off from an anxiety about the progressive loss of power by Christianity in the modern world, as more and more people embraced atheism, agnosticism or alternative forms of religion and spirituality. Its first notable appearance seems to have been in 1895, with a short story by the Anglican Christian Arthur Machen, entitled 'The Novel of the Black Seal'.[18] This featured the Little People, the degenerate descendants of pre-Celtic races, who dwell underground in remote countryside and creep forth in search of virgins to sacrifice in their pagan rituals.

Thereafter the storyline was more usually that of somebody who settles in a contemporary, outwardly normal, rural community, only to realize that the ancient paganism is still persisting there in secret. A trickle of such works over the succeeding eight decades produced two literary bestsellers and a cinematic one. The first of the two pieces of literature was *Witch Wood*, published in 1927 by the celebrated novelist and politician John Buchan, who remained a lifelong devout Scottish Presbyterian. It features a heroic young minister of that faith who comes to serve a parish in

Scotland's Southern Uplands in the 1640s, only to realize that most of its inhabitants still secretly adhere to a depraved and disgusting native religion centred on a Romano-British altar. He is unable to convince the authorities of its existence – which is a standard feature of the genre – or win over most of his parishioners, but does manage to destroy the high priest of the cult, aided by what could plausibly, in the context, be interpreted as a benevolent divine power accessed through his identity as a Christian. The second of the best-selling novels was Nora Lofts' *The Devil's Own* from 1960, set in a modern Essex village where the 'old ways' are secretly still carried on by most of the inhabitants. These turn out to centre on a religion celebrating ancient festivals with sexual orgies, naked dancing and gluttonous feasts, led by a high priestess; and it seems moreover to equip its devotees with genuine and malevolent magical powers. It is detected and opposed by a newcomer, an obsessive celibate spinster who, though once more given no support by official authority and no effectual help within the village, manages to wreck it and bring about the death of the priestess.[19]

Seven years after Lofts' success, an author called David Pinner published a minor contribution to the genre, a novel entitled *Ritual*, concerning a London policeman sent to investigate the mysterious death of a teenage girl in a Cornish village, who (of course) uncovers a secret pagan sect surviving there. It is worthy of remembrance only because it accidentally gave birth to the hugely popular film *The Wicker Man*, released by the British company Lion Films in 1973. Its screenwriter, Anthony Shaffer, had intended to adapt *Ritual* for the screen, but decided instead to write a similar story of his own, with a pious Christian policeman sent to investigate the apparent disappearance of a schoolgirl on a secluded Scottish island. It made two major innovations to the genre, which contributed to the film's eventual success. One was that for most of the story the usual sympathies are reversed, as the incomer is an unsympathetic character, graceless, repressed and bigoted, and the pagan fertility religion practised by the islanders is one of joyous celebration of nature, life and sex, of a kind matching the attitudes of the contemporary Flower Power generation. That is, until the final moments of the story, when the intruder is burned alive as a human sacrifice by the islanders, to restore the health of their blighted crops: suddenly the basic message of the genre is powerfully reasserted. The second innovation was that the island's religion is not one that has survived from ancient times but one that has been crafted by the Victorian owner of the land, using ancient models, and successfully introduced to the people.[20] The film drew for its effect, however, on much the same contemporary belief system as that which nurtured the idea of a long survival of paganism, summed up in the case of *The Wicker Man* by one commentator as 'the very argument of the film: that underneath a thin veneer of civility lie the still glowing embers of the "old ways", which need only a small spark to start blazing again'.[21]

Other scholarly work served to reinforce the sense of a long persistence of paganism among the common people. Some concerned medieval carved figures in British churches, especially human heads gushing leaves from mouths and nostrils and figures of nude women with their legs spread facing the observer, which became known in the twentieth century by the Irish name of sheela-na-gigs. These were not much discussed before the early twentieth century. In the 1930s, the current enthusiasm for finding evidence for surviving paganism among medieval commoners caused writers connected to the Folk-Lore Society to suggest that they had been beloved pagan deities, respectively a god and goddess of fertility. These authors further proposed that the images had been included in medieval churches by popular demand, so that people attending services could look up and see their own ancient divinities represented there even while the official icons and services in the buildings were devoted to the new religion. This interpretation of the motifs remained dominant all through the middle decades of the twentieth century.[22]

Similar trends were found in the study of Anglo-Saxon healing charms, words of power that were designed to be recited for the cure of specific ailments. A number of collections of these have survived from the tenth and eleventh centuries, apparently made originally by monks or cathedral clergy, and when they were edited in the nineteenth century it was observed that some of them contained clear references to pagan deities and spirits.[23] Most famous in this respect is the so-called Lay of the Nine Twigs of Woden, Woden being apparently the most important god in the pagan Anglo-Saxon pantheon, the equivalent of Odin in the Norse and Wotan in the German. In a set of verses which ascribe the creation of healing herbs in general to the Christian God, one couplet credits Woden with having destroyed an adder with nine 'glory-twigs'. Two more herbs are said to be creations of 'the wise Lord holy in heaven when He hung', which may be a reference to the myth of Woden's self-sacrifice on a sacred tree.[24] Then there is the 'Aecerbot', or Field Blessing, a charm for the fertility of the land, which seems piously Christian but at one point has the invocation 'Erce, erce, erce, earth's mother', to address an entity to whom or which God is asked to grant abundance.[25] Finally in this celebrated list is 'With Faerstice', the charm 'For a Sudden Stitch', which at one point calls upon 'the Lord' (in Anglo-Saxon sources, conventionally meaning the Christian God) for help. It ascribes the pains which it is designed to cure, however, to a range of non-Christian entities: 'mighty women' who ride across the land and hurl magical spears; the 'Aesir' (pagan deities); elves; and a hag.[26] These verses could be taken to prove the existence of a dual system of religion, the old continuing alongside the new, of the sort which had been suggested as evidenced by the church carvings; and by the mid-twentieth century the 'pagan' aspects of the charms were strongly emphasized by scholars.[27]

If such aspects were found in charms apparently copied and preserved by clerics, it was legitimate to wonder whether the folk healers who served the common people had an even greater component of paganism in their repertoire. That this could have been so was apparently suggested by the denunciations of reforming churchmen, above all Aelfric of Eynsham around the year 1000, who condemned healing magic as 'heathen worship'. He furthermore accused those who practised it (and whom he termed *wiccan*, i.e. witches) of teaching people to make offerings to stones and trees to achieve their needs, in 'heathen' fashion.[28] Some ten centuries later, the kind of folk magicians whom Aelfric denounced were still around, under the name of wise or cunning folk, and in 1976 a historian published a much-admired study of religious attitudes in Victorian rural Lincolnshire. In this he described any spiritual aspect of popular culture which was not clearly Christian as 'pagan', and in particular identified the wise man as the most beneficent figure in 'paganism'. He did stress that he was not using that term to signify 'a counter-religion to Christianity' or 'a cosmos to be contemplated or worshipped', but 'a treasury of separate and specific resources to be used and applied in concrete situations', by which he seemed to mean the repertoire of spells and charms used by popular magicians.[29]

Most dramatically, between the mid-nineteenth and mid-twentieth centuries, many scholars argued that a full-blown pagan cult had persisted all through the Middle Ages, across Western Europe, and been persecuted into extinction during the early modern period under the name of witchcraft. This idea had appeared in Germany, as one response to the challenge presented by the pan-European eighteenth-century movement known as the Enlightenment. One result of this movement was to make the ruling political and social elites all over Europe at least officially lose a belief in the literal efficacy of magic, and so in witchcraft. This now meant that every one of the forty to sixty thousand Europeans who had been executed as witches during the period between the fifteenth and eighteenth centuries, when witchcraft was viewed as a satanic religion, had been an innocent victim of religious delusion. This realization equipped liberals and reformers, from the time of the Enlightenment savants like Voltaire through to the early twentieth century, with a powerful ideological weapon with which to attack the traditional powers of Europe – nobilities, monarchies and above all churchmen – which they wanted to remove or reform. For most of the modern period, the dominant discourse used to describe the history of the early modern witch trials was one of a tragedy produced by ignorance, superstition, credulity and the machinations of unscrupulous clerics and politicians, brought to an end by the modernizing forces of reason and science.[30]

A reply to it was developed in Germany between 1825 and 1840, by intellectuals who were committed to defending the old political and religious order in the period of reaction following the fall of Napoleon. These suggested that early modern witchcraft had been a degenerate remnant of former pagan religion which had been carried on in secret and engaged in all the disgusting practices of sexual transgression and bloodshed of which witches had been accused in the trials. The argument was a clever one, as it recognized the probable non-existence of all forms of magic while still justifying the authorities in wiping out the cult concerned.[31] Its main weakness was that it was entirely speculative, resting on no actual evidence, which is why people who were expert in the witch trials records proceeded to disregard it, now and hereafter. It was also, however, given a different sort of response a generation later by a famous French historian, of precisely opposed – liberal and anticlerical – political attitudes,. This was Jules Michelet, who in 1862 published a passionate and colourful book entitled *La Sorcière* (The Witch). It was based on minimal research, padded out with a lot of imagination, and dealt with the challenge made by the Germans by accepting their premise that early modern witchcraft had been a surviving pagan religion but reversing the sympathies. His witch religion had kept the spirit of liberty alive through the Middle Ages and represented especially the needs of women and the working classes, being served by priestesses who venerated a fertility god. The book became a bestseller and has never been out of print.

By the 1890s its ideas had been taken up by two Americans who were both to find enthusiastic niche audiences, up to the present. One was Matilda Joslyn Gage, a feminist who adopted Michelet's model and embellished it by declaring that his priestesses had preserved the traditions of a prehistoric golden age of matriarchy, and that their persecution had been intended to destroy female independence.[32] The other was a journalist, Charles Godfrey Leland, who spent much of his life in Europe and shared Michelet's political stance, and with it his loathing of the Middle Ages and the early modern ancien régime. Through local informants and assistants, he collected a lot of contemporary Italian folklore, especially from the Tuscan Romagna, which he interpreted in the fashionable manner of the decade as being almost all or entirely of pagan origin. He noted that some of his informants termed popular magic 'the old religion', though in two of his three books on the subject he acknowledged that it was not really a religion.[33]

His third book, however, contained what he believed to be the 'gospel' of a full-blown pagan witch religion, of rebellion and liberation like that imagined by Michelet but dedicated to the goddess Diana, her consort Lucifer and her daughter Aradia (the Biblical Herodias). This had been delivered to him by the most regular and important of his local collectors, and he added that a secret society practising this religion still survived in 'fragmentary' form, and that certain villages in the Romagna remained entirely 'heathen'.[34] Nobody in or since his time has turned up any evidence for the existence of such a religion in nineteenth-century Italy: the one revealed by Leland was, rather, a fantasy developed by northern Italian witch-hunters in the early sixteenth century, with the sympathies reversed to favour its practitioners. There is plenty of genuine Italian folklore in the spells and charms embedded in his 'gospel'; it is the containing portrait of the religion which remains anomalous, outside the realm of the early modern imagination.

Only in Britain, however, was the idea taken up by scholars in the mainstream of the intellectual establishment that the people persecuted as witches had been pagan. This happened, unsurprisingly, in the 1890s, that decade when the concept of the British countryside as a refuge for enduring pagan beliefs and customs became widely influential. Its earliest articulation in British scholarship seems, indeed, to have been by a president of the Folk-Lore Society, and included the assertion that 'the witch is the successor of the Druid priestess'.[35] Later in the decade, a mathematics professor at University College London suggested that the witch religion had venerated a great goddess and her male consort, the god of nature – and that Joan of Arc had been a priestess of it.[36] It was, however, another two decades before the idea began to be given both widespread public acceptance and scholarly respectability, and that was because of the work of another London academic and Folk-Lore Society luminary, the Egyptologist Margaret Murray. Hitherto the idea that alleged witches had been pagans, though now quite widespread in the Western world, had rested largely on

11

speculation, without much basis of evidence. Murray now apparently provided this, from trial records (mostly published and mostly Scottish), pamphlets and demonologies, in a pair of books which appeared in 1921 and 1933.[37]

Her witch religion was the cult of a horned god representing the generative powers of nature, organized in groups of thirteen run by women or men which met to transact business and celebrate festivals with feasting, dancing, animal and human sacrifice and ritualized sex. She came to refer to it simply as 'the Old Religion' (having picked up that phrase from Leland) and to characterize it as one of joy and affirmation of life, contrasted with the gloom of Christianity. As such, she suggested, it retained the allegiance of the bulk of the population until the end of the Middle Ages. Her work was immediately and consistently rejected by historians familiar with the evidence for early modern witchcraft beliefs and trials, who judged at once that she had misused it.[38] These were, however, very few in number, and it won rapid acceptance among respected historians expert in other subjects,[39] novelists (it was clearly an influence on Buchan's *Witch Wood*), occultists and mystical Celticists,[40] and authors of popular books on witchcraft.[41] Some folklorists also rapidly adopted it.[42] Murray was invited to write the entry on witchcraft in the *Encyclopaedia Britannica*, and used it to state her own theory as proven fact, so taking it to a much wider public.

Nonetheless, its popularity and celebrity really took off after the Second World War, and by the 1960s it was probably the dominant explanation for the early modern witch trials among the populace in general and scholars who – however distinguished – were not expert in the subject. In 1945 one of the most respected academic historians, Sir George Clark, brought out a second edition of a much-used textbook on the seventeenth century, and incorporated Murray's explanation for the trials into it as the now most likely one.[43] The leading British historian of that century in the next generation, Christopher Hill, endorsed it repeatedly in the mid-1960s, above all in his own textbook on early modern England, which was especially popular among socialist teachers.[44] In 1962 – the year before Murray's death – Oxford University Press reissued her most scholarly book on witchcraft as a paperback, with an approving preface by Sir Stephen Runciman, probably then the dominant British historian of the Middle Ages. In that year a Canadian historian commented that 'the Murrayites seem to hold . . . an almost undisputed sway at the higher intellectual levels'.[45] Four years later, a young scholar who was to become probably the greatest living Italian historian, Carlo Ginzburg, launched his own first book with the declaration that the Murray thesis had 'ended by prevailing'.[46] At the same time, a French historian who was to achieve a similar eminence in his nation to Ginzburg, Emmanuel Le Roy Ladurie, built a religion of rebel witches into his portrait of early modern France.[47] Ten years later, the figure who towered over the field of comparative religion in the US academic system, Mircea Eliade, made medieval witchcraft a rebel faith descended from ancient paganism.[48]

Where these giants led the way, lesser academic scholars followed, either in repeating Murray's views unaltered or adapting them to produce slightly different portraits of medieval and early modern pagan witch cults, in a string of publications through the mid-twentieth century.[49] In the same period, that activity was even more characteristic of non-academic authors writing on the history of witchcraft whom she inspired prolifically to flights of fancy of varying wildness, united by the acceptance of the idea that the witch trials were directed against a pagan religion.[50] That idea was also embodied during the early 1970s in the work of the great collector of spoken history and tradition among rural English people George Ewart Evans.[51] It was adopted by some local museums in the 1960s and used to explain and contextualize exhibits relating to witchcraft.[52] In 1970 a documentary film, *Legend of the Witches*, was released, which combined the work of Leland and Murray and added some touches of its own. These included the confident statement that the famous scene of Harold Godwinson in the eleventh-century Bayeux tapestry, swearing support for William of Normandy on two boxes of Christian holy relics, actually showed him swearing on both Christian and pagan altar, because like most people of the time he would have recognized both faiths.[53]

More people probably gain an impression of history from popular works and films than academic publications, and another great source of impressions of it is historical fiction. Here, too, Murray's work was extremely influential, as its impact on novels, which commenced with John Buchan's, continued steadily through the rest of the century.[54] Its most popular and talented convert was Rosemary Sutcliff, a much loved and admired author of historical fiction designed mainly for young adults. Her books, especially in the years around 1960, when she was at the peak of her productivity, accepted in its entirety the idea that medieval England had remained pagan under an outward show of Christianity, and that this paganism had been centred on Margaret Murray's witches' god. In *The Lantern Bearers*, from 1959, early medieval Britain was shown as a place in which the inhabitants 'dance for the Horned One at Beltane' (the pagan feast opening summer) but 'listen to God's word between whiles'.[55] The same pattern obtained in *Knight's Fee*, published the next year and set six hundred years later in the Norman period, where villagers 'come to Mass on Sundays and Saints' Days, and turn at all other times to their Horned God'.[56] Those who read Sutcliff's books in their teenage years during the 1960s and 1970s would go into the later twentieth century with a firm impression that this had been so.[57] Historical novels continued to embody the same idea into the 1980s and 1990s.[58]

Margaret Murray herself continued to reinforce it with further books until the time of her death in the 1960s and by giving interviews to popular newspapers and magazines, who treated her by that period as the leading expert on the subject.[59] To a Birmingham paper in 1950 she made the assertion that not only had the pagan witch religion survived in secret into the modern period, but it continued to the present day, with murders committed as human sacrifices.[60] Four years later, however, she contributed an approving foreword to a book by a fellow member of the Folk-Lore Society and admirer of her work, Gerald Gardner. In this, he revealed what he claimed to be one of the few remaining covens of the old religion, into which he had been initiated, and the beliefs and rites of which he was now partially revealing; as she acknowledged, they consisted of a wholly benevolent worship of a goddess and god of nature, the former being the dominant partner.[61] Gardner's tradition, which became known as Wicca, grew rapidly thereafter into the senior, most important and most influential member of a family of religions grouped together under the umbrella term of modern Paganism. These naturally perpetuated Murray's portrait of medieval and early modern belief into the 1970s and 1980s with especial vigour, as during that period many of those religions claimed, like Gardner's Wicca, to have survived in secret from ancient times.[62]

It may therefore be suggested that the majority of people in the English-speaking world who were interested in medieval and early modern history approached the last quarter of the twentieth century believing that, in some form and to some extent, the ancient pagan religion or religions of Britain had persisted actively long after the introduction of Christianity as the official faith – until the end of the Middle Ages, or the early modern period, or even the present. This belief could take significantly different forms. In one, Christianity was an upper-class veneer, accepted by the social and political elite while the common folk remained mostly pagan. In another, a dual-faith system obtained at all levels of society, with both the old and the new co-existing and to some extent blending (for example in church decoration) until the great Christian remaking of the Reformation and Counter-Reformation ended the co-existence. Both, however, rested on the same foundation of an assumption of surviving paganism. What needs to be emphasized is that this assumption was not a traditional one for the British: rather, it was a late Victorian creation which had been sustained and reinforced for most of the succeeding twentieth century. It flourished within one long lifetime, between 1890 and 1970. So what was going on in that particular period which made such a belief especially attractive?

It may be suggested that the answer lies in two major developments of the nineteenth century in Britain, one ideological, the other economic and social. The former was the shift to a pluralist religious culture, in which first the Church of England lost its monopoly of public office and higher education and was forced to recognize parity in both with other Christian denominations, and then Christianity came to recognize the legitimacy of other forms of religion, and of agnosticism and atheism, as personal faith positions. The latter was the transformation of the British population from predominantly rural to predominantly urbanized and industrialized. Both processes spanned the century, and both were substantially complete by its end. Both tended in various ways to foster a wish to believe that ancient paganism had lasted a lot longer as a potent force in Britain, and perhaps in Europe in general, than had previously been thought. The religious changes tended to this result in two utterly different ways.

The first was through a desire to attack the traditional power of Christian Churches, and especially established Churches, by convincing people that the Middle Ages, which hitherto had been much represented as a time of devout Christianity, uniting society in religious harmony, had been nothing of the kind. If the public could be persuaded that the faith of Christ had been throughout the period nothing more than a veneer concentrated in the elite, covering a general population which had never really accepted it, then its claim to represent the ancestral and universal faith of the nation could be seriously weakened. This was directly the inspiration of Michelet in writing *La Sorcière*. As the book went on sale, he noted in his diary: 'I have assumed a new position which my best friends have not as yet clearly adopted, that of proclaiming the provisional death of Christianity'.[63] One scholar of his work has suggested that in his own mind, 'Michelet killed, executed, [and] murdered [what he called] "that bizarre, monstrous, prodigiously artificial condition of life" . . . the Christian Middle Ages'.[64] The same mission possessed Leland, as he explicitly used his work on Italian folklore to protest against what he thought to be an unhealthy admiration for the period expressed by 'all historians' at the time: for him there could be no mitigation for a period dominated by the Roman Catholic Church and a feudal nobility, in which 'on the whole, mankind was for a long time worse off than before'.[65] Such attitudes were also found in Britain. In 1865 a tract was appended to a new edition of an earlier book on pagan fertility religion, *A Discourse on the Worship of Priapus*, by Richard Payne Knight. It was entitled 'Essay on the Worship of the Generative Powers during the Middle Ages in Western Europe', and though anonymous was attributed to a political and religious radical and antiquary called Thomas Wright. Its argument was that a pagan veneration of fertility, and therefore of sexuality, had continued through the medieval period in various lands, including Britain: to underpin this argument it actually went as far as to print a falsified version of an entry in a major medieval British text, the Lanercost Chronicle.[66]

The model of medieval religion which suggested that paganism had survived alongside Christianity as a dual faith system in which the dominant Christian churchmen and rulers tacitly accepted and condoned it also undermined the traditional belief in the total victory of the new faith. It could, however, do so more gently, and rather than operating as an attack on Christianity it could function as a plea for a tolerant multi-faith society in the future, based on mutual respect and accommodation, and even syncretism. The Anglo-Irish poet W.B. Yeats, writing of the contemporary Irish rural population in 1897, could assert:

> Nothing shows how blind educated Ireland … is about peasant Ireland, than that it does not understand how the old religion, which made of the coming and going of the greenness of the woods and of the fruitfulness of the fields a part of its worship, lives side by side with the new religion which would trample nature as a serpent under its feet; nor is that old religion faded to a meaningless repetition of the old customs, for the ecstatic who has seen the red light and the white light of God smite themselves into the bread and wine at the Mass, has seen the exultant hidden multitudes among the winds of May: and if he were philosophical, would cry … I go inward to God, outward to the gods.[67]

Yeats's 'hidden multitudes' were the fairies, in which many Irish country folk did indeed believe in his time, and he defined that belief as paganism in itself. He himself was, or wished to be, such an 'ecstatic', and indeed he formed a blend of Christianity and paganism in his own personal belief system, as did many of the other members of the society of ritual magicians which he joined, the Hermetic Order of the Golden Dawn. So also, in the period between 1890 and 1940, did the novelists Rider Haggard,

Kenneth Grahame, D.H. Lawrence and Dion Fortune, the theosophical philosopher George Russell, and members of a movement designed as a socialist equivalent to the Boy Scouts and Girl Guides, the Order of Woodcraft Chivalry.[68]

The concept of harmony, syncretism and co-existence between medieval Christianity and paganism carried with it one of a profound and organic continuity of religion in British history. Instead of a battle for supremacy between rival faiths, with inevitable victory for the superior one, that history became a process whereby the new religion built slowly and surely upon the old, both in the physical and the ideological sense. To people experiencing the spiritual and technological disruption of the nineteenth and twentieth centuries, and reckoning with a need for co-existence and cooperation between religious traditions in the present, this vision could be deeply comforting. It was enunciated by another president of the Folk-Lore Society in 1896, who declared that, all across Europe, medieval churches had been built on or next to pagan shrines, and concluded that this supplied 'unbroken evidences of the pagan foundation, which, itself resting on barbaric bedrock, upholds the structures of classical and Christian faiths'.[69]

In the next decade this idea flowered in the work of amateur historians and archaeologists into the belief that most if not all medieval churches were built on pagan holy sites, that medieval pillar crosses were transformed prehistoric standing stones, that the old yews in churchyards had been pre-Christian holy trees, and that Christian festivals were simply those of the older religion in new dress.[70] This made an acceptance of a persistence of that older religion, alongside or combined with the new one, even easier. One of the most popular such amateur authors was Harold Massingham, a writer on the English countryside, who between 1930 and 1945 drove home the message that many Christian observances were inspired by pagan predecessors: to him, even the table tombs in churchyards were a development of prehistoric dolmens, and the traditional beating of the bounds of a Cotswold parish remained a rite of the ancient Earth Goddess. He made the Cerne Abbas Giant into the perfect symbol of an imagined reconciliation between the old and new religions, in which the medieval monks purged paganism of its grossness and cruelty but recognized its embodiment of the inherent powers of the earth.[71]

The belief that Christianity had been a religion of the medieval elite, spread thinly over the surface of a populace which itself largely remained pagan, fed off another major feature of the educated British psyche in the late nineteenth and early twentieth centuries: a sense of civilization as a fragile crust over a seething, menacing magma of primeval barbarism. In part, this was the product of the fears of the newly expanded and enriched middle and upper classes which industrial and commercial development had created, balanced on top of the huge, poor, exploited and restless new industrial and urban proletariat. The rapid contemporary expansion of the British Empire had created a similar anxiety among the new white colonial elites ruling over the mass of native peoples in the colonies. Another novelty of tremendous import, the theory of evolution by natural selection, had revealed humanity in general to be genetically connected to the beasts, and so with a presumed higher and lower nature either forever holding each other in check, or at war with each other. The old and new religions could be projected into the same relationship.

None of this, however, explains why the rural population, in particular, should be regarded as the natural, and enduring, repositories of surviving paganism.[72] The reason for this lay in a simple pair of statistics: that in 1810, 80 per cent of the population of England lived in the countryside and engaged in occupations directly or ultimately based on farming, and in 1910, 80 per cent lived in towns and cities and engaged in occupations directly or ultimately based on commerce or industry. The balance had tipped by the 1850s. This sudden and unprecedented shift created an unfamiliar and rather frightening new world, in which it seemed that the countryside might soon disappear altogether. Moreover, it made country people into unusual and to some degree anomalous members of the new society – which mattered especially for views of the historic relationship between paganism and Christianity, as most of the authors who were to write about it came from and lived in towns. It did not, however, mean that they would necessarily take the same view of rural people. Instead, the views that were taken tended to cluster around two polarized opposites, drawing on very different emotions but nevertheless tending to the same conclusion, of a massive rural continuity of traditional ways.

At one pole was a millennia-old tendency of urban people to regard their environment as the one which produced virtually all progress and refinement in human affairs and was the seat of learning, invention and social polish: the very word 'civilization' was based on this understanding. As part of this, ordinary rural people were mocked and reviled as ignorant and rough: clods, boors and yokels.[73] It was quite easy, therefore, for those who held this attitude to credit them with mindlessly carrying on, year after year, customs and beliefs which perpetuated an ancient and primitive religion. It was also easy for those who had views of country folk which spanned the affectionate and the mocking to let the term 'pagan' creep into a characterization of their religious attitudes in general. In 1860, George Eliot, in her novel *The Mill on the Floss*, could say of her imagined English rustics 'one sees little trace of religion, still less of a distinctively Christian creed. Their belief in the Unseen, so far as it manifests at all, seems to be rather of a pagan kind; their moral notions, though held with strong tenacity, seem to have no standard beyond hereditary custom'. In another place she wrote of them that 'their religion was of a simple, semi-pagan kind'. However, she also made clear that Christianity was the only religion they knew, and that they were sure to get their children baptized and were anxious to be buried in the churchyard. What she meant by 'pagan' or 'semi-pagan' was only that they did not have any strenuous personal faith or knowledge of theology, and that some believed in elementary folk magic like carrying a mutton bone to ward off cramp.[74]

When the trope of actual pagan survival emerged in British writing, it was easily assimilated to the traditional disparaging language of the urban directed against the rural. One of the most influential of the Edwardian writers who wrote of the persistence of ancient tradition in the English countryside declared that this was because 'the peasant is, in some respects, a child as truly as he is physically a healthy animal'.[75] More vicious was the Cambridge academic who became the most influential and popular of all the scholarly authors who promoted the idea of the survival of paganism through folk custom, Sir James Frazer. He believed that 'to this day the peasant remains a pagan and a savage at heart: his civilisation is merely a thin veneer which the hard knocks of his life soon abrade, exposing the solid core of paganism and savagery below. The danger created by a bottomless layer of ignorance and superstition beneath the crust of civilised society is lessened, not only by the natural torpidity and inertia of the rural mind, but also by the progressive decrease of the rural compared with the urban population in modern states.'[76] In other words, the good news was that the country people, like traditional peoples elsewhere in the world, were going to be exterminated by modernization.

There was, however, an opposite language used by city dwellers of the countryside, which was just as ancient as the disparaging one. It characterized rural places as more beautiful, healthy, peaceful and morally virtuous than towns.[77] This took on a new force in the nineteenth century in reaction to the increasing depopulation and disappearance of the English countryside, which made it seem like a precious and immemorial resource which could now be vanishing forever. Moreover, the new scale and industrialization of urban centres made the division between town and country much sharper and more dramatic than before: they were truly becoming entirely different worlds. The result, by the late nineteenth century and above all in England, was a new intensity to the idealization of the countryside, not just for all the traditional reasons but as a repository of unchanging ways and values, anchoring the English in a past from which the new cities and industries seemed to be tearing them.[78]

The later Victorian writer of non-fiction who did more than any other to portray the countryside as an unchanging and redemptive refuge from modernity was Richard Jeffries, who in 1880 could declare that 'these modern inventions, this steam, and electric telegraph, and even the printing press have but skimmed the surface of village life'. He invented the character of 'Hodge' to typify the quiet immemorial wisdom of the stereotypical ordinary countryman.[79] In the 1900s Rudyard Kipling took this persona into fiction, in the form of Hobden, the old Sussex smallholder who embodies the tradition of his valley over millennia and instinctually remembers and understands all that has happened there.[80] This view of the country both inspired and gave popularity to the work of folklore collectors over the same span of time: in the words of one of their recent descendants, they became 'the high priests and priestesses of the rural myth'.[81] Two of their leaders declared in a pamphlet designed for a popular readership that:

> in every society there are people who do not progress either in reli-
> gion or in polity with the foremost of the nation. They are left
> stranded amidst the progress. They live in out-of-the-way villages,
> or in places where the general culture does not penetrate easily; they
> keep to old ways, practices and ideas, following with religious awe
> all that their parents had held to be necessary in their lives. These
> people are living repositories of ancient history – a history that has
> not been written down, but which has come down by tradition.[82]

In vain did one of their colleagues in the Folk-Lore Society protest in 1893 that this idealization of the rural population as a monolithic, inert, unthinking and unchanging mass was bad for scholarship, and declare that 'the folk is a fraud, a delusion, a myth' and 'a name for our ignorance'.[83] The myth concerned was too beguiling, and it descended for most of the next century intact among enthusiasts for rural ways. As late as 1956, the collector of valuable spoken history George Ewart Evans could repeat that 'old people in the countryside are survivors from another era. They belong essentially to a culture that has extended in unbroken line since at least the early Middle Ages.'[84] The potential in this view for a belief in surviving paganism is obvious, and was indeed hinted at in the reference to a lack of progress in religion recorded above. It had in fact already been suggested before the foundation of the Folk-Lore Society, in the work of the novelist who was the fiction-writing equivalent in fame to Richard Jeffries in promoting the idea of the English countryside as a place of timeless tradition: Thomas Hardy. In his bestseller of 1878, *The Return of the Native*, he could describe a rural maypole dance and add 'the impulses of all such outlandish hamlets are pagan still: in these spots homage to nature, self-adoration, frantic gaieties, fragments of Teutonic rites to divinities whose names are forgotten, have in some way or other survived medieval doctrine'.[85] As was the case with other aspects of the theme of the persistence of the old religions, the idea of the timeless countryside had been proposed by fantasy writers or political propagandists before scholars made it their own.

Revisionism

In the last quarter of the twentieth century, this whole complex of ideas, and the evidence which had apparently underpinned it, was dismantled with astonishing speed. By the 1990s an apparently unanimous agreement had been reached among professional historians that there was no surviving paganism in any area of Europe for more than a short period after its official conversion to Christianity. In other words, no coherent and self-conscious pagan resistance movement, with an active and conscious retention of allegiance to the old deities in preference to Christianity, persisted anywhere on the continent once the rulers of an area had adopted the new religion.[86] A huge wave of new and detailed local research had proved all the data assembled to argue the case for persisting paganism to be either misunderstood or susceptible to different readings.

In the 1980s it was realized that there was no record of the Cerne Abbas Giant before the seventeenth century, in a valley with good previous records, and some testimony that he had been made at that period. Instead of being the figure of an ancient god, it now seemed possible, or even likely, that he was a bawdy early modern caricature. The problem of how such an apparently pagan image could have survived alongside a medieval abbey was removed if it had simply not been there in the time of the abbey.[87] During the 1970s and 1980s it became clear that there was no solid evidence of the mummers' play before the mid-eighteenth century, and that it was spread from that time onward through printed texts and seemed to have influenced the sword dance and the plough play – which accounted for the common features of all.[88] In the same period it was established that the morris dance had appeared in the fifteenth century as a fashionable new entertainment in the royal and ducal courts of France and Burgundy, and spread from them to the English ones. In the early sixteenth century it had begun to move out among the English populace, and it became a widespread craze in the second half of that century, breaking into distinctive regional forms in the Stuart and Georgian periods.[89]

The ritual animal disguises – horse, ram or bull – carried or danced around settlements at midwinter and May Day turned out to be recorded, with the single exception of the Abbots Bromley Horn Dance, only after 1800.[90] They may all be modern offshoots of the popular late medieval and early modern entertainment of the hobby horse dance, which did not have any particular season. The Horn Dance is certainly older, but is not recorded before the seventeenth century: an earlier reference to the same entertainment in the village only mentions the hobby horse. The antlers have now been dated, and are indeed about a thousand years old; but they came from domesticated reindeer, which were never kept in Britain, and so must have been imported, at some point between the eleventh and seventeenth centuries.[91] The Haxey Hood Game turned out to have grown out of a widespread East Midlands custom in which plough boys toured their district to gather donations of food and money at the opening of the ploughing season. It was put together in its present, unique form in the decades around 1800.[92] The customs collected by the folklorists between the 1870s and 1920s began to look less like a chart of prehistoric ritual and more like one of nineteenth-century popular festivity.

Some readers may be tempted to wonder whether the first recorded appearance of a custom need mark a date close to its actual development, and whether it might have been around unrecorded for centuries before then. If we were dealing with a period before 1400 then this concern would be entirely justified, because the survival of entries concerning popular festivity in this earlier time is so patchy and incidental that the initial citation of an activity usually gives no indication of its point of origin. The fifteenth, sixteenth, seventeenth and eighteenth centuries are very different, however, because the records for popular customs in them are so numerous and varied that it would be very difficult for one to enjoy any widespread or extended success while escaping all notice.[93]

As part of this sequence of discoveries, a new generation of folklorists, following directly in the footsteps of those before and usually attached to the same organizations – above all the now slightly renamed Folklore Society – rejected the conceptual apparatus of their predecessors. Two foundations of that apparatus – the belief in an unchanging and immemorial culture of rural commoners and (therefore) in modern folk customs and beliefs as living fossils of ancient religion – were comprehensively disowned. It was accepted, once proper historical research had been carried out into a large number of those customs and beliefs for the first time, that country people could be as dynamic, creative and unfettered by tradition as any other commoners, and that their cultures were in a constant state of evolution. In 1982 one of the new folklorists could already declare that 'the belief that traditional behaviour is a fading relic of former primeval cultures has long since disappeared from folklore study', and excoriate the former application of it to dances such as the morris.[94] In the same year another poured scorn on the preceding preoccupation of folklorists with the ancient origins of customs as flawed and irrelevant.[95] Conversely, half a decade later a third could lament the fact that 'the belief that all calendar customs have their origin in pagan fertility ritual is well established in public consciousness, and is still defying most academic attempts to shift it'. She went on herself to condemn the patronizing attitude which was implied in earlier scholars' views of 'the folk' as unthinking and amorphous inheritors of tradition.[96] At the opening of the 1990s, a fourth of the new practitioners of the discipline could declare that 'the way forward for British Folklore Studies must surely be . . . the study of the real country and the real town, outside the confines of a world of dreams and shadows'.[97]

In the same period, the idea that certain carved figures in medieval churches represented pagan deities came into question. The sheela-na-gigs were shown to have a place in a fashion for church images preaching moral messages which originated in France as a package of designs associated with

Romanesque architecture and spread outwards through Western Europe in the twelfth century. The foliate heads were a later fashion, mostly from the fourteenth and fifteenth centuries, and found mostly in buildings constructed by fashion-conscious elites rather than by and for the common people. Their first appearance seems to lie in manuscripts produced by monks. All this makes a pagan origin and association seem very unlikely.[98]

A parallel shift of attitude occurred towards the apparent references to pagan deities and spirits in Anglo-Saxon healing charms. It was pointed out that these were very few, within the whole corpus of such works, and were almost always interspersed with pious references to the Christian God, to Jesus and to saints. Moreover, the words with which they were associated were often garbled, as if the copyists no longer really understood their significance. There was no indication of how the gods and other supernatural entities concerned were viewed by the people using these recitations: whether still as actual deities, as lesser spirits subservient to the Christian Lord, as legendary human physicians or as demons. Early English medicine contained notable Greek, Roman and Arab elements as well as native tradition, so drew eclectically on all knowledge that seemed to be available. The scholar who has written most extensively on these texts since 1990 has concluded that they 'indicate a strong Christian sense of God's presence governing over the natural world: they have incorporated their folk sense of nature into the Christian cosmology quite neatly, in a holistic view of the world'.[99]

Did the folk healers of Anglo-Saxon England preserve a more reverential attitude to the old deities, and a better understanding of them? We simply do not know, as no evidence survives to determine the matter; but it is now certain that we cannot take at face value the denunciations of them as heathens by the likes of Abbot Aelfric, who were a most unusual, puritanical and evangelical breed of reforming churchmen, inclined to condemn all magic – and indeed all elements of folk Christianity of which they personally disapproved – as non-Christian.[100] What is most significant in this context is that references to pagan Anglo-Saxon and Scandinavian deities disappear completely from English magical recipes after the eleventh century.

There was no enduring tradition of calling upon them – or on any other of the old deities – among folk healers and sellers of other magical remedies. There are good records for the activities and beliefs of these people – those commonly called wise or cunning folk – from the sixteenth century onward, increasing in volume to the nineteenth, and they display the cross-section of religious attitudes held by most people in their society at each stage of this span of time.[101] In other words, they ranged from a fervent Christianity (in different denominations) to apparent religious indifference, but none showed any allegiance to pagan deities. The only religion which appears in their charms, spells and conjurations is the Christian, though it was often of an increasingly old-fashioned kind, embodying a medieval cult of the saints which had been officially abolished in the Protestant Reformation.[102]

In the late twentieth century, also, the belief that the people prosecuted for the alleged crime of witchcraft in early modern Europe were practitioners of a surviving pagan religion collapsed completely among professional historians. From 1970 onwards a steady process of systematic and detailed research began into the trial records and associated documents and published literature, in one region after another, and it revealed absolutely no evidence for the belief. The pagan ancient world still played a part in the story of the witch trials. Everybody agreed that ideas and images originating in that world helped to formulate the novel concept of the satanic witch which propelled those trials. In many areas, also, popular beliefs which either definitely or possibly had ancient origins played a part in the accusations and confessions associated with the trials, and the demonological literature that justified and encouraged them. Those accused of witchcraft were, however, drawn from the same social and cultural groups as their accusers, and seemed to have shared the same religion, in each case the local variety of Christianity. There remains a slight chance that a few of them may to some extent have embraced the Satan-worship of which they were accused (though as an individual action and not as part of an organized counter-religion as was alleged of them), but this is nowhere firmly proved. The witch hunts between the fifteenth and eighteenth centuries were generated by an unhappy combination of a general fear and anguish produced by uncanny misfortune, blamed on malicious magic, and a new elite belief in a satanic conspiracy to subvert Christianity. The worship of old deities played no part in it. This shift of scholarly perspective was the more final in that it was brought about not by a few iconoclasts but by studies produced by scores of academics, covering in the end every part of Europe.[103]

What brought about this wholesale revisionism, at such speed and at this particular time? It was certainly not the product of a Christian backlash against the earlier propensity to see paganism as surviving far into the Christian centuries. The period concerned was, on the contrary, that in which Christian hegemony broke down across most of the Western world and a massive apparent secularization took place. More relevant was the great expansion and professionalization of the academic system in Western nations between the 1960s and 1980s, resulting in a much larger number of full-time scholars supported by public money and expected to engage in constant research and publication. This in itself would have shaken things up considerably, especially as many of the scholars recruited came from outside the upper-middle-class and gentry social groups which had produced most previous historians, and so were less inclined to defer to received opinion. Among folklorists in particular, however, most of those at the forefront of rejecting former approaches were not academics at all, and yet they were seized by the same fervour to re-examine prevailing orthodoxies. That fervour embraced all areas of history and prehistory, from the Neolithic to the recent past. Clearly something profound was going on.

It may be suggested here that the source of this wholesale jettisoning of received assertion and supposition was that the latter was, as has been noted, itself a creation of the period between the late nineteenth and the mid-twentieth centuries. As such, it was bound up with a particular set of social and cultural attitudes rooted in the physical, economic and intellectual environment of that period which ceased to obtain once that environment disintegrated. A heated questioning of received belief and custom, especially by younger generations, was a feature of the entire Western world from the 1960s onward. In the British context, it responded to the progressive disappearance of the national characteristics which had obtained since the late nineteenth century and remained stable until the period following the Second World War: an economic reliance on heavy industry and a male workforce mainly engaged in manual labour; great power status on the world stage linked to the possession of a large colonial empire; religious diversity within the bonding framework of an official and public Christian dominance which relegated other faith positions to the margins and especially discouraged newly appeared belief systems; and a restrictive and prescriptive set of attitudes towards race, gender and sexual preference which operated strong social and political prejudices against those who failed to conform. That package of phenomena had accompanied, and for many people had seemed to produce and sustain, a story of outstanding national success during the period concerned. By the 1960s, however, British industry was starting to collapse, and the empire, great power status and Christian hegemony almost gone; and there now seemed no further need for the restrictive cultural, moral and social prejudices which had accompanied them, especially as social and technological changes made those both less relevant and less practicable. The historian who proposed the term 'revisionism' for the resulting wholesale questioning of historical orthodoxies, Conrad Russell, suggested that those involved in it were the intellectual equivalent of contemporary urban planners, needing to renew the decaying late Victorian and Edwardian infrastructures of British cities.[104]

In the case of pagan survival, this work of wholesale reappraisal was made easier by the evaporation of most of the emotional impetus which has been suggested above as being behind the popularity of the idea. With the end of Christian cultural hegemony, there was less need to undermine the credentials of Christianity as the national religion – it had effectively ceased to be one – and there was less need to acclimatize to genuine religious pluralism, because it was now a familiar fact. The slowing and at times cessation of urban expansion, the greater healthiness and familiarity of city life, the decline of heavy industry and the greater accessibility of rural areas because of the motor car – so that increasingly people were commuting from homes in villages – made the countryside seem less endangered, detached, remote and mysterious than it had done earlier. A wish to believe in pagan continuity and survival deep into the Christian period or through it just seemed less relevant than before, like organized religion in general.

Pagan Survival and Pagan Survivals

By 1990, as said, professional historians seem to have been unanimous that paganism – as a fully formed set of religions devoted to the old deities – did not persist long after the conversion of a given region to Christianity. They were, however, apparently equally unanimous that large numbers of ideas, figures, stories, magical techniques, customs and motifs were taken into medieval and early modern culture from ancient paganism, and that some proved remarkably enduring. They spanned the fields of architecture, art, literature, operative magic, medicine and folk tradition. Scholars were not unanimous regarding the extent of this importation, the spirit in which it was conducted or whether specific phenomena should be assigned to it or not. Nonetheless, the general principle was accepted. The Christian religion itself adopted extensively the trappings of pagan worship for the core elements of its own. All that its founder had prescribed was a code of ethics, a direction to hold a commemorative meal in his honour and (apparently) a cult of his own figure as a saviour and redeemer, set within the ritual and theological structure of the Judaism of his time. On making the transition from the Jewish to the Gentile world, the new religion borrowed from pagans the shape of its first churches, and the use of candles, incense, wreaths and garlands, altars, images, formal liturgies, hymns, vestments and choral music. Into these familiar structures it poured a radically different theology.

In 1991 the present author suggested a working distinction between 'surviving paganism', signifying a persisting pagan religion, and a 'pagan survival', meaning a custom, belief or object taken into Christian religion, culture or society from ancient paganism and redeployed in the new religious context.[105] It was very clear from the beginning that the boundaries of this latter category were always going to be blurred, that there would be contention over its contents and that there would be semantic problems in implementing it. For example, until the nineteenth century a church at Enna in Sicily housed statues of the Christian Madonna and Child which were actually once the cult images of the Roman agricultural goddesses Ceres and Proserpina from the ancient temple on the site of which the church was built.[106] So were they or were they not 'pagan images'? The answer seems to be yes and no: yes, in origin, but not in the purpose to which they were subsequently put. The same ambivalence extends to the allied question of whether they could be called 'pagan survivals'. They were certainly surviving relics of ancient paganism, and could physically be said to have survived in their original context, but theologically they had not done so. If, however, they had been preserved by nominally Christian peasants on a farm, where they were regarded as lucky objects which guarded the fertility of the land, then that would have been a less equivocal pagan survival.

The work published in 1991 which distinguished 'surviving paganism' from 'pagan survivals' also identified four direct lines of connection between ancient paganism and the present which acted as particularly effective conduits for the latter.[107] The first consisted of ceremonial magic, the summoning and control of supernatural forces by the use of invocations and specialized equipment, both solid (as in the case of swords, knives, vessels, censers and animal parts) and geometric (as in the use of circles, triangles and pentagrams). This was first apparently developed in ancient Egypt and has formed a continuous tradition ever since, permeating Judaism, Islam and Christianity even though all three religions (and especially the last) formally condemned and sometimes persecuted most forms of it. Although it could be entirely assimilated to all three, it also at times carried along with it some relics of paganism. Among the lists of spirits to be summoned in particular late medieval and early modern handbooks of magic appear the garbled names of Egyptian deities, and a charm 'to see visions and cause dreams' by calling on the goddess Isis and the god Bes is apparently found both in an Egyptian papyrus of the Roman period and a sixteenth-century English manuscript.[108] More importantly, in the twelfth century the Arabic system of astral magic, the harnessing of the arcane influences of the sun, moon and planets, reached Western Christianity and inspired the idea that the indwelling spirits of those heavenly bodies had been placed there by the Christian God to rule over aspects of the world. As they were identified with the Graeco-Roman deities associated with these bodies, this was effectively a way of bringing back most of the Olympian divinities into the Christian cosmos. For a time, this idea came close to being accepted as respectable theology, and though by the fourteenth century it was clearly rejected by orthodoxy, it persisted until the seventeenth century as a clandestine learned tradition.[109]

At a more fundamental level, the pagan ancient world supplied the European tradition of learned ritual magic with a basic framework which was to sustain it until modern times, consisting of complex rites which unify actions, materials and words, conveyed in written texts; an emphasis on the power of special names and of invocations in unknown languages; a stress on the purification of the magician and the working space before the rite, and on measures to protect and strengthen the magician during it; the use of special equipment, often made particularly for the purpose, and the choice of an especially propitious time at which to work; the compulsion or attraction of spirits or deities to join and assist the rite; and an eclectic and multicultural range of source material. All these features first appear together in Egypt during late antiquity, and would supply ceremonial magicians with a list of actions and artefacts from which they could choose according to taste and need until the present day.[110] They also provided the twentieth century with a structure within which, once the pagan deities were put back, a viable modern Paganism could easily be created.[111]

The second significant line of connection between ancient paganism and the present consisted of popular service magic, of folk magicians serving clients in return for payment. These were the wise or cunning folk of English tradition, also known by many local names. Their charms and spells were, as said, far less successful than learned ceremonial and textual

32

magic in preserving the names of pagan deities in the longer term (though the two types of magic merged at their boundaries). Nonetheless, they did preserve from ancient times some basic principles and practices. The underlying one was the belief that humans – or at least especially gifted humans – had the right to work rituals to manipulate the hidden powers of nature or to seem to transcend nature, and so to exceed the normal span of human ability, in order to remedy practical problems. There was also the recognition that this magic could be sympathetic, operating through similarities and attractions between different parts of the natural world, or contagious, directed at or employing substances generated by or associated with particular people and animals. Some of the specific techniques involved, such as the making of an image of a person to represent them, or the manipulation of a presumed link between particular plants, colours, times and planets, descended directly through the whole history of popular magic from ancient to modern times.[112]

The third line of connection between ancient paganism and modernity did indeed consist of folk customs, especially seasonal rituals, although to nothing like the same extent or in the same way that the early folklorists supposed. The genuine connections take two forms. One is that there are a few customs which when tested by proper historical research have turned out indeed to descend from pagan antiquity to recent times or the present. The lighting of sacred fires to bless and protect people and livestock at the opening of summer and at midsummer is one example of these, and the giving of gifts at midwinter (formerly at New Year, now at Christmas) another.[113] These survived so long because they were not mere entertainments but served what seemed to be a vital purpose: to protect herds and their keepers at the opening of the summer pastures, and communities in general facing the threat of epidemics, storms and raids in late summer, and to bless and encourage people at the opening of a new yearly cycle. The other form of genuine connection is more general, and best explained by reversing the traditional metaphor of throwing out the baby with the bathwater. During the past fifty years, as described, a lot of babies have been removed from the bathwater of primeval seasonal festivity, in the shape of customs which proved to be a lot less old than had previously been supposed. It may now be suggested that, once all of them have been dried off and safely tucked up in eighteenth- and nineteenth-century, or early modern, cots, then it is the bathwater itself which becomes interesting: in other words, the background seasonal environment to particular pastimes.

Thus, the mummers' play, sword dance and plough play may indeed be developments of the Georgian period, but there would always have been folk plays and dances at midwinter in Britain: the three named were just the favourite nineteenth-century forms. The morris may be a late medieval courtly entertainment popularized in England under the Tudors, but dances had always formed an important part of the festivities that celebrated the coming of summer, even if the form of them changed over time. In this manner there have always been rites of divination concerning death and the mocking of spirits of dark, cold and fear at the beginning of winter; rites centred on light, warmth, greenery and feasting, and blessing for the coming year, at midwinter; rites focused on driving back darkness and cold in early spring and on rebirth and reopening in late spring; rites of fire and flowers at midsummer; and rites which embodied thanksgiving, community, remeeting and closure in autumn. Their actual nature changed every few centuries, but the basic pattern of the wheel of the year endured, and was truly prehistoric.

The fourth, and perhaps the greatest, line of continuity consisted of the ongoing relationship of Christian cultures with the deities and spirits of the pagan ancient world, as embodied in art, literature and folklore. At the elite level, an admiration of and love for the mythology of pagan Greece and Rome remained a constant feature of European civilization. Botticelli, Titian, Velázquez and Lord Leighton were only the most famous of a succession of artists to paint pictures of the goddess Venus, as an embodiment of female beauty and allure. Her more austere counterpart Minerva was evoked as a patroness by intellectuals and civic leaders from the twelfth to the twentieth centuries, just as Apollo remained emblematic of the arts and Mercury of communication. The Irish and Norse deities were remembered with the same affection, and indeed we depend entirely for our knowledge of them upon the tales recorded of them by medieval Christians. When a Highland Scottish chief, the earl of Argyll, marched off to join an invasion of England in 1513, his bard compared him to the former Gaelic god Lugh.[114] At a popular level continuity with a pre-Christian supernatural world was maintained most obviously in the sense of an environment populated by non-human intelligent beings, some visible and some not, which could interact with humanity sometimes to its advantage and mostly not. These beings were encountered both in and out of the home, and known variously as fairies, elves, pixies, goblins, pucks, hobs and by many other names. Whereas the pagan goddesses and gods remained largely figures of mythology, allegory and entertainment to the cultured elite, to ordinary people these lesser beings often seemed very real, and were blamed for a range of physical ills and other misfortunes. Their persistence in Christianized societies is a global phenomenon.[115]

All these categories of belief and action could be thoroughly Christianized, and for around a thousand years, at least, the people who believed and enacted the contents of them were at least nominally Christians. Fervent and pious followers of Christ could be ceremonial magicians and have a love of Greek and Roman (or Norse or Irish) mythology, while cunning craft, seasonal rites and a belief in fairies were common components of folk Christian culture. To many scholars concerned with particular periods or aspects of medieval and early modern history, their pagan origins can hardly seem relevant at all. Once a longer perspective is taken, however, things look rather different. While all of these areas of belief and operation could be assimilated to Christianity, all of them were in both origin and essence unconnected with and different from it, and all of them caused Christian churchmen and magistrates grave misgivings at times: in the case of both kinds of magic, this normally took the form of sustained official hostility. Furthermore, looking across the span of two millennia, it is apparent that all four of these lines of connection were recombined in the twentieth century, with an active regard for the deities put back, to produce modern Paganism.

An early and celebrated application of the concept of pagan survivals was made in 1971 by a leading French historian, Jean Delumeau, in a manner which actually spanned the gap between it and the earlier one of surviving paganism. With special reference to France, he repeated the view that Catholic Europeans, at least, had only truly been made Christian in the seventeenth century, by that movement traditionally known as the Counter-Reformation. He did not claim, however, that they had been converted from paganism, or that any of the latter had survived anywhere near that time. Instead, he characterized medieval Christianity as a hybrid, in which many pagan elements survived in the forms of a great variety of folk magic and popular superstition, practised in and out of churches and often embodying a view of the natural world as animated by spirits. In his formula, 'Christianity camouflaged rather than suppressed the beliefs and actions transmitted by millennia of obscure history'. The Counter-Reformation, he suggested, drove many of these customs and beliefs away from the Church and suppressed many more altogether, thereby providing a purer and more authentic kind of Christian religion.[116]

Between the 1970s and 1990s, the distinction between surviving paganism and pagan survivals was deployed with particular effect in the study of the early modern witch trials, where surviving paganism had been most commonly and thoroughly assumed to be a major element by earlier authors. Three scholars in particular made an international impact by operating that distinction and indeed it might be said in general that those authors who were most explicit in distancing themselves from a belief in surviving paganism – especially as expressed by Margaret Murray – were also the most active in acknowledging and working with the concept of pagan survivals. One was British, Norman Cohn, who in 1975 attacked and refuted Murray's interpretation at length, but suggested instead that the stereotype of the satanic witch drew on two ancient sources of inspiration. The first was a construct of what evil religion should be, combining human sacrifice, cannibalism and sexual promiscuity, and the other was a complex of traditions concerning night-roving spirits.[117]

The second scholar was Carlo Ginzburg, publishing in 1989, by which time he was probably the most internationally renowned of Italian historians. He too was savage about Murray, describing it as 'justified' to call her work 'amateurish, absurd, bereft of any scientific merit' and terming her use of evidence 'obviously absurd'. He was adamant that the descriptions of early modern witches' activities were mythologies, not portraits of an actual cult. He insisted, however, that it had a 'core of truth', in that popular traditions ultimately based in ancient pagan beliefs had contributed to the stereotype of the witches' sabbath, as Norman Cohn had argued. He went further, to argue that these traditions were remnants of an ancient pan-European shamanistic fertility religion.[118] The third scholar was a Hungarian folklorist, Éva Pócs, who from the 1990s published a series of works in which she demonstrated the apparently archaic folk elements in the belief systems which underpinned the witch trials in her nation, and in the world of popular magic throughout south-eastern Europe. She praised Cohn for having drawn attention to the importance of such elements (though later Ginzburg became a greater influence), and carefully distanced herself from Murray and the other proponents of the idea that the alleged witches had been pagans. Nonetheless, she thought it likely that memories of genuine societies, or at least bonding traditions, of popular service magicians had partly lain behind the images of the witch religion, combined with tales about demons and concerning good and bad magicians who sent out their souls to fight each other at night.[119]

In 1991 a distinguished collection of essays by continental European scholars was published which appeared in English as *The Pagan Middle Ages* and exemplified the 'pagan survivals' approach to the period.[120] Its concern was with the way in which medieval societies assimilated, rejected or disputed the cultural heritage of pagan antiquity. The editor later wrote as his contribution to a subsequent, similar collection that the sheer otherworldliness of Christianity had forced medieval people to retain memories of ancient pagan beliefs in order to cope with the present world. This in turn provoked intermittent Christian movements of reform and purification in which a more literal reading of the Bible inspired attempts to remove these elements from the religion and the wider culture, but they generally survived or returned after these interventions. He concluded that 'the result was syncretism in which very often the pagan origin got lost'.[121]

The apparent consensus which had formed by the 1990s around this model provided great potential for the historian. It was apparent that all over Europe the older religions had bequeathed a rich inheritance of beliefs, practices, remedies, symbols, images, ideas and forms to Christian culture. The result was indeed a constant process of adaptation, negotiation, disputation, utilization and condemnation, taking place at all social levels and within and without formal ecclesiastical structures, as different states, communities and individuals made their own relationships with this inheritance. Intellectual, religious, political and social elites attempted to define and police what could be adopted directly from paganism, what needed to be remodelled and redefined before absorption and what had to be rejected and forbidden outright. Having made these decisions – which often embodied some inconsistencies and involved subsequent changes of attitude – the elites concerned then had the often formidable job of ensuring that anybody else paid attention to them.

Post-Revisionism

The apparent consensus among historians and allied scholars over the model of 'pagan survivals' did not prove lasting, although many of them, as shown, found it a useful one, and continue to do so. From the 1990s, however, the current that had been carrying scholarship away from the idea of surviving paganism continued to move some authors further on to reject the term 'pagan' altogether for any aspects of medieval culture, including those inherited or borrowed from a pre-Christian antiquity.[122] In 1996 an expert in Anglo-Saxon charms, cited earlier, defined as erroneous two previous assumptions about 'With Faerstice': that 'the lack of Christian elements (and the presence of "magic" as we see it) means it was not Christian and, second, that if the origins of the material predate Christianity or represent an older tradition, the remedy was therefore pagan'. In the terms set by the present argument, that seems correct, but she went on to assert that 'these so-called magic or pagan elements represent areligious folklore, transferable from one religious tradition to another'.[123] Those elements may have *become* a religious folklore, but that does not diminish the status of the references to pagan figures as pagan survivals, and significant and interesting as such.

In the new century the movement among professional historians to get rid of the term 'pagan' in any connection with the Middle Ages has strengthened. In 2009 an eminent British medievalist declared that 'what the rigorists of the early medieval Church did have to face . . . was the fact that traditional rituals of varying origins survived everywhere routinized into local Christian practice'. He went on to note, equally correctly, that the surviving Anglo-Saxon healing charms were preserved in monastic or cathedral copying schools. He then went further to add the importance of stressing that 'the village wise-woman, too, would in most cases have seen her powers as operating in an entirely Christian context, and so would her clientele'.[124] In an impressive study of the relationship between science and magic in medieval Europe, an American scholar agreed that 'much that has been pointed to among the religious practices of the populace as evidence for a persistence of paganism or as a pagan residue should instead be regarded as not substantially different from the broad spirituality promoted by the official Church'.[125] A young Cambridge scholar, in his (generally very good) first book, went furthest, to attack Jean Delumeau, Norman Cohn, Carlo Ginzburg and the present author, together, for speaking of pagan survivals at all in the medieval context, calling the term completely unhelpful because it merely reflected the ruses of language employed by an unrepresentative minority of reforming churchmen to condemn forms of Christianity of which they disapproved. He thundered the conclusion that 'the strongest evidence for residues of rival pagan belief and practice in the central Middle Ages does not survive close scrutiny', thereby missing the point that the four colleagues whom he was denouncing had not argued for residues that were *rival* to Christianity, but against this idea.[126]

At the same time a current in the different discipline of religious studies was carrying a few scholars in the opposite direction. This was to define paganism as comprising any cultic behaviour that involves a veneration of the natural and/or features 'worship at an unreflective and spontaneous level' and/or derives ultimately from an animist, polytheist, pantheist or shamanic world picture. It could involve subliminal and unconsciously automatic activities such as tossing a coin in a fountain, wishing somebody good morning or proposing a 'toast' in alcohol. This formulation views it as an intrinsic part of religious activity in itself, so that identifiable pagan practices variously infuse all faiths, though they can be developed into full religions in their own right (among which this definition would include not just the pre-Christian traditions of Europe and the Near East and Modern Paganism, but Chinese folk religion, Shinto, primal tribal religion, Amerindian spirituality and Afro-American Spiritism). This is essentially an ahistorical view, a timeless and global exercise in comparative religion. Whatever its merits as such, it has little relevance to a study of medieval and early modern European cultures, where the adoption, exclusion and contestation of the pre-Christian heritage went far beyond the embodiment of 'an underlying subliminal, organic and natural apprehension'.[127]

Revisionism, therefore, like most reformations, has shattered a former near-unity but not produced a new one, generating a number of competing positions instead. The present book is intended as a contribution to the resulting debate, with the intention not of directly refuting any of the voices in it but of recasting the basic terms of the discussion. It is designed to look at a set of figures in the medieval and early modern European imagination which do not seem to fit very well into the categories of pagan or Christian. One of them was found in learned and elite culture, and three in popular culture. Between them, they may be suggested to challenge the religious polarities and dualities around which discussion has been centred, perhaps, for too long.

CHAPTER 2

MOTHER EARTH

T he first figure to be discussed in this context is the one found in learned and elite culture, at least until the late modern age. She consists of a mighty female being thought to represent the whole of the natural world, or at least the terrestrial realm of it. Sometimes she functions as a mediatrix between heaven and earth, and correspondingly between a greater divinity than herself and human beings. She has variously been named Natura, Mother Nature, Mother Earth and (in recent times) the Great Earth Mother, the Mother Goddess or simply the Great Goddess.

The Ancient Context

The pagan ancient world could conceive of such divinities, representing the whole of nature and the earth, but they tended to be marginal to actual cult practice. Some ancient goddesses acted as the patronesses of particular kingdoms and peoples, and sometimes were regarded as giving fertility to their lands as well, most notably a trio in Asia Minor: Cybele in Phrygia, Artemis in Lydia and Hecate in Lycia. Others embodied or protected parts of the landscape, such as Ninhursaga in Mesopotamia, who cared for the wombs of creatures and was married to the paramount sky god – but was herself the indwelling spirit of the deserts and mountains that ringed the region, while the Mesopotamian landscape itself was in the hands of other deities.[1] The Greek Gaia and the Roman Terra Mater, on the other hand, did approximate far better to the later universal Earth Mother. Gaia certainly represented the whole terrestrial realm and was a maternal figure in that she produced the principal family of Greek deities, while Terra Mater was literally 'Mother Earth' or 'The Earth Mother'. Here, however, the problem of worship kicks in. Most references to Gaia feature in literary texts, such as the poems of Hesiod and the Homeric and Orphic hymns, which use her as an emblematic figure. In 1985 the dominant authority on ancient Greek religion, Walter Burkert, could conclude that her true place was in the literature of 'speculation', adding that 'in customary religion the role of Gaia is exceedingly modest', confined mainly to the pouring of libations.[2] Since then, more evidence has been turned up, and the current position seems to be that most Greeks seemed to know about her, but that her worship consisted only of a statue or a place for offerings in a few temples of her son or grandson Zeus, and an annual offering in two local religious calendars.[3]

Terra Mater is even less well attested in religious practice. The emperor Augustus included her near the end of a long list of deities to receive sacrifices during one cycle of state-provided games. She was accompanied in this honour by the Fates and the goddesses who protected childbirth, as forces that guarded fertility.[4] There seems, however, to be not a single temple or shrine or even a statue dedicated to her anywhere in the Roman Empire, and no private inscriptions or dedications to her throughout the western half of the empire, which was the region in which such a figure was later to become prominent. Instead, Rome had a much more important goddess of earth, Tellus, who was specifically the power who quickened the fertility of cultivated soil, and to whom temples certainly were raised. In actual worship, Tellus was paired with the grain goddess Ceres, and the latter's shadowy husband, Cerus, and both were accompanied by twelve lesser figures with particular responsibilities for different aspects of the farming cycle.[5] Ancient religion tended to be localized, in specific regions, cities and people, and also practical, in that deities were invoked because of the particular aspects of life over which they wielded power. It seems that the Greeks and Romans could conceive of mighty figures which encompassed the whole of the earth and the natural world, and put them into their literature as symbolic and allegorical figures, but they did not have a lot of use for them in actual worship.

It may be that this began to change towards the end of the ancient world, in the mystery cults which were appearing as a feature of late Roman paganism: closed cults of initiates dedicated to one or two divine figures, with whom members were able to form especially intense personal relationships. One of these was dedicated to the Egyptian goddess Isis and is the subject of one of the most famous novels to survive from antiquity, that from the second century by Apuleius of Madaura which has long been popularly known as *The Golden Ass*. Towards the end of it, Isis herself manifests in response to a plea, and is portrayed as associated with the full moon and addressed as 'blessed queen of heaven'. She then introduces herself as 'nature, mother of all, mistress of the elements, primordial daughter of time, ruler of all spiritual matters, queen of the dead, queen also of immortal beings, the single manifestation of all gods and goddesses'.[6] This is truly a universal deity, claiming to speak for all and represent the entire cosmos, and it may be exactly how the initiates of this mystery religion actually regarded her. On the other hand, it is not clear how far Apuleius was intending a genuine, and serious, representation of the cult, and how far his representation of the goddess is an inventive and literary one, intended for non-initiates.

Bobbing alongside these unequivocal deities, from the classical Greek period onwards, were more abstract figures employed by philosophers and poets to personify the natural world, the Greek Physis and the Roman Natura. To Aristotle, Physis was the power which generated and animated living things and fashioned and embodied the elements and primary materials of the world. As such, she (or it) had domain over the changeable terrestrial environment below the level of the changeless heavens which were the seat of the highest and purest divinity.[7] This meant that she (or it) could be associated with Plato's concept of the world soul, an entity endowed by the creator god with the role of linking his own eternal and ideal realm with that of material and mortal beings and acting as ruler over them.[8] For the rest of antiquity philosophers elaborated and combined these figures, as cosmological abstractions, in different ways, with Physis translated into Latin, and the Roman world, as Natura.[9] Roman poets of the imperial period subsequently picked up the concept of nature as a cosmic power, led by Ovid, who declared that order was first established in the world by 'divinity and nature', and Lucretius, who called 'creatrix nature' the maker and governess of all things.[10] At some point later in the period of the empire, one of the Orphic hymns addressed Aristotle's Physis as a deity, in a collection which honoured not only familiar goddesses and gods with long-established cults but also abstractions such as Night which had never been worshipped. Physis belonged to the latter category, hailed as a bisexual and timeless spirit, connecting heaven and earth and ruling over and giving life to the world.[11]

The Antique–Medieval Transition

The literary tradition of a mighty goddess representing the whole natural world developed further in the transitional period between the ancient and medieval worlds, the fourth and fifth centuries. The Roman emperors were now almost all Christian (and all those who ruled for more than a brief period were), and Christianity was becoming first the most favoured religion in the empire and then – by the 390s – the only legally permitted one. At the same time, admiration for the literary heritage of pagan Greece and Rome remained almost as strong as ever, knowledge of it still representing a qualification for membership of the social elite. As a result, in the decades around 400 it is sometimes difficult to tell whether a particular author belonged to the old or new religion, as his enthusiasm for pagan mythology would suggest the former, but his position in the imperial court or hierarchy would seem reserved for the latter.

One such is Claudian, the last great classical Roman poet. In one of his works, he repeated the theme of how 'Mother Nature' (as he now firmly called her) produced an ordered world out of chaos, and hailed her as the generous provider of crops for humanity. In another he provided the first real visual portrait of her to date, as a divine being, seated 'immensely old yet ever beautiful, with spirits crowding and flying all around her'.[12] An author from this period whose Christianity was certainly not in doubt was Augustine of Hippo, the most influential of all the theologians of late antiquity, who felt obliged to consider the figure of Natura given her place in philosophy. On the whole, his conclusions were favourable, as he declared the natural world to be a teacher and guide to humanity, appointed by the Christian God to carry out his will. He wobbled over whether that nature should be considered an animate being, with a personality, first endorsing the idea and then withdrawing it without actually condemning it.[13] That opened a path whereby belief in such a being could be expressed, at least poetically and allegorically, by the orthodox.

Other Christian writers of the fourth and fifth centuries picked up the question of the place of nature in the cosmos and answered it in much the same way, drawing as Augustine did on the answer provided by Aristotle and the pagan philosophers whom he and Plato had inspired. They tended to do so for a particular polemical purpose: to condemn the pagan belief in an animate natural world, presided over by deities who often embodied particular aspects of it. Against this, they asserted that their own true God had created the whole universe and governed it in person ever after, so that the natural world was his product and servant. A spin-off consequence of this argument, however, was that they tended to personify nature as an animate being, of female gender, instructed by the Christian God to provide for humanity and to act as a teacher and guide for it. At times they made her speak in her own voice.[14]

A very good example of how such an entity could make the transition from paganism to Christianity, and from abstraction to active invocation, is provided by the Latin poem *Praecatio terrae matris*, which was composed by an unknown author, probably but not certainly pagan, towards the end of the Western Roman Empire. The opening section of it has survived, and is a very sophisticated and polished literary composition, eulogizing the fertile land as 'Earth, Divine Goddess, Mother Nature', who offers protection and nourishment: it fits into the salutation of this being in poetry during this period. What is significant about it in this context is that it was preserved by being incorporated into early medieval medical works as a charm to be used when collecting plants for medicinal purposes. It was glossed in the earliest extant of these, from the sixth century, as 'the beginning of the prayer to earth employed by the pagans of old when they wished to collect herbs': it is possible that what had originated as a glittering piece of literature had indeed became used for this purpose by pagans, or that the later Christian author of this gloss was in error. At any rate, it became popular in this context, being found in several Continental manuscripts, and also an English one from the eleventh or twelfth century. It was adapted to a Christian model by the addition to it of a similar prayer directed to the Christian heavenly powers, so bringing the divine spirit of earth into the domain of those powers, much as Augustine, taking his cue from Aristotle and Plato, had suggested.[15]

A similar theology was manifested in an Anglo-Saxon charm, which may possibly have been influenced by the *Praecatio*. This is the *Aecerbot*, or Field Blessing, already cited in the present book. It is known from a single manuscript of the late tenth or early eleventh century, with its cry of 'Erce, erce, erce, earth's mother'.[16] It is a long and elaborate act of magic to increase the fertility of a piece of land, involving the consecration of pieces of earth from it, with both various natural substances and Christian masses and prayers, and the invocation of the Christian Trinity and evangelists. All this takes place before 'earth's mother' is addressed, and she is treated not as an active power in her own right but as one to whom 'the eternal lord' must grant prosperity. Thereafter that 'God' is implored again repeatedly, and the ceremony ends with a triple repetition of the Lord's Prayer. The term 'erce' has been the object of much scholarly speculation. It does not work grammatically in Anglo-Saxon, and may possibly be the name of a former pagan goddess, though one attested nowhere else and who would be an odd addition to such a liturgically inspired text; a neat solution recently proposed is that it functions perfectly as a form of a contemporary Irish verb signifying 'may you be abundant'. Anglo-Saxon medical texts show many other imported Irish words and phrases, so this would fit the context well.[17]

It seems, therefore, that, on making the transition to the Christian era, a being who had operated in pagan literature as a philosophical and allegorical abstraction had become one who could be supplicated for aid within a firmly Christianized theological setting. This development was doubtless made the easier by the lack of any apparent existing cult centres or iconography of her; but it is also telling that she seemed to fill a conceptual gap within the Christian cosmos so neatly.

The Medieval and Early Modern Periods

The next great development in the figure took place in that major efflorescence of Latin Christian culture, produced by a mixture of political stability, economic prosperity and a large-scale recovery of ancient texts, which has become known as the Twelfth-Century Renaissance. In particular, it was associated with one of the most notable schools which embodied this movement: that attached to the superb cathedral which was being constructed in the French city of Chartres, south of Paris. The scholar connected to it who took up the figure of Natura, and in spectacular fashion, was Bernard Silvester, working around 1150, who gave her a major role in an epic for the first time. He portrayed her as a divinity created by the Christian God who initiates the formation of a beautiful world from the crude matter of primal creation. In his allegorical fable, she persuades the divine intellect (also personified as a goddess, and identified with the Roman Minerva) to undertake the work of making an ordered and lovely universe. The resulting achievement is then animated by Plato's world soul, likewise represented as a female being, and Natura fashions the bodies to contain the souls engendered by the world one. The divine intellect then gives her the task of creating and instructing humanity, which she does with the help of two other goddess figures, Urania, representing the heavens, and Physis, representing the earth, under the overall authority of the Christian Trinity.[18]

Bernard's work was immediately followed up by another scholar associated with Chartres, Alan of Lille, between 1160 and 1184, in a pair of works which begin by saluting Natura as the ruler of the world on behalf of the Christian God and the maker of humanity. Under her master's instructions, and emphasizing her utter dependence on his authority, she makes humans the gift of procreation to continue their species, enlisting the aid of the pagan goddess of sex, Venus, though Venus mars the work by investing humans with sinful and sensual desires as well as the healthy and preordained one of producing children. Alan supplies a vivid visual portrait of Natura, her crown glittering with jewels representing the heavenly bodies and her clothing embroidered with images of animals and plants. She travels in a glass coach, drawn by peacocks and driven by a handsome male giant. At her arrival on earth, the birds and fish come to greet her, the sun shines more brightly and the fields sprout flowers.[19] She is also the heroine of his second work, a poem in which Natura sets out to make a new and better kind of human, lacking the flaws in the existing one. It gives her a home, a columned palace set in a forest and painted with images of famously wise and brave people, to which she calls the virtues, personified as her sisters, to assist her. God sanctions the project and creates the soul of the new being, while Natura models its body, and so a new and better era begins.[20] Both Bernard Sylvester and Alan of Lille knew the poems of Claudian and were influenced by them.

Their books, though philosophical and theological allegories, were wholly or partly in verse, and, just as in antiquity, genuine poets now followed where philosophers had led. Already in the 1180s another Frenchman with connections to Chartres, Jean de Hauteville, composed a work in which a young man goes on a quest to find Natura and be healed of his woes and learn from her the meaning of the world and the best way to live in it (which he does, and she gives him a wife, Moderation, as well).[21] During the following two centuries, the greatest poets of their time in both France and England made use of her. The French one was Jean de Meun, in his version of the *Roman de la Rose*, a quest romance embodying a discussion of erotic love, which he wrote in the 1270s. Once more, Natura has responsibility for the making of mortal beings and the continuity of life on earth, as God's chamberlain there and queen of the world. De Meun does not provide a portrait of her, commenting only that her beauty is beyond description, but equips her with a palace that comes complete with a Christian chapel. He reveals that those who keep her laws go after death to an especially delectable pastoral paradise caught in a perpetual springtime.[22] The Englishman, a hundred years later, was Geoffrey Chaucer, in the poem commonly known as *The Parliament of Fowls*. His Nature is a goddess fairer than any other earthly being, enthroned in a palace of green boughs set upon a hill covered with flowers. She presides over the annual springtime assembly of birds, at which they choose their mates for the year: Chaucer references Alan of Lille for the idea that she represents the God-created world and acts as God's deputy there, and he was well acquainted with *Le Roman de la Rose*.[23]

This celebration of her at times provoked counterblasts. One of the most notable was a long poem composed by a fourteenth-century French monk and translated into English early in the following century. It was at least in part a reply to *Le Roman de la Rose*, and portrayed Nature as a quarrelsome old woman, in order to elevate the spiritual and eternal over the material and changeable.[24] Generally, however, late medieval representations of her were admiring, largely due to the great influence of *Le Roman*. One of the most delightful was in a French quest romance, composed around 1400 and rapidly turned into English, in which Nature manifests to the princely hero on a spring morning as a bright goddess clad in a robe woven with pictures of all earthly things. She fills his bedchamber with the scents of ambergris and roses and sends him on his search for worthiness.[25] Her appearances became rarer as the Middle Ages ended and allegory became less popular as a literary form, although she resurfaced when it was adopted: notably, for example, in *The Faerie Queen*, the epic produced by the Elizabethan Englishman Edmund Spenser. His Nature is a radiant, ageless and mighty supernatural being, invested with divine authority to carry out her tasks. A pavilion of trees spontaneously grows up to receive her, flowers spring up beneath her feet and the spirits of rivers pay her homage, even as the classical deities of Greece and Rome recognize her as much greater than they.[26]

Early modern scholars, however, were more inclined to envisage a great female entity embodying or superintending the earth on behalf of the Christian Almighty in the form of the Platonic world soul, which underwent a revival at this time in accordance with the revival of interest in Plato's works in Western Europe. The seventeenth-century Jesuit polymath Athanasius Kircher, publishing in Rome, prefaced one of his books with a woodcut of the goddess Isis in this role, as described by Apuleius.[27] A Jacobean English occultist, publishing in Germany, also made Isis the Soul of the World, this time using ideas from another author working in the Roman Empire, Plutarch. In his frontispiece illustration she stands nude, with flowing hair and a crown of stars. A crescent moon covers her pudenda, another her left breast and a star her right one, though it is clear that rays or seeds are streaming to earth, like mother's milk, from the nipple beneath the star. The hand of God holds a chain attached to one of her arms, while in turn she holds another attached to an arm of Man. She has one foot on land and another in water.[28]

It may thus be seen that the concept of a mighty female figure embodying and ruling over the terrestrial world was embedded in Christian intellectual and literary culture all through the periods in which Christianity most completely dominated Europe, the medieval and early modern. The idea that this being could be supplicated as part of fertility and medicinal rites seems to be confined to the earlier Middle Ages, as no more is heard of it after the eleventh century: it appears to have functioned as a transitional notion. Allegorical use of a goddess-like entity called Nature or the world soul, however, only gathered strength thereafter, to become an enduring component of elite Christian thought.

The Modern Nature Goddess: The Literary Personification

The main effect of the advent of true modernity on the figure of Nature, Mother Earth or the world soul was to strip away the empowering and dominating figure of the Christian God from her cosmos and leave her to reign in her own right. This could be done with all the more enthusiasm in that one of the main features of the Romantic Movement, that great cultural current that swept Europe in the late eighteenth and early nineteenth centuries, was to eulogize the natural world as a fount of wisdom, beauty and redemption from the more corrupting and debilitating aspects of civilization and urbanization. It was achieved with the greatest drama and violence, though also the greatest brevity, in the French Revolution, where a national cult of Nature was instituted by the revolutionary government to replace Christianity. It lasted only long enough to stage one festival, on 10 August 1793, the anniversary of the final overthrow of the French monarchy, upon the site of the now-demolished royal fortress-prison of the Bastille. At sunrise a chorus of girls dressed in white performed a hymn to the goddess by one of the revolutionaries' favourite composers, François-Joseph Gossec, and then a cantata was sung based on a text by their favourite philosopher and eulogist of Nature, Jean-Jacques Rousseau. The president of the National Convention next ascended a flight of white steps to a statue of the goddess, enthroned between two lions, with water pouring from her breasts into a tank below. He hailed the deity, asked her to bless and fructify France, and poured a libation of the water in the name of liberty. Eighty-six old men then followed his example, each representing one of the new administrative departments of the nation, and each being announced with drum rolls and fanfares of brass and his action followed by the firing of cannon. A huge crowd watched the ceremony.[29]

Within a year the regime which had instituted this cult was overthrown, and the new observance fell with it. Instead, a reverence for a personified natural world proved to be more enduring, if less dramatic, in England, which not only became as deeply imbued with Romanticism as any other country but responded to its adulation of that world with the more intensity because of its sudden, extreme and unprecedented degree of urbanization and industrialization.[30] Of the first major generation of English Romantic poets, in the late 1810s, two in particular articulated aspects of it. One was Percy Shelley, who introduced the classical deity Proserpine, daughter of the Roman corn-goddess Ceres, with an invocation to her mother as:

> Sacred Goddess, Mother Earth,
> Thou from whose immortal bosom
> Gods, and men, and beasts have birth,
> Leaf and blade, and bud and blossom,
> Breath thine influence most divine
> On thy own child Proserpine.
>
> If with mists of evening dew
> Thou dost nourish these young flowers
> Till they grow, in scent and hue,
> Fairest children of the Hours,
> Breathe thine influence most divine
> On thy own child Proserpine.[31]

This is much more the divine nature as described by the medieval authors than the Roman grain goddess. The association of that greater being with the night sky also endured in the work of these poets, most vividly in that of the other poet who is especially relevant here, John Keats. He also celebrated Nature as donor of a delightful store of luxuries and patroness of deities and nymphs.[32] It was, however, when he turned his eyes towards the celestial that his invocation became most passionate:

> What is there in thee, Moon! that thou shouldst move
> My heart so potently? when yet a child
> I oft have dried my tears when thou hast smiled.
> Thou seemst my sister: hand in hand we went
> From eve to morn across the firmament.
> . . .
> And as I grew in years, still didst thou blend
> With all my ardours: thou wast the deep glen;

Thou wast the mountain's top – the sage's pen –
The poet's harp – the voice of friends – the sun ;
Thou wast the river – thou wast glory won;
Thou wast my clarion's blast – thou wast my steed –
My goblet full of wine – my topmost deed:
Thou wast the charm of women, lovely Moon![33]

At times the former Christian pattern of a cosmic feminine force subject to a patriarchal sky deity lingered among creative writers. Charlotte Brontë's 1847 novel *Jane Eyre* was the work of an author who was herself the daughter and wife of clergymen, and made her heroine consider a life as a missionary abroad. It is, however, the moon and not Jesus that appears at moments of especially intense emotion in her life, and at one of these takes the form of a white divine female in a dream, to give her advice: she addresses this being as 'mother'. Having run away from her previous existence and finding herself alone and penniless, sleeping rough on a moor, she is comforted first by the thought of Nature, again conceived of as maternal, and next by that of a loving God, as creator of Nature.[34] At times, the same heavenly–earthly divine relationship could be blended with traditional classicism, as in the work of another celebrated mid-Victorian writer, the poet Robert Browning. For his representative of the natural world, he chose the Greek goddess Artemis, patroness of wild places and animals and of the night, and elevated her status to the greatest female divinity next to Hera, the latter being wife to the patriarchal sky god Zeus and so queen of deities. Once more, the equation between wild nature, the moon and the divine feminine was articulated, and Browning gives this goddess dominion in the sky, the earth and the underworld as well:

I am a goddess of the ambrosial courts,
And save by Hera, Queen of Pride, surpassed
By none whose temples whiten this the world.
Through heaven I roll my lucid moon along;
I shed in hell o'er my pale people peace;
On earth I, caring for the creatures, guard

Each pregnant yellow wolf and fox-bitch sleek,
And every feathered mother's callow brood,
And all that love green haunts and loneliness.[35]

Another course was, however, possible for mid-Victorian writers of a more radical or counter-cultural turn of mind, and one of these was Algernon Swinburne. In 1867 he introduced his readers to a mighty female deity, embodying and creating the universe herself, to whom he gave the Germanic name Hertha, to signify a goddess representing the whole earth. Her declaration commenced:

I am that which began,
Out of me the years roll,
Out of me, god and man,
I am equal and whole;
God changes, and man,
And the form of them bodily;
I am the soul.

Before ever land was,
Before ever the sea,
Or soft hair of the grass
Or fair limbs of the tree,
Or the flesh-coloured fruit of my branches,
I was, and thy soul was in me.

First life on my sources,
First drifted and swam,
Out of me are the forces
That save it or damn;
Out of me, man and woman,
And wild-beast, and bird;
Before god was, I am.[36]

Few were yet prepared to go that far, and later Victorian creative writers tended to want their earth goddess still to share her power. The medieval Christian role for her could be found consistently, for example in the poetry of George Meredith between the 1860s and 1880s. His passionate love of the English natural world shone through it across all these decades, and he often personified that world as 'Great Mother Nature' or 'Earth, the mother of all'. Meredith held that only by loving and understanding her could humans be truly led to an understanding of 'her just Lord', the Christian God, who presided over heaven and the afterlife even as the goddess presided over the earth and the mortal existence. His attitude was summed up in the verse:

And are we the children of Heaven and Earth,
We'll be true to the mother with whom we are,
So as to be worthy of Him who afar,
Beckons us on to a brighter birth.

Meredith found a place for the classical pagan deities in this scheme, declaring that Aphrodite, Apollo and Pan still had a place on earth and deserved respect there as a part of Nature, serving, loving and honouring her. He thus envisaged a divine hierarchy descending from God to Mother Nature or Mother Earth and through her to the Graeco-Roman goddesses and gods.[37] Another writer in this tradition was George Russell, who like his friend and collaborator William Butler Yeats (who has been cited earlier) made an eclectic personal mixture of religions. To him, the goddess of nature and earth was above all maternal, 'the Mighty Mother', 'ancient mother' or 'Virgin Mother', sometimes given the name Dana, from a presumed earth goddess in medieval Irish literature. His verse could be fired up with love for her:

Mother, thy rudest sod to me
Is thrilled with fire of hidden day
And haunted by all mystery.[38]

Ah, when I think this earth on which I tread
Hath borne these blossoms of the lovely dead,
And makes the living heart I love to bear,
I look, with sudden awe, beneath my feet
As you with erring reverence overhead.[39]

That last line reads like a rebuke to those who looked to a heavenly father, but in his poetry Russell referred indiscriminately to 'God', also called 'the Mighty Master' or the 'Heavenly Wizard', or to the earth goddess as the presiding power of the universe, without any sense of contradiction. He even found a place for Christ, though as an aspect of the Hindu god Krishna.[40] When he finally came to publish a formal synthesis of his cosmology, he firmly made the 'Lord and King' the creator and master of Nature, also called 'Earth the Mother of Us All', and the Olympian and Irish deities subservient to her, a hierarchy much the same as Meredith's.[41]

During this later period, however, some authors were prepared to follow Swinburne and grant the earth goddess independent and dominant power. The fantasy novelist and creator of short stories Algernon Blackwood in *The Centaur* (1911) sends its hero on a spiritual quest which culminates in a rediscovery of the Garden of Eden, as 'the heart of the Earth, his mother', where he knows 'the Great Atonement' of perfect union with Nature and so self-realization. His deity is explicitly 'his great Earth Mother'. From the time of the First World War, creative writers were less inclined to be concerned with deities in general, save for that minority which self-consciously represented traditional denominational positions. Instead, to more hard-bitten modernists, the qualities hitherto associated with the world goddess, namely the green earth and the night sky, became treated as hallmarks of the feminine in general. One very clear illustration of this is in the novels of D.H. Lawrence. In *The Rainbow* (1915) his heroine repeatedly seems to empower herself mystically by relation to the celestial lights of the night. In one passage she 'stood filled with the full moon, offering herself. Her two breasts opened to make way with it, her body opened wide like a quivering anemone, a soft, dilated invitation touched by the moon. She wanted the moon to fill in to her, she wanted more, more communion with the moon, more consummation.' In another she makes love with her boyfriend on chalk down turf at night and as she does so 'her eyes were open looking at the stars, it was as if the stars were lying with her and entering the unfathomable darkness of her womb, fathoming her at last'.[42]

Another of his heroines, Lady Chatterley, manifested the aspect of the nature goddess as the greenwood, this time after sex, when 'she was like a forest, like the dark interlacing of the oakwood, humming inaudibly with myriad unfolding buds. Meanwhile the birds of desire were asleep in the vast interlaced intricacy of her body.'[43] In *Women in Love* (1921), one of his male anti-heroes lashed out repeatedly at this image of transcendent womanhood, railing against 'the Great Mother of everything, out of whom proceedeth everything and to whom everything must finally be rendered up . . . He had a horror of the Magna Mater, she was detestable.' Later the same man symbolically threw stones into a pond to smash the reflection of the full moon in it, reviling 'the accursed Syria Dea' (one ancient great local goddess). Later still he found 'horrible' the idea that woman was 'the perfect womb, the bath of birth, to which all men must come'.[44] A piece written by Lawrence in 1924 contains the outburst 'Oh woman, wonderful is the craft of your softness, the distance of your dark depths. Oh open silently the deep that has no end and do not turn the horns of the moon against me.'[45]

By the twentieth century, therefore, the medieval image of a natural world personified as a single mighty goddess had retained its potency in response to modern needs and proved resiliently adaptable. To some creative writers, the earlier Christian concept of a ruling and empowering creator God still had traction, whereas to others, the goddess had been cut loose from it to function as a dominant entity in her own right. To yet others, she had become a repository of symbols and associations which could be used to inform a sense of female divinity in general, or even of femininity itself. It was not creative writers, however, who were to be the main fount of interest in such a figure during the modern era, but scholars, who were to project her into the remote past and across the globe, in a manner which supercharged her apparent importance and significance as a universal human concept.

The Modern Nature-Goddess: The Scholarly Personification

It seems to have been a German classicist, Eduard Gerhard, at Berlin in 1849, who first suggested that before the dawn of history the ancient Greeks had venerated a single great goddess, of whom the various female deities recorded in historic times had been aspects and derivations, who took individual form as the original belief disintegrated and localized.[46] It made sense that this idea should surface then and there. A generation of German Romantic thinkers, notably Johann Herder, Ludwig Tieck and Friedrich Schlegel, had argued that primitive human society had generally held religious beliefs which embodied sublime truths concerning the processes of nature and of human life. This was advanced in opposition to the dominant view taken by leaders of the French and Scottish Enlightenments that primeval religion had been a compound of superstition, ignorance and fear, from which civilization had rescued humanity: the Germans held instead that the closer to creation humans had been, the nobler their instincts. Tieck and Schlegel, the two younger men, had worked together in Berlin, the city of Gerhard. One of the sublime truths that ancient human intuition had attained was assumed to be monotheism, and in constructing an imagined single great goddess for the ancestors of the Greeks, Gerhard was giving specific expression to this idea.

During the later nineteenth century it was taken up by a few prominent French and German scholars, the former being classicists who were also experts in the growing field of Near Eastern archaeology, and the latter concerned with comparative mythology, as supported by archaeology.[47] The Frenchmen were able to point to the divine patronesses of the kingdoms of Asia Minor and the maternal nature-goddesses of Mesopotamia as models for what such an imagined prehistoric supreme deity might have been like. This strain of thought was given additional impetus at the end of the century, when prehistoric sites in south-eastern Europe and the eastern Mediterranean islands began to reveal large quantities of figurines, most apparently female. There was no evidence that these represented goddesses, let alone a single great one, but also no disproof of that idea, and so they began to be enlisted in support of it.[48]

By now, some British scholars were becoming converts, and one of the most notable was Sir Arthur Evans, discoverer of the Minoan civilization of ancient Crete. Those Cretan sites were also revealing prehistoric female figurines, and while in the 1890s Evans did not associate them with any specific deity, in 1901 he identified them firmly as being the same one as the Mesopotamian mother goddess, whose cult he believed had spread to the Levant.[49] In the next year he declared that all of the apparently different goddess images found in Minoan Crete were actually aspects of one great deity, whom he termed the Virgin Mother.[50] Goddesses who conceived offspring apparently spontaneously were known in the ancient world, but were rare. Evans's elevation of the type to dominance allowed him to unite female deities of apparently varied kinds, but it in addition is hard to imagine that it would have had such traction on him without the example provided by the Christian Virgin Mary, which would have operated also in the case of George Russell's use of the same term for his universal goddess. By 1931 Evans had extended the realm in which this deity form was venerated to include all of Greece, Asia Minor, Syria and Egypt.[51] By the time that he first became convinced of her prehistoric existence, another element was entering the construct, which had emerged from a debate between lawyers over the origins of society and the human family. It was supplied first by a Swiss jurist and academic, Johann Jakob Bachofen, in 1861, who, relying largely on ancient Greek myth, proposed that the earliest human societies had been run by women, altering to a male-led form before the beginning of history. Naturally, he suggested that the prehistoric woman-centred culture had a religious focus on an earth mother goddess.[52] This was imported into Britain in 1875, in J.F. MacLellan's *Primitive Marriage*. A female-dominated society could readily be paired with a religion of a great goddess. That pairing was made influentially in Britain in 1903 by a Cambridge academic, Jane Ellen Harrison, and once more in the particular case of ancient Greece. This was for the Victorians and Edwardians a culture of particular exemplary power, because not only was the evidence for it so rich but it was regarded with some justice as the foundation of all succeeding European civilization, and with more subjectivity as the most admirable in the ancient world. Harrison suggested not only that prehistoric Greek society had been matriarchal but that it had been centred on the cult of a single great goddess who had three aspects, of which the first two were Maiden and Mother (she did not name the third). She portrayed this being as functioning to the subordinate male deities as 'somewhere between Mother and Lover, with a touch of the patron saint'. Her rule, according to Harrison, was overthrown before history began, with the imposition of male dominance in both the human and divine spheres, the goddess's role in the latter being supplanted by the celestial father-god Zeus, to whom she referred, rather charmingly and with a very apparent eye on her contemporary society, as 'an archpatriarchal bourgeois'.[53] Harrison relied especially on German lexicons and dictionaries which drew attention to those Greek goddesses who appeared in triple form, such as the Fates, and Hekate and Diana. Poets and philosophers under the Roman Empire had sometimes compared the three faces of the last two deities to the phases of the moon. These ideas were developed further by scholars commenting on famous classical texts, in that boundary phase between paganism and Christianity that had produced Claudian: notably Servius in the fifth century, who declared that the goddess known as Diana on earth had been known as Luna above it and Proserpina below it, and that her three aspects had respectively presided over birth, life and death.[54]

In the following twenty years, a set of leading classicists at Oxford and Cambridge endorsed the idea of a single prehistoric deity, a goddess associated with the earth and motherhood, as the focal point of the oldest Greek religion.[55] By this time, the range of that deity's worship was being greatly extended by some scholars. In 1903 a distinguished British scholar, of medieval and early modern drama, spoke of an earth mother goddess, associated both with fertility and death, as having been worshipped under various names and forms in many ancient civilizations as the fundamental form of ancient female deity.[56] Three years later, a German one declared that such a goddess had been found universally throughout humanity, as one of the most ancient and primordial of human religious conceptions.[57] Over the following decades more and more anthropologists picked up this idea and interpreted the beliefs of indigenous peoples in conformity with it; indeed, it has been alleged that these researchers actually erroneously convinced some of those peoples, especially in the Americas and Australia, that they had formerly held it. Thus, some native Australians did apparently believe in a divine mother figure, but had not connected her to the earth until white academics persuaded them to do so.[58] In 1908 a French archaeologist declared that a Great Goddess concerned with death and fertility had been worshipped by all the Neolithic peoples of Europe and the Near East, and that her cult had been focused above all on images of her eyes and breasts. This enabled him to use any figure or symbol on a Neolithic site which *could* be interpreted as representing an eye or a breast as proof of that cult.[59] Two years later an Italian medical scientist who wrote on prehistory asserted that matriarchal religion had held sway across Neolithic culture and had been brought to an end by an invasion of patriarchal barbarians whom he identified with the Indo-European peoples.[60] Finally, in 1929 a British archaeologist projected it backwards effectively to the beginning of human time by suggesting that the feminine figurines found on a scatter of Palaeolithic sites across Europe had also been images of the Great Goddess.[61]

As the twentieth century entered its central decades, a belief in a primeval human propensity, and especially one of Neolithic Europeans and Near Easterners, to venerate a great earth mother was spreading further, and especially in the English-speaking world. Hitherto it had made little impression upon experts on the prehistory of the British Isles themselves. Their Neolithic had produced spectacular stone monuments but was remarkably aniconic, free of symbols, images and figurines which could be interpreted as evidence for any kind of deity.

British writers who were not experts on prehistory, by contrast, had no such inhibitions, being carried away by the attraction of a nature-goddess figure which had been sweeping the West for a century. In 1898 a medical doctor with a mystical attachment to the Celtic past declared that ancient Ireland had been ruled by a high queen representing the land's Great Mother Goddess, whom 'the Celtic Church' turned into the Christian saint Bridget.[62] In 1932 a popular writer on the English countryside, Harold Massingham, produced a book on the Cotswold Hills in which he showed particular interest in their Neolithic chambered long mounds, which had been brought to public notice by an archaeological survey a few years before. That survey had scrupulously avoided commenting on the possible nature of the religion which had inspired the construction of these monuments while suggesting that they had been united by a common worship, but the popular author had no hesitation in declaring confidently that it had been devoted to Mother Earth. He seemed to elide this figure with what he termed 'the Sleeping Beauty of the countryside', who would be reawoken when 'the English recover their appetite for natural beauty and natural living'.[63] Yet, all the while, specialists in British archaeology held their peace.

That was broken after 1939, when a remarkable discovery was reported at the complex of Neolithic flint mines in Norfolk called Grimes Graves. At the bottom of one mine, a female chalk figurine was allegedly uncovered, seated on a crude altar and with a vessel, apparently for offerings, placed before her. This was sensational, and apparently decisive: none of the other Neolithic (or Palaeolithic) figurines from the rest of Europe and the Near East had been found in a context so clearly indicative of worship. The statuette accordingly appeared in books on the British Neolithic as a deity, and the Ministry of Works put it on the cover of its official guide to the site and reconstructed its 'shrine' for visitors to see. Not until the 1980s did doubt begin to be expressed publicly about the authenticity of the find, and not until the 1990s was a proper investigation carried out into the circumstances of discovery and the nature of the objects. That was not conclusive, because chalk artefacts cannot be chemically dated, but the discovery turned out to have been announced by the director of the excavation, without his having recorded it in the site note-book and after he had asked all other experienced archaeologists to leave the area. The figurine and vessel looked freshly carved, and somebody on the team was an expert sculptor and had made other objects during the dig from the same local rock.[64] As a result, and in view of the fact that nothing like this 'shrine' has been found anywhere else in Europe, it can no longer be accepted as reliable evidence.

At the time of its announcement, however, it opened the way for anybody who wished credibly to add the British Isles to the domain of the Neolithic Great Goddess. Two respected archaeologists to accept this invi-tation were a young married couple, Jacquetta and Christopher Hawkes, who proceeded in the course of the 1940s to publish textbooks in which they proposed that the builders of the megalithic monuments of Western Europe had been converted to the worship of a single great fertility goddess by missionaries moving up through the Mediterranean from her older cult centres in the Balkans and Levant. This religion had been replaced in turn, they argued, by new cults of sky gods introduced by the Beaker People, conquering westwards from Central Europe.[65]

At the end of the decade, Jacquetta abandoned both Christopher and professional archaeology to marry the playwright and novelist J.B. Priestley and become herself, throughout the 1950s and 1960s, a prolific writer of novels, plays, poetry and (above all) popular surveys of prehistory and the history of religion. The latter earned her an enormous readership, and she became one of the two first British members of the new United Nations cultural organization, UNESCO. The vision of the European Neolithic which she propagated was one of a woman-centred, peaceful and creative set of cultures, united by the worship of Nature, embodied as a single goddess, with whom they lived in harmony. This religion united the whole continent between the figurine-makers of the south-east and the megalith-builders of the west, with a series of specific cult centres between, such as the temples of Malta. In her version, which built directly on that devel-oped in the 1900s, it was destroyed by the Indo-Europeans, of whom the

Beaker People were the western spearhead, a horde of warlike and patriarchal invaders who substituted a religion centred on aggressive sky gods – so
rupturing permanently the harmony between peoples and sexes, and
between humans and the land.[66]

The belief that Neolithic Europe had venerated a single great goddess
representing mother earth now at last became something like a general
orthodoxy among the leaders of British archaeology. During the 1950s it
was adopted by four of them: Gordon Childe, O.G.S. Crawford, Stuart
Piggott and Glyn Daniel. Crawford made something like a dramatic personal
conversion to it during a holiday in Brittany in 1953 and devoted a large and
euphoric book to propagating the idea to the general public.[67] He and
Childe projected the image into later ages, the latter asserting that memories
of the prehistoric goddess lay behind the medieval Christian veneration of
female saints, and Crawford finding traces of her in a range of folk customs,
including corn dollies. In a circular process, the interpretation of newly
discovered ancient sites was made in conformity with the belief in her cult,
and so appeared to reinforce the evidence for it. The most spectacular
example of this effect was probably James Mellaart's revelation and excavation of a Neolithic town in Turkey dating from 6500 to 5700 BC, at Catal
Höyük, in the early 1960s: this was the biggest urban settlement yet found
for the age. He immediately interpreted the female figurines there, and some
wall paintings and plaster reliefs, as images of 'the Mother Goddess' or 'the
Great Goddess', a deity of fertility and abundance of whom the later
goddesses of historic Greece were mere aspects. Male representations were
taken as those of her son and consort, as they had been by Evans in Crete:
this was a relationship found in two historic goddess cults in Anatolia.[68]
Mellaart also suggested that religious and social life had been dominated by
women. He then publicized these views both in reports for fellow experts
and popular textbooks.[69] He acknowledged to fellow archaeologists that his
own readings of his finds were 'speculation, not scientific fact', but declared
that 'at this period there was no doubt that the supreme deity was the Great
Goddess'.[70] In his popular works, his interpretations were generally presented
without even these qualifications, and as established truth.

To a great extent, the vision of a prehistory in which human society had been violently altered from being led by and centred on women to being dominated by men, and in which religion had changed its focus from an earth goddess to a sky god, was an obvious response to modern anxieties about gender roles in changing Western social orders. Nonetheless, the divine relationships being envisaged preserved a memory of the medieval origins of the two figures. In those, the earth goddess had a harmonious interaction with the sky god, as his creation and his deputy in caring directly for the earth and for generation. In the newly imagined past, the two were placed at odds with each other, the goddess initially both dominant and in a superior position to her own male consort as his parent, mate and leader. It was the sky god's cult which then overthrew and replaced her worship. The utility of this vision of the remote past was that it could be used to equal effect by both extremes of modern gender attitudes. To feminists of different hues, prehistoric social and/or religious matriarchy could be turned into an earthly paradise of peace, harmony within society, sound ecology and benevolent political and judicial structures. In this version, its violent overthrow turned the condition of humanity into one of war, oppression, exploitation and pollution, a new version of the Christian Fall or the ancient pagan myth of the human decline from a Golden to an Iron Age. To those who wanted to retain the traditional gender roles of Western society, at least as conceived in the nineteenth and early twentieth centuries, a female focus in religion and society could be disparaged and dismissed as a hallmark of the primitive and underdeveloped, a child-like phase from which the human race progressed as a first stage in its climb to the benefits of civilization and modernity. The same basic model of prehistory could thus be made to satisfy a range of modern ideological positions.

With this advantage, and the increasing endorsement of so many professional archaeologists, it is not surprising that it was taken up by a widening range of other writers between the 1920s and 1960s. In 1927 a medical doctor in London, Robert Briffault, published a large book to support the belief in prehistoric matriarchy and the rule of the Virgin Mother Goddess, with her son as her partner, worldwide. He developed the image of the goddess further from that supplied by Harrison, into a triple deity who appeared as young, mature and elderly, to match the phases of the moon.[71] This image, of a universal moon goddess who was simultaneously Maiden, Mother and Crone, was taken further by one of the greatest poets and novelists of the century, Robert Graves, in his celebrated publication of 1948, *The White Goddess*. It was specifically aimed at the general public, on the grounds that scholars were too timid and blinkered to recognize its truth, and consisted of a personal interpretation of texts taken from a very wide range of cultures, bridged by personal assertions of faith. Like Harrison and Briffault, who exerted a great influence upon him, he accepted completely the existence of prehistoric matriarchy in both society and religion, but his goddess was more particularly the patroness of poetry, as was natural enough to a poet.[72] Graves's book had an impact on Jacquetta Hawkes, and also on George Ewart Evans, the eminent collector of oral information on traditional rural crafts and lifestyles, who adopted the Great Earth Mother into the hinterland of his impression of history and declared that she had been revered in Britain long after the official triumph of Christianity.[73] James Mellaart interpreted the images at Catal Höyük in conformity with Briffault's and Graves's concept of a universal goddess who was at once Mother, Maiden and Crone.[74] In view of her prominence in the professional texts of archaeologists, as well as in the work of Briffault, Graves and Hawkes, it is not surprising that when the modern Pagan religion of Wicca was revealed to the public in the 1950s, its principal female deity was characterized as the Great Mother who rules the natural world and gives birth to all life.[75]

Moreover, scholars in other academic disciplines were persuaded by the archaeologists to adopt the same concept as an established feature of remote prehistory. During the 1950s an expert in medieval Welsh literature declared that prominent female characters in it were echoes of the Great Mother Goddess, preserved in immemorial, orally transmitted, myths.[76] Experts in the history of religion now routinely incorporated her worship into their accounts of its early development, as a now proven fact.[77] One of the most important and fruitful interdisciplinary impacts of the concept was on the relationship between archaeology and psychology, which likewise peaked in the middle of the twentieth century. Sigmund Freud himself had apparently said nothing directly about the primeval divine feminine, although his work did emphasize the universal importance of mother figures. Carl Jung, in view of his famous emphasis on the crucial role of archetypes, was likewise also surprisingly reluctant to embrace the idea of the ancient goddess. While declaring that the essential archetype was that of the mother, he saw the goddess as merely one derivation from it, and not of immediate concern to psychologists because her image was rarely encountered in the modern world. Indeed, he seemed to imply that he only considered her at all because historians of religion were making such a fuss about her.[78] It was left to one of his disciples, Erich Neumann, to argue in 1963 that the evidence for the universal ancient goddess indicated that the archetype of the Great Mother had been a constant 'inward image at work in the human psyche'. He developed this belief into an elaborate theory of worldwide spiritual development, in which the goddess stood for the 'archetypal unity and multiplicity of the feminine nature' and even now determined 'the psychic history of modern man and of modern woman'. The system of symbols which he proposed by which to recognize ancient images of the universal goddess, and the different aspects in which she was supposed to appear, was based directly on the interpretations made by archaeologists of the evidence from southeastern Europe and the Levant.[79] A perfectly circular process was now set up, whereby psychologists such as Neumann used material provided by archaeology, and writers such as Jacquetta Hawkes could declare that psychology had proved that the archetype of the Great Mother was inherent in the human mind.[80]

Belief in the universal human worship of a great prehistoric goddess representing Mother Earth or Mother Nature was therefore dominant by the mid-twentieth century among both academic and popular writers; and its trajectory had exactly paralleled that of the belief in the survival of ancient paganism through the Middle Ages. Both had been deeply influenced by nineteenth-century German and French ideas, while becoming eventually especially popular in the English-speaking world. There, both had followed exactly the same chronology of acceptance, becoming fashionable in the 1890s and established by the Edwardian period, before being elaborated and reinforced still further through the first half of the twentieth century, to reach an apogee in the 1950s and 1960s. The concept of the Great Goddess was therefore, like that of surviving paganism, ripe to meet the wave of reassessment and revision of established ideological orthodoxies which swept the West from the late 1960s onwards.

Revision and Restatement

There had always been authors who were not convinced by the evidence for the prehistoric goddess. Both significantly and ironically, the Germans, who had done so much to pioneer the idea of her, were also the first national group of scholars to retreat from it, and that process started in the discipline which had launched them: Classics. In the 1920s some who were emerging as leaders in it there started to question Evans's attempt, in particular, to reduce all Minoan goddess images to a single one, a nature deity with a youthful male son and consort. They thought it more likely that these representations were of a multitude of different deities like those venerated by other ancient peoples.[81] In the English-speaking world, even as the opposite belief became dominant in the mid-twentieth century, there were still isolated experts who questioned it. A leading authority on the archaeology of Neolithic Malta, which had been taken as providing some of the most famous images that had been used to bolster belief in the Great Goddess, could still publish a textbook on it in 1959 which pointed out that this interpretation of them remained unproven, as did accompanying visions of ancient matriarchy on the island.[82]

From the late 1960s, such scepticism became general across most of the scholarly world. There was no great onslaught on the concept, just two pieces by young archaeologists focusing on different artefacts at opposite ends of Europe: Peter Ucko on the Neolithic figurines of the Levant and Andrew Fleming on the megalithic monuments of the north-west. Each pointed out that the evidence used to support the belief in veneration of a single great deity was not conclusive and could all be interpreted in other ways.[83] They emphatically did not *disprove* the veneration of such a goddess in the Neolithic, but showed that there was no solid basis for a belief in it; and that was enough for virtually all archaeologists. Nobody came forward to defend the departing orthodoxy, and it duly vanished from textbooks on prehistory in the English-speaking world during the 1970s. Even Jacquetta Hawkes mounted no defence, only referring to the change in passing in an article in which she condemned the whole of the so-called New Archaeology of the late 1960s and which drew heavily on structural models taken from sociology and anthropology and tended to ignore religion as too intangible a phenomenon to understand in pre-literate societies.[84] She subsequently declared that she would continue to believe in a Neolithic cult of the goddess as a personal opinion.[85] Though she lived for another three decades, she wrote no more popular studies of prehistory after 1968. Subsequently, some anthropologists, especially in the United States and Australia, attacked the manner in which they asserted that their predecessors had distorted the beliefs of indigenous peoples to bolster the idea that the veneration of Mother Earth was natural to all humanity.[86]

These developments were, as said, part of the wholesale inspection and rejection of former orthodoxies which was a feature of the period between 1967 and 1980. It was certainly not an antifeminist backlash, because (as said) the related constructs of the goddess and prehistoric matriarchy could be employed as readily for feminism as against it. However, there were features of the concept of the prehistoric Great Goddess which did seem unpalatable to many academics from the late 1960s and ran counter to aspects of intellectual culture from this time. There was something disturbingly essentialist, as an image of femininity, in the presentation of her that had been made by previous generations. It was all about womanhood as focused on fertility, pregnancy, motherhood and nurturing. There was nothing there about leadership in technology, public affairs, intellectual pursuits, creative arts, commerce or industry, absences which were the more striking in that the genuinely attested cults of historic ancient goddesses frequently did reference such roles. Moreover, the twentieth-century concept of the ancient Great Mother seemed essentialist in its sharp polarization of gender as well as its associations for femininity. This especially mattered because by the 1970s anthropology had brought in large quantities of new information about the way in which gender relations had been constructed in other human societies. It displayed the wide range of possibilities which were open to humans in this respect. In 1975 the British anthropologist Shirley Ardener could pose the question of whether Western categories of 'men' and 'women' might not be entirely an intellectual creation which some day could disappear.[87]

In this context, it was significant that previous prominent champions of the concept of the prehistoric goddess had often themselves been inspired by social and cultural conservatism. Jane Ellen Harrison had been a lifelong Tory who had opposed the suffragette campaign to secure women the parliamentary vote, holding that their influence should be confined to the cultural sphere.[88] Harold Massingham loathed modernity for its industrialization and urbanization, which he called an 'utter darkness and savagery'.[89] His favourite period was the Middle Ages, and his most admired institution the Roman Catholic Church, at least in what he imagined to be its medieval form in England.[90] Robert Graves's eulogy to the universal triple goddess as muse of poetry embodied a wholesale condemnation of modern poets, especially T.S. Eliot, Ezra Pound, W.H. Auden and Dylan Thomas.[91] Jacquetta Hawkes hated modernity as much as Massingham, and for the same aspects, though her most admired age in England was the eighteenth century, the Georgian period, which she saw as an apogee of beauty, civilization, order and hierarchy.[92] In many respects her books provided a prehistoric dimension to the sentimental conservatism represented in the same period by the histories of Sir Arthur Bryant and Sir Winston Churchill and the guides to English counties provided by Arthur Mee. A major feature of Erich Neumann's work was that it instinctually presupposed that the mass human psychology which was being created in his story was a male one, with the female archetypes as auxiliaries to its development.[93]

It mattered also that the whole construct of the downfall of the goddess religion in Europe, and the often associated one of primeval matriarchy, was bound up with a model of European prehistory as driven by successive invasions by newly arrived conquering races equipped with superior technology. This had been developed in the mid-nineteenth century, and was clearly inspired by the contemporary phenomenon whereby European settlers were occupying larger and larger areas of North America, Australasia and northern and central Asia at the expense of indigenous peoples. In the early twentieth century, the sweep of German and Soviet armies across large tracts of the continent during the world wars, and especially the second one, with its much greater component of ethnic displacement and massacre, made the model continue to seem familiar and relevant. The Hawkeses, writing in the early 1940s, drew an explicit parallel between ancient and modern to produce a sense of Britain as an island always threatened by attackers from the east. In the postcolonial, stable and increasingly united Europe of the late twentieth century, such a view came to seem much less instinctively obvious. Moreover, it did not seem to match a lot of the archaeology either, as processes of cultural change came to appear a lot more gradual, piecemeal and extended than had been formerly thought.[94]

There were, however, two qualifications to the quiet abandonment of the Great Goddess concept by authors on prehistory after 1970. One was that popular writers sometimes continued to put her cult into their works as an established orthodoxy of the Neolithic, simply because they were not aware of the change. The most prominent of these was Michael Dames, a lecturer in the history of art who during the late 1970s wrote a pair of widely selling books which interpreted the ritual landscape around the spectacular late Neolithic site of Avebury in Wiltshire in terms of that cult.[95] His ideas were based on those of Briffault, Graves and Jacquetta Hawkes, but his reading of archaeology itself was flawed, so that he assumed that monuments which actually belonged to different millennia were part of a single system – even though to Hawkes they had been separated by the great divide in her imagined past which had separated the era of the goddess and matriarchy from that of the sky gods and patriarchy.

Nonetheless, aided by his deep knowledge of the modern Wiltshire land-scape and the sweep and daring of his imagination, he both propagated the idea of the Neolithic goddess further among general readers, especially among the new counter-culture of the 1970s, and concealed from them the disappearance of belief in her among experts.

The other qualification is that the idea of the Neolithic Great Goddess was given a powerful new academic endorsement in the years around 1990 by a single front-rank academic archaeologist, Marija Gimbutas, at the University of California. She was the foremost Western expert in the prehistory of Eastern Europe, and between the 1950s and the 1970s produced a standard series of publications which at first paid no particular attention to ancient religion and then, when she turned to it, treated the evidence from the Greek and Balkan Neolithic as suggesting a range of different deities of both sexes.[96] After then, however, she moved to California and formed a personal association with the evolving US spiritual feminist (or 'Goddess') movement of the 1970s and 1980s, which sought to substitute the worship or honouring of a female deity for the male one of the Abrahamic faiths. This had already drawn upon some of the apparent evidence for prehistoric matriarchy and the veneration of an ancient great goddess produced by previous generations of writers.[97] Gimbutas's own work now gradually mutated to serve the beliefs and ideals of this movement, culminating in a pair of large and excitingly illustrated books at the end of her life, in the years around 1990, which were explicitly aimed at a popular and inexpert audience.[98] In these she fully restated, with complete and unqualified confidence, the view of the European and Near Eastern Neolithic as woman-centred in society and religion, (and so) peaceful and creative, and devoted to the worship of a single great goddess, this having been brought to a violent end by patriarchal, brutal and destructive invaders, the Indo-Europeans.

There was a paradox at the heart of this later work of hers. On the one hand, it was deeply traditional, drawing upon the ideas of predecessors as those had developed through the first seven decades of the twentieth century, down to and including Jacquetta Hawkes, James Mellaart, Erich Neumann and Michael Dames. In major respects – the goddess and the invasion – it was a continuation of the view of European prehistory taken in her youth, in the 1950s and 1960s, enriched with her own detailed knowledge of the south-eastern European material.[99] At the same time, she concealed this inherent conservatism of approach and interpretation by presenting her own restatement of the old model as something radically new, and concealing its debt to forebears. She emphasized instead that she had been the first to reveal 'the pictorial "script" for the religion of the Old European Goddess' and allowed Joseph Campbell, the well-known psychologist and author on the history of religion, to state in a foreword to one of her books that she had deciphered Neolithic symbolism even as the French scholar Champollion had discovered the meaning of Egyptian hieroglyphics. She declared herself the first scholar 'to bring into our awareness essential aspects of European prehistory that have been unknown or simply not treated on a pan-European scale'.[100] This approach had the important tactical benefit of concealing the extent to which the former deployment of the concept of the Great Goddess had been bound up with reactionary, restrictive or sexist attitudes to society and gender. By emphasizing instead the value of the goddess figure as one of general female majesty and empowerment, and jettisoning its especial association with fertility and motherhood, she refashioned it for a new and politically radical audience. A large part of the power of the concept of the primeval Great Goddess, for over a hundred years, had been that it could be equally used for radical and reactionary purposes, to topple the foundations of a patriarchal society, or to denigrate and confine womanhood. Marija Gimbutas was the latest scholar to attempt the former project. The problem was that to fit the concept for her purpose she had remodelled it, whereas her professional colleagues, especially in Britain, had discarded it. Both were effective approaches to the problem of a figure with inconvenient trappings: unhappily, they were also mutually incompatible.

For a moment it looked possible that Western archaeologists might divide over the issue, with Americans on one side and Europeans on the other, or feminists on one and the rest of the professional community on the other, but it was not to be, as Marija Gimbutas, while attracting a fervent public following, won no allies among her peers and left no successors. Her dogmatic approach to evidence and use of what seemed to many to be outdated interpretative models alienated colleagues, and especially other self-consciously feminist archaeologists, including fellow Californians. These argued that a proper feminist archaeology should consist of a celebration of the ambiguity of the archaeological record and the plurality of interpretations possible from it, enabling a genuine diversity of vision.[101] When an Anglo-American team, led from a Californian university, commenced a systematic re-excavation of Çatal Höyük in the 1990s, it soon made a very different reading of the evidence from that of Mellaart – and thereby found itself in a sometimes uneasy interaction with (mostly American) feminists making pilgrimages to the site as a Goddess centre because of his works and those of Gimbutas.[102] One consequence of the latter's championing of the idea of the Neolithic goddess was, indeed, an abandonment by archaeologists in the English-speaking world of the earlier policy of ceasing to express belief in it without mounting much of a direct attack. In the two decades following 1993, there was an outpouring of publication from professionals, directly opposing the interpretation of Neolithic material as evidence for such a being and covering between them all the main sites in Europe and the Near East which had supplied it.[103] As a result, the figure of a single mighty goddess representing the natural and terrestrial world now seems to exist mainly as a component of a particular branch of contemporary spiritual feminism, with some crossover into traditions of modern Paganism.[104]

She has enjoyed a very long career, in which she has repeatedly demonstrated an ability to adapt to different ages of the world and their changing cultural needs. Drawing on ancient philosophical and poetic roots, she became a major figure in the European imagination virtually as soon as Christianity became dominant, as though there was a gap in Christian theology which demanded, for many thinkers and writers, such a figure. As that religion began to lose its hegemonic status among Europeans (and their descendants in other continents) with the onset of full modernity, she remained just as relevant, retaining her status as a powerful literary metaphor, allegory or personality and acquiring a new and very extensive back-projection as a component of the human past. She may have fresh glories before her yet.

CHAPTER 3

THE FAIRY QUEEN

The maternal earth goddess was, as shown, essentially a figure of high literary culture, although she eventually got into popular culture towards the end of the twentieth century in societies in which literacy had by then virtually become universal. The second being to be considered in this book spanned both ends of the cultural spectrum, apparently originating among the cultural elite but rapidly becoming well known at all levels of the social order. She was conceived of as being the queen of a parallel realm of human-like beings with superhuman powers, usually known as fairies. Unlike Mother Earth or Mother Nature, she did not appear until the later part of the Middle Ages, and was a distinctively British phenomenon, whose popularity ended with the early modern period.[1]

The Elvish Anarchy

Early and high medieval Britain did not have fairies, because the term had not yet been imported, but the parts of it which spoke English and Scots had roughly equivalent beings called elves, who were later to be elided with the category of fairy. The best extant study of the belief in them in Anglo-Saxon England has (inadvertently) revealed how little actually we know of it.[2] It is very clear that they were regarded as a menace, being held responsible for the infliction of sudden and mysteriously originating illnesses, rashes and pains in humans and their animals. Early English medical texts had various remedies for these, and protections against elf attack. It is also possible, though much less certain, that they targeted particular individuals, perhaps because the latter were in some way transgressive of human social norms, and so were not a habitual menace to society as a whole. A few authors increasingly equated them with demons or monsters, but there are strong linguistic hints in other texts that they could be beautiful and seductive (if dangerous), especially in female form, and these also seem to get stronger as the Anglo-Saxon period went on. There may in addition be some association of them with diviners or prophets, but there is no unequivocal evidence that they taught skills to or shared their powers with favoured people. There are no extant stories about them in Anglo-Saxon, or references to any, and no sense of a coherent tradition of them seems to emerge from the evidence. They certainly seem to have been regarded as existing within no parallel political or social system of their own, being treated instead as individual and capricious operators.

It must be emphasized, however, that these reflections are based on a very sparse and patchy survival of texts, all of which were created by a small, learned, clerical, male elite, and this may badly have skewed our impressions. Moreover, because our knowledge of context is so cloudy, confusion and ambiguity remain concerning specific bits of linguistic evidence. One example which may be chosen here is the Anglo-Saxon personal name Aelfwine, 'elf-friend'. Does it indicate that special people were expected to enjoy warm and mutually beneficial relationships with elves, by which the latter helped and aided them? Or was the name a gesture of propitiation to flatter and mollify elves, and so make the bearer less vulnerable than others to their attacks? We simply do not know, and that lack of knowledge is one illustration of our general ignorance concerning the ways in which these beings were regarded.

THE FAIRY QUEEN

The probability that no coherent view of elves was held in early medieval England is increased by the evidence provided by famous texts from the twelfth and thirteenth centuries, which have become more or less canonical in studies of British fairy tradition: those of Gerald of Wales, Ralph of Coggleshall, Gervase of Tilbury, Walter Map and William of Newburgh.[3] These dealt with alleged encounters of humans with non-humans in a human-like form who could not easily be fitted into conventional Christian concepts of angels or demons. Some of these occupied a parallel world to the human one, usually accessed through portals in hollows, mounds, lakes or hills, where they had a complete society, and were longer-lived and in other ways superior to humanity. Sometimes they were especially associated with the colour green, and some lived in or near people's homes, which they could enter to disrupt the occupants with mischievous tricks or assist them by performing useful tasks. Some blessed individual people who treated them graciously and generously, but some were apparently hostile to all humans, and afflicted them especially by leading them astray at night into pits or bogs. In one of the anecdotes recounted by Gerald of Wales, a boy in the Gower Peninsula went underground into a beautiful realm populated by a blonde race of small human size who were ruled by a king.[4] No real interest was shown in the tale, however, concerning this potentate, and the motif of a parallel kingdom was generally missing from the accounts furnished by these scholars.

Those accounts lack, indeed, any sense of a coherent belief system within which to contain and explain these stories. They cannot represent more than a portion of popular belief, because they entirely lack accounts of the infliction of injuries on people by such beings, without direct provocation, which are so prominent in the Anglo-Saxon sources and would be again later in the Middle Ages. On the other hand, the anecdotes strongly suggest that the beliefs and anecdotes concerned were shared by different social classes. As a number of modern scholars have pointed out, the intellectuals who recorded them struggled to create both a meaningful category within which to group them and a language for the beings described, as the range of Latin terms available did not quite seem to match the latter.

Collectively, they failed in both enterprises and often candidly admitted their puzzlement.[5]

There was, in addition, a tradition widely distributed across Western Europe, which like the Anglo-Saxon elves must derive from pre-Christian culture, of woodland beings which could take the form of beautiful people, of either gender, and have sexual intercourse with the humans whom they encountered and seduced. These seem to have been equivalent to the classical Greek and Roman nymphs and satyrs, and were variously described by clerical authors as *silvani* (wood beings), Pans, *agrestes feminae* (wild women), fauns or *Dusii*. The authors concerned naturally equated them with demons, and wrote to condemn the belief in them. Such authors spanned the fifth to the eleventh centuries and included such prominent ecclesiastics as Augustine of Hippo at the opening of that period and Burchard of Worms at its end.[6] It is not clear whether this belief extended to Anglo-Saxon England. One eleventh-century medical English text prescribes a salve 'against elf-kin and against a night-walker and against (or for) people who have sex with a (or the) devil'.[7] Once more, however, our ignorance of context fogs an understanding of the sense. The sex concerned could be voluntary (and so involve such sylvan beings) or involuntary and so probably refer to erotic dreams leading to orgasm (which medieval churchmen usually ascribed to incubus or succubus demons), in which case the salve repels a succession of uncanny nocturnal menaces: elves, incubi (or succubi) and whatever 'night-walkers' were. If the belief in seductive woodland entities did include Britain, it would make a very good fit with the likely beautiful and alluring associations of Anglo-Saxon elves, but again these associations are not absolutely certain.

What is sure is that by the late twelfth and the thirteenth centuries a tradition had crystallized in England of beautiful non-human women, and sometimes men, who appeared dancing at night in wild places, and with whom humans could mate. Walter Map, writing in the 1180s, told of a Welsh landowner who caught a woman in a group which emerged nightly from a lake to dance by moonlight, and had sons by her, until he hit her with a bridle (so transgressing a taboo) and she returned to the lake. He also provided a parallel story of an eleventh-century Shropshire lord who encountered a set of ladies, taller and nobler than humans, dancing in linen shifts in a house beside a forest at night. He seized one and married her, and she gave him a son before he broke the condition she had laid upon him for remaining – that he would not speak of her sisters, with whom he had found her – and she too vanished.[8] At times these beings could be more aggressive or sexually predatory. An account of the miracles that occurred at the shrine of St Swithun in Winchester included the curing of a man who had been crippled by three dark, naked women whom he had encountered in a lonely place near a river one evening. They had attempted to speak to him and he had run away, so provoking their anger that one caught, struck and blighted him before they vanished into the water.[9] Gerald of Wales heard of a Welsh sage who had lived into his own lifetime in Monmouthshire who had acquired powers of prophecy and lie detection, and power over demons. He had gained these after recovering from a bout of insanity, into which he had been plunged by making love with a beautiful girl one evening, who then turned into a shaggy, rough and ugly creature. Gerald also told of another Monmouthshire demon which made love with young women and revealed the future, and hidden secrets, to the local people.[10]

By the end of the thirteenth century, these figures had fused, at least in western England, into a composite image of beautiful beings who lived in the woods and on high hills and could be seen dancing and playing – and who lured humans to make love. The old name 'elves' was applied to them. This idea is found in a pair of texts produced in or near Worcester or Gloucester between 1270 and 1300, and the point made in these was that such beings were actually demons, former angels who had remained neutral during the rebellion of Satan and been punished with banishment to the earth (while the rebel angels went beneath it, to hell), and that people who coupled with them were usually afflicted with illness, and sometimes died.[11] Still, however, there was no sense that these were organized into a single society with a particular leader or leaders. That idea seems to have come from a very different source.

QUEENS OF THE WILD

Faierie

In the course of the twelfth century a new genre of literature emerged in Western Europe, and especially in its French-speaking lands: the romance. It was produced by and for a newly established social class, of militarized feudal landholders – nobles and knights – and their families and households, and featured the exploits of members of that class in deeds of martial and moral prowess. Its main purpose was to uphold and expound the nature of gentility as professed by this class. A strong element of marvel and magic ran through it, and this was partly embodied in beings which featured in the stories concerned who were often called fays. These had human forms and sumptuous lifestyles which mirrored those of the contemporary noble and knightly elite, but they disposed of apparently superhuman powers. They formed relations with people in the tales, acting as lovers, counsellors and protectors for them, or sometimes being exploiters, rapists, seducers or seductresses. Whereas the scholarly texts mentioned above dealt with incidents which were supposed to have happened in the real world, the romances were uninhibited works of fiction and fantasy. Those written in French supplied the genesis of the word 'fairy' itself, associated with the term *fai*, *fae* or *fay*, applied to these beings.

The origins of these glamorous characters may lie in three different, though not mutually exclusive, sources, to none of which they may be attributed with certainty. The first, which was popular among literary scholars during the early and mid-twentieth century, is in ancient Celtic cultures.[12] It is certainly true that medieval Celtic literatures are populated by beings who seem remarkably similar to the fays, set in more primeval, early medieval societies. Those in the Irish stories are fairly clearly former pagan deities, reimagined as aristocratic superhumans inhabiting a parallel world located within hills or ancient burial mounds or on islands and making much the same relations with human beings as the fays. The stories concerned certainly much predate the romances, being recorded from the eighth or ninth centuries onward, though the composition of them continued though the Middle Ages; latterly the entities concerned were given the collective name of the Túatha dé Danann.[13] The Welsh equivalents are also very similar to the fays, and may also be transformed ancient native goddesses and gods, though this is more speculative and none of the stories that feature them can themselves securely be dated before the twelfth century.[14] The second possible source for the fays is in the predatory and seductive rural beings mentioned by early medieval churchmen, and the third consists of a projection of wish fulfilment by the high medieval Western European elite itself. Fays are after all glamorized versions of twelfth-century barons, knights and ladies, equipped with magical powers and greater knowledge.

In recent years scholars of medieval literature have generally abandoned the quest for origins as fruitless because no hypothesis is apparently susceptible of proof; interest in Celtic progenitors has been dismissed with especial force.[15] Instead, experts have concentrated on the far more practicable goal of studying the roles of fays as vehicles for plot devices and as mirrors of contemporary social and cultural preoccupations.[16] As such, they could be used as channels for prophecy, as they were neither bound by human limitations nor demonic. They could act as arbiters of justice when human forms of that failed and acknowledge virtue in a hero or encourage it to develop. Most often, they embodied, both for good and bad, power without responsibility, and represented classic sexual fantasy, shot through with allure and danger. They could indeed be used to express female physical desire and fulfilment with a frankness hard to employ when dealing with human ladies of the time, and to serve with equal facility as dream lovers or evil temptresses.

Recent scholars have also collectively emphasized the lack of an attempt in most of the stories to locate fays within a theological framework, or indeed to explain who they are at all or to explore their motivation: they are usually just assumed to be mysterious. Partly as a consequence, the romances often leave in doubt their status as human or non-human. At times it is explicitly stated that they are people who have learned magic and so gained extraordinary powers, but in most cases they are not consigned to any specific category of being. Nonetheless, they represent, as said, the linguistic root of the whole concept of fairies. The word *fay* or *fai* itself may possibly derive from the Latin *fata*, meaning the classical goddesses known in English as the Fates. This term was indeed to be used in Latin works to translate 'fairies', but it may have converged with them rather than given birth to them. 'Fay' actually functioned more often as a verb than a noun, in both Old French and the Middle English texts into which the French themes were transposed. It denotes the working of something magical or uncanny. Its derivation or parallel term, *faierie*, was used in both French and English to describe magical events, wonders and marvels, or a place where fays dwelt. Only in English, and not until the mid-fifteenth century, did it come to mean a type of human-like being who wielded magic, a 'fairy'. Before then the expression 'fairy knight' did not indicate a knight who was a fairy, but a knight who came from fairyland.[17]

The male exemplars of this sort of character are masters of shape-shifting, deception and seduction. One romance, *Yonec*, features one attired as a wealthy knight who emerges from a hillside and changes into the form of a great bird to fly into a human lady's bedchamber. In *Tydorel*, another of the same kind, handsome and richly dressed, comes out of a lake at midsummer to become the lover of a queen of Brittany, so siring the hero of the tale, who eventually returns to his father's home in the lake. *Tyolet* features a stag who turns into a knight on horseback and instructs the hero. The addition to *Guy of Warwick* which features the adventures of that hero's son has him at one point rescue a friend of Guy's from the prison of a fairy knight 'hard as marble'.[18] During the thirteenth century the character who was to be the most famous and enduring of these magical males made his appearance in the romance of *Huon de Bordeaux*. This is Auberon or Oberon, whose story grew by instalments into one of an ageless hunchbacked dwarf ruler of a forest kingdom with a capital city of white marble, located vaguely in the Middle East, who is possessed of great powers as an enchanter as well as great wealth. The audience for the story is assured of his illustrious parentage, as the son of Julius Caesar and an immortal 'Lady of the Secret Isle', and also of his religious orthodoxy, as a devout Christian who is taken to heaven by angels when at last he chooses to die. He was given his magical powers by superhuman beings who attended his birth, while his one defect, his physical deformity, was the result of a curse bestowed upon him by another such being. Huon, the hero of the tale, eventually succeeds Oberon as the ruler of his realm, over which he will preside with a queen, Esclaramonde, until the end of the world: happily ever after, indeed.[19]

Generally, however, it is the female fays who are the most striking characters in the category of *faierie*, and who provide memorable examples of feminine personalities who take the initiative in their own and human affairs and wield considerable political and magical power with a full sense of personal autonomy and agency. Typical of these would be the 'Maiden of the White Hands' in Renaud de Beaujeu's romance *Le Bel Inconnu*, who is mistress of 'the Golden Isle' and becomes the beloved and helper of the young hero of the tale, having seen his destiny beforehand. The hero is himself the son of the Arthurian knight Sir Gawain and a fay whom his father had met in a forest. Two fays in particular were to enjoy long careers in medieval literature. One was Morgen, later named Morgan or Morgaine and to be given the defining nickname 'Le Fay'. She appears in Geoffrey of Monmouth's Latin poem *The Life of Merlin*, from around 1150, in which she features as the most beautiful of nine sisters who rule an earthly paradise of abundant natural crops called the Isle of Apples or the Fortunate Island; the description of this is taken from one of an archipelago by the early medieval scholar Isidore of Seville, which most probably refers to the Canaries.[20] She is skilled in healing, using herbal remedies, and in astrology, can change her shape, and flies around the world on 'strange wings' which may be her invention. People from Britain are taken to her to be cured of their ills, the most distinguished being the wounded King Arthur after his final battle.

The origin of Morgen's name has been much debated, as there are many possibilities, but there is more consensus that the original inspiration for her as a figure comes from ancient Greece, and above all from Homer's demi-goddess Circe and her enchanted island.[21] Indeed, classical enchantresses like Circe and Medea exerted an influence on conceptions of medieval fays in general. From Geoffrey's text she leaked out through Western

European literature in haphazard fashion. Sometimes she retained her character and context but changed her name, such as in the reworking of Geoffrey's version of British history into English verse by the Worcestershire priest Layamon in the late twelfth or early thirteenth centuries. There Morgen is called Queen Argante and her island is known as Avalon, and Layamon uses the English term 'most beautiful of elves' for her, though she is still a healer presiding over an enchanted isle where she takes Arthur into her care.[22] At other times she retained her name and context but changed her nature, as she does in the first Arthurian romance in German, Hartmann von Aue's *Erec*, from the 1180s. Here she has the same home and function as in Geoffrey, but also enhanced magical powers and a streak of unpleasantness. With an extra dose of character from the classical Circe, she can change men into animals and back, and command animals, including fish, dragons and demons. Her power over demons is explained when it is revealed that she is aided by the Devil. At yet other times Morgen (more or less) kept her name but changed both character and context, as in the thirteenth-century French romance *Claris et Laris*, where, now under the name of Morgana, she has spent a period at Arthur's court and then retired in middle age to set up her own realm in a Breton forest. There she maintains a sumptuous castle with a retinue of humans and spirits, walled in by spells, and imprisons and seduces handsome young men who enter her territory: she has become unequivocally wicked, and the Isle of Apples has turned into Sunset Boulevard.[23] Thereafter she was to have a career as a (mostly) villainous human enchantress in the Arthurian legend, which lasts until the present.

The other fay of the early romances who was to have notable staying power was the one who features in Marie de France's *Lanval*, composed – perhaps for the Plantagenet royal court – in the late twelfth century. She is a beautiful young woman, or woman-like being, of great wealth and magical prowess, who somehow comes to perceive and fall in love with a young knight at King Arthur's court, a Breton, who suffers neglect and penury through no fault of his own. She waylays him with her attendants, makes him her lover and turns his luck around, her one stipulation being that he keeps her identity a secret. He manages both to break this promise and to offend Arthur's queen, by insisting that his beloved is more beautiful than her or any other lady at court. As a result of the latter blunder, he is falsely accused and put on trial, and is saved when his fay lover arrives at court with an entourage to vindicate him, before carrying him off behind her on her horse to live with her in Avalon.

All of these works were composed between the mid-twelfth and mid-thirteenth centuries, showing how luxuriant a growth the concept of the fay proved in Western Europe at that time. For the purposes of the present chapter, it may be pointed out that the Maiden of the White Hands, Argante and Morgana are all literally fairy queens, in the sense that they both work *faierie* and dwell in it. On the other hand, they are all disparate characters, alongside the other fays of early romance, with no common otherworldly allegiance or homeland. The appearance of those factors was going to be the next development in the concept of fairies.

The Coming of the Kingdom

It is in the years around, or just after, 1300 that a sense begins to develop of a single established fairy realm which interacts with the human world; and it does so in two romances written at that time. Both were marked by a further injection of ideas from classical Graeco-Roman literature which helped form that sense. One was the English *Sir Orfeo*, which retold the ancient story of the attempted rescue by the heroic musician Orpheus of his wife Eurydice from the pagan underworld realm of the dead, putting the tale into medieval dress.[24] In this version, he has to retrieve his wife from the land of a nameless 'King of Fayre' or 'Fare' or 'Fairy' (the spelling varies between versions) who takes the role of the Roman god Pluto as ruler of a kingdom of the dead, although in this case they are those who have met untimely ends: a preoccupation with the fate of such people had been a mark of Western European thought in the previous two hundred years.[25] It is not, however, a ghostly underworld but a pleasant green land, where the king reigns from a huge castle with his queen and sometimes leads a retinue on white horses into the human world to hunt animals and abduct chosen people, including Orfeo's wife – who is, unlike her ancient predecessor, successfully rescued. In addition to the Roman foundation, the cultural materials that may have been used to create the work were very diverse, including Old Irish, Anglo-Saxon, Middle English, Old French, Breton and medieval Latin and Italian works.[26] The result is a complete picture of a fairyland with a presiding royal court.

The other romance is the French *Artus de Bretagne*, which displays another potential of an identification of a land of fays with the classical Graeco-Roman underworld. Instead of emphasizing its king, it foregrounds its queen, the ancient goddess Proserpine, and makes her a sovereign of *faierie*. She first appears to one of the heroes of the tale around midnight, predictably beautiful, crowned with gold and attended by bright torchlight, to tell him how to accomplish a quest, and then vanishes. Later he meets her again at the entrance to a fair forest, with two pretty attendants, and she offers him her love, which he refuses. Understandably, she now abandons him, leaving him to lose his way.[27] Not surprisingly, with all this cross-referencing between the realms of fays and of the dead, a preacher's manual from the early fourteenth century, *Fasciculus Morum*, could condemn a current belief that elves could carry off humans to their own land, where heroes of the past dwelt.[28] This may have been an old aspect of native belief, or a product of the equation between fairyland and the ancient underworld, or a result of the developing legend of the Isle of Apples or Avalon.

These works made possible the major leap taken by the end of the century, when Chaucer could speak, famously, of how in the days of King Arthur, Britain was 'fulfilled of fayerye' and of how 'the elf queen, with her jolly company, danced full oft in many a green mead'.[29] He had taken the classic image of a royal fay, blended her with the tradition of nocturnal revels of beautiful female beings and – in a vital step – given her the definite article. This turned her into a personality in her own right, on the way to becoming a standardized archetype. This process, however, was incomplete and the result uneven, because in another tale, in a more satirical mood, in which he was prepared to parody the whole stereotype of the fay and the knight, he makes the hero decide that he must win the love of '*an* elf-queen'. He subsequently enters the land 'of Fairye so wild' and encounters '*the* queen of Faierye, with harp and pipe and symphony'.[30] In yet another story Chaucer embraces the classicizing tradition to make Pluto, the Roman god of the underworld and dead, 'King of Faierye', with Proserpine as his queen. Together and accompanied by attendants, they enter the human world to view the affairs of its inhabitants and intervene in those using their divine powers, which equate to magic. Proserpine acts independently of her spouse and according to her own morals and impulses, thereby counter-acting the effects of his decisions.[31] Thus concepts remained fluid, but a set of associations was starting to form and settle around the notion of elf and fairy monarchs and realms which defined an increasingly familiar pair of characters, who might operate independently and of whom the queen was a being of genuine might and agency in her own right.

The same process can be seen at work in the case of an old friend to this chapter, the generous and anonymous fay who was the heroine of *Lanval*. Around 1300 the romance of Marie de France was translated into Middle English as *Sir Landevale*, with no significant alteration to her as a character. Near the end of the century, however, the story was told again by Thomas Chestre, as *Sir Launfal*, and by now she has undergone a makeover. Her disposition and actions have remained the same, but she has acquired a name, the emblematic one of Dame Tryamour, and a point of origin, as daughter of 'the King of Faërie, of occiente fair and nigh, A man of mickle might'. As part of this association, she now dresses in the increasingly distinctive fairy colour of green, whereas in the twelfth-century version she was clad in white, and sometimes in ermine and purple to emphasize her royal status, while her attendants wore purple liveries. When she and the hero depart at the end, it is 'into the faërie' whence she came (also still glossed as the 'Isle of Olyroun', which seems to be Avalon).[32]

During the early fifteenth century, the idea of a single fairy kingdom spread with remarkable rapidity, not just through English society but across Britain. By the middle of the century, it was well enough known in south-eastern England to be a worthwhile guise for confidence tricksters or maniacs. In 1450 'one calling himself Queen of the Fayre' was recorded as touring Essex and Kent, 'but did no harm'.[33] The next year a gang of poachers around a hundred strong, armed and attired in armour, fake beards and blacked-up faces, raided the deer park of the duke of Buckingham in Kent. They called themselves 'servants of the queen of the fairies', presumably as a mocking expression to indicate that they were outside of human law.[34] The French word derived ultimately from the fays of chivalric romance had become thoroughly naturalized among the English and freighted with a set of royal associations not given before to the native 'elves', whom it had largely replaced. The same period saw the appearance of the romance as a Scottish literary form, and the fairy kingdom immediately manifested with it. The earliest and most famous such story was that of *Thomas of Erceldoune*, composed somewhere between 1400 and 1430. It tells of a Scottish laird who encounters and becomes the lover of a lady of 'the wild fee'. She takes him back with her to her land, where she turns out to be the wife of its king. He eventually returns to his own world with gifts of prophecy and of the detection and telling of truth.[35]

The portrait of her and her country is richly drawn. He meets her in a wood when she rides up to him wearing rich silk clothes and carrying a horn and a lyre, on a grey horse harnessed with gold, crystal and precious stones. A pack of eleven hunting dogs follows her. He persuades her to have sex with him on promise of everlasting fidelity, but the bargain is bad for both, because lovemaking transforms her into an aged and unattractive being in poor clothes, and he is now bound to leave 'Middle Earth' for her realm and remain a year. They pass through the side of a hill and journey three days through darkness to a green landscape full of fruit trees and birds, where her fine looks and raiment are restored. There she and her husband dwell in a stately castle with a retinue of knights and damsels, given up to music, dances and games. Thomas joins it (keeping the secret of her infidelity with him) until three days have apparently passed. She then informs him that this period has represented seven years in his world, and that he must leave as the following day a fiend would come from Hell to choose a victim to take back there as a regular tribute, and that as a handsome stranger he would be the obvious one. She leaves him in the place where they had met, equipped with his uncanny new powers.

The concept of such a realm also appeared in Wales around the same time, and, just as the French and English drew on classical sources to frame it, so the Welsh had an older figure, and otherworld, of their own as ready-made materials. The figure was Gwyn ap Nudd. He first appears in what seem to be two twelfth-century texts, the prose tale *Culhwch ac Olwen*, 'Culhwch and Olwen', and the poem 'Taru Trin Anuidin Blaut', 'A Bull of Battle Was He', as one of Arthur's warriors, and a great fighter. He has magical gifts in the tale, to be sure, but so has almost everybody else in Arthur's retinue as depicted in it. By the fourteenth century, and the poems of Dafydd ap Gwilym, he had been detached from the Arthurian legend and located in the present, as the pre-eminent spirit of darkness, enchantment and deception, abroad by night.[36] The owl is his favourite bird, the mist is conjured up by him and he sports in marshes. He is associated with Annwn or Annwfn, a realm known earlier in Welsh literature, especially in the prose tale *Pwyll Pendeuic Dyuet*, 'Pwyll Prince of Dyfed', as a parallel world with its own king and queen and magically gifted people. By the time of Dafydd, however, it was very clearly an underworld with creepy, if not diabolic, associations like those acquired by Gwyn. Those associations fitted the latter perfectly for the part he played in *Buchedd Collen*, 'The Life of St Collen', a late medieval Welsh hagiography written in the style of a romance. In this, Gwyn has become 'King of the Fairies' as well as of Annwn, with a beautiful castle crowning a hill and filled with courtiers, musicians, maidens, servants in his livery of red and blue, and fine tables covered in provisions. There he presides from a golden chair. However, all this is an illusion of the classic demonic kind which vanishes when the saint sprinkles it with holy water. It leaves behind only green mounds of the sort associated with fairy-like beings as meeting places and portals.[37]

The idea of a fairy kingdom did not, however, put down roots in Wales, and no more is heard there of one, aside from in this one text, in either an elite literary context or a popular one. Fairy-like beings are recorded as widely believed in by ordinary people there during the early modern period, but without monarchs, and there is no apparent reference to a queen.[38] Likewise, she does not feature in the whole late medieval and early modern Gaelic world, embracing most of Ireland, the Scottish Highlands, the Hebrides and the Isle of Man. It is possible that the existing mythology there, of the Túatha dé Danann, filled the conceptual space available for fairy monarchs. It may likewise be suspected that something similar happened in Wales, where the mythology of Annwn and its beings could have been ample and well established enough to render the newcomers from *faierie* superfluous.

Things were very different in Lowland Scotland and at the Scottish royal court, which was situated in that region, and between 1450 and 1550 the fairy kingdom was a regular subject for treatment, or at least reference, by poets there. One was a notary, Robert Henryson, who flourished in the late fifteenth century and was associated with Dunfermline. He made another treatment of the Orpheus legend in the dress of medieval romance, in which Proserpine features simultaneously as the 'goddess infernal' and the 'queen of fary'. So Orpheus's wife Eurydice is 'with the fary taken', though the realm to which she is carried is a classical underworld.[39] Henryson was also credited with an extraordinary piece of whimsy called 'King Berdok', i.e. burdock, in which fairy-like beings are miniaturized, an idea which was a one-off for the time and place. The tiny king concerned, whose realm is improbably given as Babylon, is said to live in summer in a cabbage stalk and in winter in a cockle shell. He woos the daughter of the 'king of fary', and, when the latter discovers his suit and drives him away, the classical god Mercury saves him by hiding him in a bracken bush.[40]

In his masterpiece from 1535, *Ane Satyre of the Thrie Estaits* (A Satire of the Three Estates), the great court poet Sir David Lyndsay played repeatedly with the idea of fairy monarchs, and usually did so with fear or aversion. One character expostulates 'We will have no more deal with thee / Than with the Queen of Farie'. A demon declares 'I pray the alrich [uncanny] Queen of Farie to be your protection', and at another point occurs the taunt 'I will recommend you to the Queen of Farie'. A sinner admits that

'I must pass to the King of Farie, / Or else, the right to Hell'.[41] In another of his satires, *The Testament and Complaynt of our Soverane Lordis Papyngo* (The Testament and Complaint of our Sovereign Lord's Parrot), from 1530, the bird is made to declare: 'But when my spirit must from my body go, / I recommend it to the queen of Fary, / Eternally in her court to tarry / In wilderness among the lonely dens.'[42] Once more, the sense of fairyland as a place of the dead, or at least special kinds of dead (heroic or untimely), which was either engendered by or reflected in the input from the classical underworld and Avalon, is sustained. A leading poet of the previous generation, William Dunbar, had kept up the disturbing associations, by reviling a fellow courtier as the offspring of a giant and 'a farie queen, gotten by sorcery'.[43] In a tableaux of classical deities he described Pluto, god of the underworld, as 'the elrich incubus, / In cloak of green'.[44]

There is therefore a distinctly darker hue to the fairy monarchs in sixteenth-century Scots verse than there had been during the previous century, and the Reformation seems to have confirmed the association of fairies with the diabolic in elite Scottish culture. In a satirical poem by Alexander Montgomerie from around 1580, the host of the 'King of Pharie' and the 'elf queen' includes overtly demonic figures such as incubi.[45] Montgomerie's patron was King James VI, Scotland's first Protestant monarch and himself an author, who in the next decade condemned all apparent manifestations of the fairy kingdom as demonic illusions intended to ensnare souls and formerly encouraged under Roman Catholicism – excoriating beliefs 'that there was a King and Queen of Phairie, of such a jolly court and train as they had, how they naturally rode and went, ate and drank, and did all other actions like natural men and women'.[46] This sectarian hostility was compounded by the absence of media in which other views might have been explored in Scotland, with the decline of Scots poetry after 1600 owing to the removal of the court to England and the increasing influence of English print, and the lack of a vibrant theatre. It built, however, on a strong existing trend, which was not denominational: the wariness of the fairy sovereigns of pre-Reformation poets has been noted and Montgomerie was himself a Catholic. In 1567 James's

Catholic mother, Mary, Queen of Scots, had been entertained by a comic play in which 'the Farie' was again an alternative destination to Hell.[47]

One of the most remarkable aspects of this outright formal hostility on the part of the Scottish elite was that it did not wholly translate into an equivalent attitude on the part of ordinary Scots, many of whom retained a belief not merely in the fairy realm but in its essential benevolence. King James himself complained of some who had asserted that they had been transported by 'Phairie' to a hill, and seen it open and found therein 'a fair Queen' who gave them 'a stone which has sundry virtues'.[48] The court records of his reign and those following amply bear him out, by recording the cases of folk magicians who claimed to have had this sort of experience and ended up accused of dealing with devils as a result. A succession of such cases has become famous in the annals of Scottish witchcraft beliefs, especially over the past thirty years. The earliest and one of the less known is that of Jonet (sic) Boyman in 1572, whose trial was indeed the first for witchcraft in Scotland for which a detailed indictment has survived. An Edinburgh magical healer, she allegedly confessed to invoking spirits to aid her in her work, at a well with an uncanny reputation on the side of the volcanic outcrop outside the city called Arthur's Seat. She did so in the names of her own personal pantheon, 'Father, Son, King Arthur and Queen Elspeth', the last apparently being her name for the fairy monarch. Subsequently, a host of fairy-like beings appeared to aid her.[49]

Much more celebrated is the trial of Bessie Dunlop, from Ayrshire at the western end of the Central Lowlands, in 1576. She allegedly confessed that she had been helped in her career as a folk magician, serving clients, by a spirit guide in the form of the ghost of a man who had been killed at a famous battle in the 1540s. He turned out to be one of the servants of 'the Queen of Elfame' (Elf Home), who eventually came to visit Bessie herself at home when the latter was 'in child bed' (preparing to give birth or just having done so), being described rather prosaically as a 'stout woman' who asked for a drink and then informed her that her sick husband would survive but the baby die, which proved true.[50] A dozen years later a Fife healer, Alison Peirson, was recorded as confessing to having frequently visited the court of the 'Queen of Elfhame' and learned her skill there: she claimed to have relatives at that court who were in high favour with the queen.[51] At least one of the factors that got her into trouble with the authorities had been her treatment of an archbishop of St Andrews, who had made political enemies, and a poem satirizing him had great fun with these alleged exploits of hers, including the detail that she rode across the Highlands at Halloween with 'the Queen of Phareis' and her entourage. Again, the detail is added that the fairy court included certain dead humans.[52]

Still more intimate was the relationship claimed by Andro Man, a wandering healer who had worked all over north-east Scotland and was tried at Aberdeen in 1597. He allegedly testified that he had first visited the 'Queen of Elphen' as a boy, sixty years before, when she had come to his family home to be delivered of a child. He brought her water and she promised that he would 'know all things', have healing powers and be well looked after, though he would still have some hard times. He subsequently became her lover and fathered several children on her, and yet the interaction between them remained uneasy and capricious: at one point she killed one of his cattle on a mound called 'Elphillock' (presumably a portal to her realm onto which the beast had strayed) but told him good things would happen to him after that. In Man's personal mythology she shared her power with an angel in white clothes called Christsonday. Again, their retinue included famous dead people such as Thomas of Erceldoune and King James IV of Scots, who had been killed in battle over eighty years before. Christsonday sometimes appeared in the form of a stag or horse, while the queen always resembled a human and rode on white steeds with her followers; he added that like Satan in contemporary mythology, she required homage to be paid to her by kissing her anus. Her courtiers looked and dressed like ordinary people but had more vitality and loved dancing and games. She was attractive, could look young or old as she desired, could make anybody she chose king of Scotland, and had sex with whomever she pleased.[53] This was the most detailed portrait of the fairy monarch to emerge from any of the trials.

After Andro Man, most testimonies of interaction with fairy monarchs seem anticlimactic, but the continuing succession of them far into the seventeenth century, and from all over the Lowlands, testifies to the vitality of their reputation. A servant called Jonet Anderson was questioned in 1617 for having tried to cure a sick woman at Falkirk, apparently by threatening the fairy monarchs to get them to rescind a blight they had put on her patient. Her charm asked in the name of Father, Son and Holy Ghost that the 'earthless king and earthless queen' should have no rest until they restored the woman to health.[54] John Stewart, an itinerant juggler and fortune-teller tried at Irvine in the following year, claimed to have acquired the ability to see the future when he met the fairy king in Ireland one Halloween. The king had touched his forehead with a white wand, which had the side-effect of making him dumb and blind in one eye, but they had met again in Dublin three years later and then Stewart had been healed. Thereafter he met the fairies weekly, celebrated Halloween with them on special hills and learned more magical skills at their court; once again, the latter was also attended by humans who had suffered untimely deaths.[55] To Margaret Alexander, interrogated at Livingston, west of Edinburgh, in 1647, the king had behaved more like a conventional early modern devil, having sex with her and getting her to renounce her Christian baptism.[56]

As a storyteller, the equal to or superior of Andro Man was Isobel Gowdie, of Auldearn on the coastal plain beside the Moray Firth, whose confession taken in 1662 is the longest, most spectacular and most famous from any Scottish witch prosecution. She claimed acquaintance with both 'fearie' monarchs, who had entertained her at their palace inside local hills with good and ample food, although the 'elf bulls' bellowing and stamping in the place scared her. It was the queen who provided her with the food and who was 'brawlie [bravely] clothed in white linen and in white and brown clothes etc', while the king was 'a braw man well favoured and broad faced etc'.[57] No lasting relationship or gifts resulted from the visit, however, and it was an incidental episode in an account which concentrated more on her dealings with the Devil and her coven, and her various acts of magic. She seems to have included it because of a feeling that contact with the fairy court was the kind of thing that a true witch ought to have in her portfolio of achievements.

All of these testimonies come to us mediated through the legal records, and we cannot tell how much the clerks who wrote them omitted (the one who took down Isobel Gowdie's made clear that much more was left out) or reshaped. Nonetheless, they are individual and idiosyncratic enough to make it reasonably certain that the accused in each case was drawing upon her or his own experiences and imagination and not being fed stereotypical images and actions. What emerges from the collective sample is a clear impression that ordinary Lowland Scots of the age had a general belief in the existence of the fairy kingdom, without any common sense of its components or nature, or of the appearance, trappings and personalities of its rulers. Put on the spot – as a legal interrogation would do with more brutal efficiency than virtually any other situation – they supplied those elements for themselves.

The English Apogee

In England during the sixteenth and seventeenth centuries, there were many writers who shared the official view of the Scottish elite that fairies were actually devils and their royal court a demonic illusion. There, however, this was not an orthodoxy ratified from the top of the state, but a single opinion among several others aired in print. The most common of the latter were that a belief in fairies was a contemptible falsehood propagated under the old, Roman Catholic, religious regime; that it was a harmless and amusing superstition of common folk; and that it was a valuable and long-established literary theme which could be a powerful stimulus to the imagination and a useful means to entertainment. As a result, the fairy queen and her spouse were represented and reimagined in a great range of different ways, as one aspect of that great European reconsideration of the world which took place under the various pressures of the Age of Discovery, the Renaissance and the Reformation, in the context of an unusually vibrant English literary and theatrical culture.[58]

Part of the impetus behind this more favourable and diverse attitude to fairies consisted of the continuing popularity of medieval romances in Tudor England as texts of them were put into the new medium of print, and sometimes translated into English for the first time in the process. A classic example of the chain reaction of creativity which could be set off by this process is that of the reception of the romance *Huon de Bordeaux*. Its final, and most developed, medieval version was translated and published in print in the 1530s by a noble enthusiast for romances, John Bourchier, Lord Berners.[59] It was very popular, going through a number of reprints before 1601 and introducing the Tudor English to its charming and virtuous fay hero Oberon.[60] By 1593 it had been dramatized and a new comedy written as well in which a 'King Egereon' enters to music with his court, followed by 'three antic fairies dancing one after another' to rescue two characters from execution.[61] In the following year a minor Elizabethan dramatist, Robert Greene, purloined the character of Oberon for a play of his on Scottish history. This commences with the entry of 'Aster Oberon, King of Fayries, and Antiques who dance about a tomb'. This king is clearly small, exists in a realm apart from the human one, is gentle, kind and wise, and loves dancing. His role is to hold the play together, providing a commentary on the nature of human affairs.[62]

That was apparently a cue for a far from minor playwright of the period, William Shakespeare, to appropriate him for a work which has passed into the world literary canon, *A Midsummer Night's Dream*. Here Oberon, master of a nocturnal woodland realm set in ancient Greece, has travelled very far from the medieval hunchbacked dwarf to become an obviously imposing figure, intelligent, authoritative and capable of anger, duplicity and generosity by turns, while remaining essentially benevolent towards his own kind and humanity. He is, of course, given a queen worthy of him, strong-willed and independent and with her own fairy retinue, and sharing most of his qualities of character (even though the play punishes her for arguing with her husband). Tellingly, Shakespeare innovates by calling her Titania, a name not used for any fay or fairy hitherto but known from the ancient poet Ovid as one for Diana, the major Roman goddess of woods and moonlight. Indeed, she and her husband resemble classical nature deities more than any other sort of being, and this Oberon is more like Ovid's orchard god Vertumnus than any of the male fays of medieval literature.[63] As such, they act as patrons to human royalty, and Shakespeare takes a swipe at the diabolic interpretation of fairies by making Oberon emphasize that, unlike ghosts and 'damned spirits', he and his court can endure sunlight.

Shakespeare did not use him or Titania again, and his treatment of fairies remained extremely varied. In *Romeo and Juliet*, as will be discussed, he turned them into figures of whimsy, while in *Hamlet* they are destructive beings equated with witches, and in *The Merry Wives of Windsor* the 'fairy queen and her retinue', now anonymized, are one entry in a list of nocturnal beings which includes a satyr and a hobgoblin. Here the queen is said to dress in white and has become a folk figure who directs her followers to pinch and bruise sleeping maids who have made a bad job of housekeeping – a popular belief (at least among people who kept servants) which was being propagated at this period. Her king has disappeared, but she retains her function of blessing homes, especially those of royalty.[64]

Oberon was, however, now assured of an honourable and benevolent role in the work of English writers. In 1597 Christopher Middleton published a new Arthurian romance, *The Famous Historie of Chinon of England*, in which 'King Oberam' acts as patron to the hero, testing his courage by assuming a monstrous shape on first meeting and then presenting him with rich armour, a magic sword and a dwarf assistant. Oberam rules an underground realm full of elves and leads a fairy troop on sallies into the human world. A few years later, towards the end of Elizabeth's reign, a new play had Oberon enter with 'Fairyes dancing before him and music with them' to tell a maiden her fate, sympathetically, and assure her that there will be a place for her in fairyland after her death. She wonders if they are disguised devils, but their predictions come true.[65] Thereafter Oberon's good character was to continue into the new century, as will be described.

During the Elizabethan era, the fairy queen enjoyed one unusual and considerable advantage among the English elite: the presence of an actual female monarch, ruling in her own right, Elizabeth I. This gave hosts who met and entertained the latter on her progresses a limited range of role models and precedents which could be summoned up from history and legend to apostrophize her; and the queen of fairies was a handy one. As in Shakespeare, she could be elided with the goddess Diana, whose chastity made her an obvious divine point of comparison for the unmarried Elizabeth. The latter therefore became accustomed on arriving at the rural seats of gentry and nobility to have her fairy counterpart emerge from woods or lakes, suitably costumed and accompanied, to salute her and make gifts to her.[66] Fairly typical was her experience at the appropriately named seat of the earl of Hertford at Elvetham in 1591, when she was seated at a gallery window overlooking a garden, into which the fairy queen came dancing with a retinue of maidens, carrying a garland in the shape of the crown. That queen gave her name as Aureola (so identifying herself with a classical dawn goddess) and claimed to have an underground realm where nightly she called Elizabeth's name 'in rings of painted flowers'. She explained that her garland had been made for Elizabeth by her royal husband, Auberon, and then sang and danced about the garden in praise of her with her maids. The real queen was so delighted that she wanted the performance repeated twice and bestowed a rich reward of money on the players.[67]

This loyal idiom was sometimes transferred to the realm of literature, with inevitably varied success. At one end of the scale was Thomas Dekker's laboured dramatic allegory *The Whore of Babylon*, which features Elizabeth as the 'Farie' queen of England (here called Titania after Shakespeare) vanquishing the Whore and her supporters (the Roman Catholic Church and its adherents).[68] Less predictably, 'good King Oberon' is her father, Henry VIII, a conceit taken from a work at the opposite end of the spectrum of merit and indeed the only one of this kind to enter the international canon: Edmund Spenser's allegorical romance *The Faerie Queene*. Published between 1590 and 1596, it sustained on a huge scale the idea of Britain as a fairy realm ruled by an Elizabeth-figure, though she herself stays mostly in the background of the long and complex action.[69]

THE FAIRY QUEEN

The death of Elizabeth and the accession of the officially fairy-disowning James VI of Scotland as James I of England raised the question of whether this allegorical posturing could be sustained; but that was soon resolved. As James's wife Anne of Denmark was travelling south from Scotland to take up residence in her new English home and court, bringing their eldest son Henry, they were entertained at Althorp in Northamptonshire, seat of the Spencer family (as it still is). Ben Jonson, whose name stands only second to Shakespeare's among the dramatists of the time, devised a pageant to receive them in which a queen of the fairies led in her retinue to dance before the royal duo. Jonson then cleverly cast the good character of this queen into doubt, having a hostile satyr call her a petty-minded deceiver who robbed dairies of cream and sometimes immobilized butter churns out of mischief, so acknowledging a more hostile contemporary attitude to fairies. An elf, however, then defended her, saying that she punished lazy maids with pinching (as has been noted) and rewarded good servants and children by leaving them gifts. The satyr was duly punished, leaving the fairy sovereign to praise the real queen and present her with a jewel, before dancing away.[70] Anne and Henry were clearly pleased, because about seven years later Jonson designed a court masque in which the prince himself was represented with a retinue of young gentlemen as Prince Oberon and his knights. They emerged from a sumptuous palace carrying torches and singing, with Oberon riding in a chariot drawn by white bears and guarded by wood nymphs. The knights are described as former human heroes, 'preserved in Faery land'. The whole company danced and praised their leader, and – in a backward glance to Althorp – distinguished itself from the coarse country fairies who haunted hearths and dairies.[71] The king was clearly not inclined to dispute the distinction, or to disapprove in any way.

Thereafter for the rest of the early Stuart period, elite literary culture and popular print alike made respectful representations of the fairy monarchs. A sub-genre of fairy mythology, embodied in simple chapbooks, dealt with the adventures of Robin Goodfellow, alias Puck, who had appeared in the fifteenth century as a lone prankster spirit wholly independent of the fairy kingdom. Shakespeare, however, famously brought him into it as a henchman of Oberon's, and he subsequently retained that role in cheap print (with the king as a benevolent background figure).[72] A similar fate subsequently befell another essentially independent folk hero, the diminutive Tom Thumb, whom another pamphlet made into the godson of 'the Fayry Queene', who attends his christening with a train of 'goblins grim' and receives him into her realm on his death with a retinue of 'dancing nymphs in green' and musicians.[73] In more highbrow culture, the musician Thomas Campion published a song in which Proserpine makes a reappearance as the queen, holding revels by moonlight 'in myrtle arbours on the downs', but also, in folksy English fashion, sending her minions to 'pinch black and blue' human transgressors.[74] The queen and Oberon together continued to preside over their courts in dramatic performances, represented in lyric verse.[75] By 1635 an anthology of such references, from both elite and popular sources, could be put together in a manner designed to appeal to both audiences, and illustrated with woodcuts.[76]

The fairy monarchs, and especially the queen, could take their place in popular print works the more easily in that they remained major figures in the imagination of the English common people, just as in Scotland. As there, too, a strong connection was perceived between fairies and the service magicians – usually called cunning or wise folk – who provided spells and charms for clients at the popular level.[77] This connection features much more seldom in trials south of the border, because English law focused more on alleged magical injury and much less on transactions with spirits than Scottish, and so service magicians tended to be accused of witchcraft less often and their relations with fairies were less a subject of interest to authorities. Nonetheless, there was an occasional exception, and one of the best recorded is the trial of Susan Swapper at the Sussex coastal port of Rye in 1607. She claimed to have had a series of visits from fairies who came to her by night in her home, starting when she was ill in bed; they began by telling her a means by which she could be healed, but later the focus of their proffered services extended to revealing buried treasure. Eventually, at noon one day, a tall male figure led her to a valley where she saw a man in black and a woman in green meeting. Her guide informed her that the woman was the fairy queen, and that if Susan knelt to her 'she would make a living'. Instead, Susan went home. She subsequently claimed to have seen a total of eighteen fairies at different times, making a regular contact of the tall male, but the queen was not mentioned or seen again (and of course no treasure was found, and she got arrested as a witch instead).[78] In Scotland she would probably have been publicly executed, by strangling, after which her body would have been burnt: such was the fate of Jonet Boyman, Bessie Dunlop, Alison Peirson, Andro Man, Margaret Alexander and probably Isobel Gowdie, while John Stewart committed suicide in prison. Susan was indeed sentenced to hang, but pardoned after four years, because in English eyes it mattered crucially that she was not apparently guilty of harming anybody.

Also relatively fortunate was a northern English service magician, tried in the years around 1650, who had made a living by treating sick people with a white powder that he claimed to have been given by the fairies. He obtained it by meeting a female one on the road, who offered to help him out of poverty and took him to a little hill, which opened to her. Inside he came to a fine hall with a queen seated in state and many attendants about her. She welcomed him and bade the woman who had brought him to present him with the powder in a small wooden box. He subsequently knocked on the hill again when he needed a fresh supply, and was once more admitted and granted his wish, after another audience with the queen. Once again, it counted in his favour that he had harmed nobody, and indeed seemed to have cured many, so the jury acquitted him of calling on evil spirits. The judge, however, ordered him to be whipped as an imposter instead.[79]

The world of popular magic shaded imperceptibly at its boundary into a different realm of magical operations, that of learned practitioners who carried out rituals for personal gain – material, intellectual or spiritual – and relied on written texts, clandestinely produced, in which the necessary operations were prescribed. These operations depended heavily on the conjuration of spirits, but fairies were seldom among those invoked, and their monarchs were mentioned in these texts even more rarely. In this respect, the world of the educated sorcerer was different from that of the common service magician. There seems to be one exception to this rule, in that during the fifteenth and sixteenth centuries a spirit called Oberycom in the former period and Oberion in the latter was regularly mentioned as a desirable servitor for such magicians.[80] This is probably our old friend Oberon from *Huon de Bordeaux*, of whom the practitioners seem only to have known that he was reputedly a being of mighty magical powers. By the end of the sixteenth century Berners and Shakespeare had made Oberon so familiar as a fairy king that on his rare subsequent appearances in the context of ritual magic he was clearly identified as such: for example, the doctor and occultist Simon Forman, around 1600, recorded an opinion that Oberon's realm extended to the centre of Europe, where he guarded precious metals in the rocks of Silesia from miners.[81]

Invocations by learned magicians of the fairy queen were even rarer, though one is recorded in an early modern English manuscript, while another such compilation has a call to 'Oberyon' as fairy king and another to 'Micob, Queen of Fairies', with a retinue of female sprites bearing classical Roman names. Oberyon is described in detail as wearing a royal crown and teaching humans healing, the properties of stones and herbs and the abilities to tell the future and locate buried treasure. This work even has a drawing of him in a turban, which may refer to his roots in *Huon de Bordeaux* as a Near Eastern potentate.[82] The queen also made a promising early appearance in a verse tract on alchemy from fifteenth-century England, cast as a dialogue between a famous thirteenth-century scientist and the 'queen of the elves', called Elchyyell. She is 'bright', 'fair and free' and encountered under a tree, and teaches him the vital alchemical trick of turning lesser metals into gold.[83] Alleged attempts to contact her by would-be conjurors were reported into the seventeenth century: the famous astrologer William Lilly related in his memoirs how he had heard of a virtuous parson who went to a wood with a friend to invoke her, after which she appeared looking glorious.[84]

One of the most striking proofs of the wide extent to which belief in the fairy monarchs existed among the Tudor and Stuart English populace is the occurrence of cases of fraud perpetrated or attempted by confidence tricksters on gullible victims whom they promised to introduce to these sovereigns. It can probably be presumed that the true number of such occurrences was higher, because some of those duped would have been too embarrassed to prosecute, or the criminals may have successfully disappeared, so that the incidence of such reports is telling. They commence in 1595, possibly in the aftermath of the new prominence given to the fairy kingdom in the metropolitan theatre, most successfully by Shakespeare. In that year a London gun-maker's wife and fortune-teller called Judith Phillips, alias Doll Pope, was arrested for having obtained a turkey and a chicken from a wealthy widow, whom she had persuaded to offer these things to 'the queen of the fairies'. Having thus gained that potentate's favour, the widow was invited to put all her gold objects in one place in her home, after which the queen would draw to them money which had been hidden in the house by a previous occupant. The intended dupe, however, realized in time that her own possessions were likely to disappear.[85] Phillips was whipped through the city for this offence, and the investigation uncovered that she had already been punished for a similar scam in a Hampshire village. There she had set up as a service magician and convinced a rich inhabitant that she could summon the fairy queen to him by a rite in which he laid gold coins under five candlesticks in his largest room. Judith herself appeared attired as the queen in a white smock and headdress, carrying a wand, and engaged in 'some dalliance'. She had then made off with the gold, the sticks and some linen.[86]

In 1613 Alice and John West were flogged and pilloried in London for persuading a wealthy couple at Hammersmith to part with £120 as a gift for the king and queen of the fairies, who would then reveal a hidden treasure to them. The Wests staged a show in a vault at which the couple's maid saw two people dressed like the fairy monarchs, 'and by them little Elves and Goblings'. They were also charged with having persuaded a servant girl to sit naked in a garden through a night with a pot of earth in her lap which the queen would have turned into gold by dawn. As she did so, they made off with her money and clothes. Farmers had been talked into giving them more money, and livestock and farm produce, for promises to have the fairies at their service, and an old woman had handed over £80 to buy from the queen the secret of how to turn silver into gold. Alice practised as a service magician, and told fortunes to people on whom she had already obtained information, informing them that her apparently remarkable insights had been vouchsafed by the queen. She had cheated an apprentice out of four pieces of his master's finest plate, which he had been instructed to place in the corners of a close as a ceremony to entice the queen to meet him.[87]

Around these semi-professional repeat offenders were more isolated and opportunistic cases of a similar kind. In the winter of 1609–10 the Court of Chancery tried the case of a young Dorset squire who while in London encountered two more predatory gentlemen. These got an accomplice to offer to introduce him to the fairy queen and gain him her hand in marriage, if he handed over £516 in gold, to be distributed among her subject fairies, in the manner of a person seeking royal favour at the contemporary court of James I, who would be expected to deliver bribes to well-placed courtiers.[88] In the 1620s a writer upon religious scepticism and false belief recounted how he had met a man who had been persuaded by a magician to try to obtain some of the fabled seed of the fern plant, which allegedly conferred superhuman powers. He had been brought to believe that the seed was kept by 'the King of the Fayries'. The author added that his informant had forgotten the king's name, 'till I remembered it unto him out of my reading in *Huon of Bordeaux*'.[89] It was, of course, Oberon, again.

These real-life stories made enough impression to inspire fictional imitations. Ben Jonson himself put into his play *The Alchemist*, launched in 1610, fraudsters who coax a man into giving them money to meet the 'Queen of Faery', whom they promised would make him rich. Again, the initial outlay of cash is to get courtiers of hers to arrange the introduction. The dupe is blindfolded and persuaded that he is surrounded by fairies.[90] A lesser play from the same period, *The Valiant Welshman*, is set in ancient Britain but still features a stupid knight in love with the fairy queen who seeks a service magician who can contact her. Of course, he finds a con man, who makes the knight creep on hands and knees to a woman dressed up as the queen, who then leads him into a ditch.[91]

The longest and most elaborate of such charades to appear in the actual records was also apparently the last, in the 1680s, and was the work of a London service magician called Mary Parish, who dealt in a variety of cures and charms. One of the clients to whom she sold a charm for success in gambling was the son of a lord, and when it failed she revealed that she had enjoyed contact with the fairy realm since the age of eight, and especially with its queen, whose stately palace she visited within a mound on Hounslow Heath, west of London. She and her royal husband presided there over a court populated by beings who were, like themselves, in human form but only about a yard high, though they could swell to normal human size at will. They gave her rings, money and jewels, and sometimes appeared to her in turn with their train and attendants in her room in the city. They were Christians who practised a form of Roman Catholicism. The king had shown less interest in her after she had refused to become his mistress and bear him children, in lieu of his barren wife, but the queen kept weekly contact for several years, until she died, after which the king married a sister of the fairy king of Portugal. In the real world this was the reign of Charles II, who had married a Portuguese princess who was herself barren, while Charles had many children by mistresses: Mary did not look far for her inspiration.

All this, she explained to the thrilled nobleman, had taken place long before, and for eight or nine years she had had no contact with the fairy realm. He pressed her to renew her acquaintance with it and introduce him, and there ensued a process, itself lasting for years and in many ways richly comic, whereby she repeatedly arranged an audience for him and then informed him that it had been called off because of unforeseen developments. She seems all this time to have been living off his money, as his mistress. After almost a decade he settled down as a landed gentleman and apparently lost his interest in other worlds, while retaining an affection and respect for Mary. Our knowledge of their relationship comes from his autobiography.[92]

The combination of the Scottish and English records leaves no doubt that a belief in the fairy kingdom formed a lively part of the culture of early modern commoners from the south coast of England to the Moray Firth. Both of its rulers were generally regarded as potential helpers of humanity, and both normally operated with equal agency, the queen having an independence of action and an effective power of will that would be unusual (or, in some representations of her, unheard of) in the wives of reigning human kings. As such, she was regarded as acting as an effective patroness in her own right of ordinary people who made a relationship with her, of a kind denied them with earthly rulers. What emerges most strongly from the aggregate of the accounts is her essential benevolence to devotees, despite all the centuries of tradition of blighting elves and of demons masquerading as beautiful and seductive beings. Her apparent origins, in the figure of the protective and inspiring fay, had served her well.

There is, therefore, the greater contrast between this widespread belief system among commoners, which extended (as shown) to the more gullible kind of gentry and aristocracy, and the attitude adopted by most creative writers, the poets and playwrights. These treated the fairy kingdom simply as a fictional resource that could be manipulated in various different ways for fun and profit, much as the original medieval composers of romances about fays seem to have done with their subject matter. One striking illustration of the flippancy with which they increasingly treated it was the fashion for miniaturizing it which set in from the 1590s. Once more, it was Shakespeare who set the fashion, at some point in the first half of the decade, when he wrote *Romeo and Juliet*, and as a comic monologue introduced the character of Queen Mab.[93] Despite her title, which is never explained, she is not a fairy sovereign but the 'fairies midwife', herself the size of an agate stone and travelling in a hazelnut shell drawn by ants, with wheel-spokes of spiders' legs, furnishings of grasshopper wings and reins of spiders' webs. Her driver is a gnat, wielding a whip of cricket bone. Her main role as described in the speech, however, is not to deliver babies but dreams, to sleeping humans over whose bodies she rides. She is also blamed for weaving horses' manes into tangles in the night. The speaker himself, a madcap young noble, admits his description to be pure fantasy, and indeed both the figure and her name seem to have been Shakespeare's own invention. No fairy or fay was called 'Mab' before he wrote, and the derivation is uncertain; the great queen of medieval Irish legend, Maeve, has no resemblance to the tiny fairy except the slight similarity of name, and it is not clear how or where Shakespeare would have encountered the Welsh *mab*, signifying childhood or youth.

Nonetheless, both the figure and the name were immensely influential. 'Mab' became used by poets and playwrights in the following few decades as one of the names of the fairy queen herself. At the same time the concept of tiny fairies rapidly became popular. In a play from around 1600, such beings have names like Penny, Cricket and Little-Little Prick, leap on flower tops, ride on flies, play under the skirts of unsuspecting girls and dance and sing in honour of their 'brave queen'.[94] This image of them was not entirely unprecedented: the Scottish King Berdok may be remembered, and back in the twelfth century Gervase of Tilbury had told of a kind of English demon called Portunes, who were six inches high, roasted frogs for food and looked like old men wearing patched coats.[95] These, however, were one-offs, and neither Berdok nor the Portunes were actually identified as fairies.

During the early seventeenth century, the concept of a royal court of tiny fairies caught on among lyric poets, until it became something of a craze by the 1620s, driven by a competition to come up with yet more inspired and sophisticated uses of miniature materials as props and trappings. Michael Drayton conjured up a palace of King Oberon and Queen Mab, from which Oberon sallies in an acorn cup, to fight a wasp, a glow-worm and bees, and catches Mab and one of his knights, Pigwiggen, listening together to a bumble bee minstrel. Fleeing his king's jealousy, Pigwiggen hides in a nutshell, and then arms himself with cockleshell, plant stalk and horse fly's tongue to fight Oberon.[96] Thomas Randolph entertained the real King Charles I and Queen Henrietta Maria with descriptions of Oberon and Mab enjoying an anti-masque performed by flies and a jig danced by ants, hunting snails and living in a palace built of precious stones, nutmegs and ginger, with palisades of teeth.[97] Robert Herrick's verses returned repeatedly to the conceit. His 'Oberon's Feast' is served on a mushroom, and consists of a wheat grain, butterfly horns, cuckoo spit, fuzz ball, a bee sac, and so forth, consumed while insect minstrels play. 'The Temple' of fairies is made from a kingfisher's nest, and the gods or saints worshipped within are a beetle, a cricket, a fly, a will-o'-the-wisp and so on, the most important being 'The Lady of the Lobster'. The priest serves communion wine in half a nutshell and uses a psalter of trout-fly wings.[98] A miniature fairy royal court also featured in a masque by Inigo Jones and literary works by John Day and Sir Simon Steward.[99]

Even in the hothouse atmosphere of early Stuart lyric poetry, there was only so much of this stuff that a reasonable person could stand, and by the middle of the century the fashion had waned. Its project of literally trivializing the fairy queen and her spouse seems to have destroyed interest in them altogether as personalities among poets and playwrights; and in the later Stuart period they virtually slipped out of English literature. Even more striking, and as a sign of how interdependent the two spheres could be, they seem to have ebbed out of the imagination of ordinary people as well, all over Britain. By the Georgian period they were gone. The rich folklore collections of the late nineteenth and early twentieth centuries showed little interest in them among commoners, and no service magicians between 1740 and 1940 seem to have claimed them as a source of knowledge; instead, it was books which were cited as the fount of skill and power for such practitioners, as for learned magicians through the ages.[100]

The nineteenth century, by contrast, saw a considerable revival of interest in fairies as a subject for literature and art which persisted into the twentieth, and this was linked in part to a revival of admiration for Shakespeare which elevated him to the historical position of the greatest British author.[101] However, the fairy queen and king did not share in this rebirth, with the exception of their incarnations as Titania and Oberon in paintings or poems based on *A Midsummer Night's Dream*. As figures of creative and emotive power for poets, playwrights and novelists, they belonged to the increasingly remote past. When one of them did suddenly appear in a new work of fantasy fiction it was a striking one-off: Galadriel in J.R.R. Tolkien's *The Lord of the Rings*, written in the 1940s and published in the 1950s. She is a classic medieval royal fay, ruling a realm of loyal human-sized elves set in an enchanted forest, stately and wise and possessed of formidable powers of magic. She has a spouse and consort whom she treats with respect and formal equality, but she is clearly the more impressive, effective and respected figure. Tolkien himself, unsurprisingly, was a professional medievalist. An active belief in fairies persisted among English, Welsh and Scottish commoners until the twentieth century, as is clear from those extensive collections of folklore; but they seemed to have lost their monarchs.[102] The recent recrudescence of enthusiasm for fairy encounters, across the English-speaking world and associated especially with a New Age and pagan milieu, seems mostly to have left the queen and king behind as well.[103] An exception is the character of Mab, from Shakespeare, who has in some renderings shed her diminutive stature and comic associations and become a goddess of the land, seemingly by strengthened association with the Irish Queen Maeve.[104]

All these are mere echoes of the fairy queen's late medieval and early modern glory. For about three hundred years she held a potent place in the English and Lowland Scottish imagination, which covered more or less the whole of both regions and spanned society from top to bottom. For elite writers she was a dynamic literary figure with potential to be represented in many different ways, sympathetic, admiring, mocking, hostile or ambivalent. She could be brought into a story alone or with her royal spouse (who had his own, almost as prominent and fertile, place in poetry and drama) and/or a retinue of followers of different kinds. By commoners she was more often represented as a patroness, teacher, helper, counsellor and (occasionally) lover, supplying roles that were apparently missing in human society for those who claimed her acquaintance. In Scotland some of those who made these claims died for her, in the literal sense that their revelations of their association with her led to a sentence of death. However, all classes, it seems, eventually tired of her and ceased to find her an effective companion of the imagination. No great changes in political, social or religious contexts had occurred to cause this – the decline had set in before the real monarchy of Britain lost any of its powers – so that it appears simply and purely that after a lengthy period people needed new figures to fulfil her roles.

CHAPTER 4

THE LADY OF THE NIGHT

The third figure to be considered makes a contrast with the last two, while having things in common with them. Unlike the fairy queen, she had a geographical range which covered most of Western Europe, and a temporal one which not only continued to the modern age but extended back to the early Middle Ages. Both those characteristics were shared by Nature and Mother Earth, but the being to be discussed now was quite unlike the latter in one very important respect: she was the focus of a genuinely popular belief system. She only entered the writings of the learned elite when its members were commenting on or investigating (usually with feelings ranging from disapproval to horror) the traditions of the common people. Her origins are far more mysterious than those of the preceding two superhuman females and her forms more diverse. She was conceived of as a mighty feminine being who travelled the night with a retinue of spirits, and sometimes included favoured human beings in it. In some accounts her company just roamed the earth, in others it stopped for feasts and revels, and in yet others it visited the houses of selected people to bless them.

Three aspects of her tradition seem consistent. The first is that it was, as said, held and propagated by commoners, and especially by poor women, though sometimes by men of the same class as well. Those who claimed to travel with the Lady thereby gained a status in their communities which normally they would not have possessed. The activities in which they engaged as part of her entourage were classic pieces of wish fulfilment for an underclass: to become favoured members of a supernatural royal court, which might admit them to feasts and games, and to gain free entry to the houses of wealthier neighbours. The second aspect of the tradition is that the women who claimed to rove with the Lady were often or mostly the service magicians of their communities. Like those in Britain who attributed their skills to the tuition of fairies, they frequently stated that they had learned their magic from her and her companions. The third aspect is that this belief system nowhere seems to have involved any actual group activity. The travels of the humans who claimed to join these phantasms were experienced in their minds, while their bodies remained static.

The Frankish Heartland

The concept first appears in one of the most famous of early medieval ecclesiastical decrees, the so-called canon 'Episcopi'. The original document of this is lost, and its earliest appearance is in a collection of canon law texts made soon after the year 900 for the archbishop of the western German city of Trier by Regino, the abbot of Prüm in the central Rhineland. It has always been thought most likely to have originated at some point in the previous century in the lands of the Frankish rulers who between them controlled most of what is now France and Germany. The author and his place of residence, however, seem likely to remain forever unknown. He asserted that 'certain wicked women, who have been perverted by Satan and seduced by illusions of devils and by phantoms, believe and profess that during the night they ride on certain beasts with the goddess Diana and an uncountable host of women; that they pass across many great lands in the silence of the dead of night; that they obey her directions as those of a mistress; and that on particular nights they are summoned to her service'. He added that this belief was held by 'an innumerable multitude', and that priests should preach against it as a diabolical illusion, and so expel 'fortune telling and the magical art' from their parishes.[1]

So what are we to make of this text? There is a strong implication in its last directive that the women who held the belief concerned and claimed to ride with Diana were the service magicians of their communities. It is more or less certain, also, that the tradition of these rides was well established by the time that the document was composed, or it would not have claimed a huge number of believers for it; although just as we do not know where it was written, so we do not know how wide an area those believers occupied at the time, or how much exaggeration it made of their number. As for the name given for the goddess whom the women claimed to follow, at first sight the Roman deity Diana, as portrayed in ancient texts, would be a very suitable leader for the cavalcades concerned. She was associated with wild animals, and the night and the moon, and so with witchcraft, was supposed to care for women in particular, and had a retinue of nymphs. Furthermore, she appears to have continued to enjoy a widespread cult in the early Middle Ages, spanning the area that the Romans called Gaul, most of which was to develop into France, and extending into what became Germany. The life of Caesarius of Arles, the foremost churchman of Gaul in the early sixth century, claimed that he exorcized from a slave girl in his diocese 'a demon, whom the peasants call Diana', which had been beating her every night. The late-sixth-century Gallic bishop Gregory of Tours described how a missionary saint whom he had met himself, Vulfolaic, had destroyed a statue of the same goddess worshipped by country people in the Ardennes region in the far north-east of Gaul. The life of another such missionary, St Killan, recorded that he had been martyred in the seventh century when he tried to convert some of the East Franks, who became the Germans, from the cult of Diana.[2]

On closer inspection, what seems to be a compelling body of evidence crumbles away. Whoever the goddess was whose devotees despatched Killan, it could not have been Diana, because the region in which he served and died, Franconia, was far beyond the bounds of the Roman world. There is not even evidence for a widespread popular cult of her in the Roman provinces north of the Alps, including Gaul, which would linger into subsequent centuries. It is just possible that there had been one in the far south, around Arles in Provence, but very difficult to credit one as far north as the Ardennes. Conversely, none of the early medieval ecclesiastical decrees or law codes from the Mediterranean basin, including Italy – which was Diana's ancient stronghold – refer to nocturnal rides led by her of the sort recorded in the Rhineland. Indeed, there is no ancient reference to Diana which portrays her as leading human devotees in this way. What seems to have been happening is that early medieval churchmen were applying her name to local rustic goddesses in general. This may have been because of their classical education, which would make them associate any female deity of the countryside with the Roman one. This solution to the problem was proposed by Carlo Ginzburg, probably the leading Italian historian of his generation, subsequently one of the luminaries of American academe and the author who dealt most inspiringly and influentially with the subject of the lady and her followers in the late twentieth century. He showed convincingly that in the later Middle Ages, when the records are full enough to contain such insights, inquisitors did indeed impose the name Diana on this figure, while those who venerated her called her by another, particular and local, one.[3] To this important suggestion may perhaps be added another: that Diana is also the only pagan deity to be named in the whole of the New Testament, and as such might readily have become a natural shorthand for a goddess in general among many medieval Christians.

The night-roaming lady next appears in another collection of canon law issued in the early eleventh century, by Burchard, bishop of Worms. Worms is, again, in the central Rhineland, but Buchard gathered his material from all over Western Europe to assemble a general body of work for the use of the Latin Church. This is as true of its nineteenth section as the others, this being a manual for the use of priests hearing confessions and prescribing penances for specific sins. As part of its remit, it listed a number of popular beliefs which Burchard's church deemed to be erroneous and harmful and to merit atonement, and after which confessors were directed to enquire. One of these passages repeats the canon 'Episcopi' but adds the name

Herodias to that of Diana as the leader of the nocturnal rides: this version of the text was to be repeated through the rest of the Middle Ages and beyond. Another reads 'Have you believed that there is any woman who can do that which some, deceived by the Devil, insist that they must do of necessity or because he commands, that is with a host of demons transformed into the shapes of women (which the deluded populace calls Holda), ride on certain animals during particular nights . . .?' Burchard included two more traditions by which women – and it was always women – were believed to leave their beds in spirit form at night and gather for different purposes, covering great distances and seemingly flying through the air: the night was, at least in imagination, a busy place for Western European females at the turn of the first millennium. The two quoted were, however, those who, clearly or possibly, named a superhuman leader for these.[4]

The bishop therefore gives us two more names, one definite and one possible, for that leader: Herodias and Holda (or in some versions Hulda). Each needs to be considered in turn. There is no apparent difficulty in identifying the origins of Herodias, who occurs in the New Testament as the woman who brings about the death of John the Baptist by prevailing on her royal husband to have him beheaded.[5] As such, she makes a very neat fit with Diana, as the wickedest woman in the Christian Bible is neatly paired with the only pagan deity in it. She does, however, seem to have been a focus for genuinely popular belief during the period now considered, to judge from a statement by Ratherius, bishop of Verona on the Plain of Lombardy in northern Italy during the early tenth century. He complained that many people, 'to the peril of their souls', claimed Herodias 'as a queen, even as a goddess', and said 'that a third of the world is her realm'.[6]

He was absolutely specific that the figure in question was the Biblical villainess responsible for the death of St John, and that both women and men made this claim for her. Tantalizingly, he does not mention any connection between her and night rides. Generally, his text was designed to chastise his fellow prelates of Italy, so it may be thought that the tradition he was recounting came from there. However, as a much-travelled churchman who himself came from Liège in the Netherlands, he might have picked up his information elsewhere. It remains inside the margin of possibility that the name Herodias was originally applied to a popular figure who had a different one, or none, by a churchman, in disdain and calumny, and then got spread into general culture by preachers. If the association did originate among the populace of some region, it is hard to imagine what would have persuaded a large number of commoners to take such a transgressive step of belief as to turn a Biblical villainess into a patroness – or at least to decide that others had done so. It may be that some garbling of the scriptural story had taken place: by the twelfth century, certainly, an apocryphal legend was reported that Herodias had been the daughter and not the wife of the king, and fell in love with John, who rejected her. It described how when, stricken by his death, she tried to bestow tears and kisses on his severed head, it blew her up into the sky, where she has wandered ever since, coming down to earth at night.[7] This account repeated the claim that she had the allegiance of a third of humanity, and would provide a back story to account for her position as a leader of nocturnal ridings, though this connection is not explicitly made.

If the source of the name Herodias is problematic in this context, then the name, or expression, Holda is even more so. In the translation of Burchard's Latin provided above, the word seems to be used to mean the cavalcade itself. It appears to be related to a set of terms in medieval Germanic languages with connotations of devotion, protection and affection, all positive associations which orbit around the idea of the roaming host as some kind of 'good company'.[8] It is not surprising that such apparent approbation was too much for one clerical copyist, who altered the term to 'Unholda' in his manuscript, to deliver the opposite message.[9] Thus far, it looks as if this is a spectral cavalcade of the same kind as that described in the canon 'Episcopi', but either lacking a special leader or with the same one. The real problem is that Burchard's text has a number of variant recensions, and one minority tradition of these has a different wording in the passage: 'a host of demons transformed into the shapes of women (she whom the deluded populace calls the *striga* Holda)'. This, therefore (if rather clumsily) gives the host an apparent leader, called Holda.

The term *striga* would have had an unpleasant resonance for medieval churchmen. Its original meaning was of a non-human nocturnal being, the *strix*, whom ancient Roman culture represented as sharing physical characteristics with an owl or a bat and credited with sucking the life from young children, causing their decline and death. The name was then transferred by Latin-writing clerks, adapted into *stria* or *striga*, to a different kind of nocturnal horror imagined by the Germanic tribes which brought down the Western Roman Empire, and is recorded in their first law codes. This was a human woman who preyed at night upon adult men, using magic to remove fat or internal organs from their bodies and then consuming it in cannibal feasts with others of their kind.[10] To conceive of Holda as a being and to apply such a term to her was to besmirch the night rides indeed and extend this to those who believed in them. Frustratingly, it does not seem possible at present securely to date the different versions of the text in relation to each other. It could be that the term Holda was first applied to the rides themselves, and that later somebody thought it more logical that it was applied to their leader and tidied up the text accordingly; or it might be that the word originally signified a superhuman woman who led the troops of beast-riders and that this was subsequently garbled into making it seem to apply to the latter. The latest thought seems to be that the earliest known manuscripts of the work are those in which the name refers to the rides.[11] It was the other usage of it, for a being, which was, however, to become dominant.

It may complicate matters still further that the name Holda is actually found much earlier, in a poem written by the scholarly monk Walahfrid Strabo, who lived on an island in Lake Constance on the border of Germany and Switzerland, in the first half of the ninth century. It was in praise of Judith, the wife of the Holy Roman Emperor Louis the Pious, leader of the Franks, and compares her both to the great archaic Greek poetess Sappho and to 'Holda'. Here the reference must surely be to the pious Old Testament prophetess Huldah, thus neatly pairing a classical with a Biblical cultural heroine; and the suggestion is strengthened by the fact that in the Latin translation of the Bible, the Vulgate, Huldah's name is rendered as Olda.[12] It would be easy to dismiss any connection between the Holda of the poem and she of the night rides as a coincidence of names, but if a Biblical villainess such as Herodias could be taken into popular culture as a benevolent patroness, then it is possible that a Biblical heroine could have been.[13]

All this is both exciting and deeply frustrating. It seems that by the ninth century a popular tradition that ordinary women rode on animals at night in the retinue of a mighty female figure was well established, but we do not really know where, let alone how or why. To judge solely from the provenance of the texts in which it is first recorded, and the silence of those elsewhere, it seems to have been a feature of the Frankish cultural zone, covering modern France and Germany, with possibly an epicentre, like the texts, in the Rhineland. It was spoken of not as a feature of societies recently reclaimed from paganism, but of those securely within the Church's embrace, with a full structure of serving priests. More cannot be said, partly because of the fortuitous effect of the survival of some sources and not others, and partly because the churchmen who wrote those sources were not interested in the matter. They had no incentive to enquire further into the origin or the details of the belief concerned because they were unanimous in dismissing it as a demonically inspired illusion. As a result, the being at its centre remains faceless and formless, and her followers anonymous and unlocated, merged into an undifferentiated mass of female commoners. To those who recorded it, it was not even an especially serious or menacing belief: a superstition held by silly and ignorant women and not a heresy or a feature of resurgent paganism. Those who admitted to it were therefore awarded relatively mild penances. The one certainty in the whole matter is that the condemnations made of it were ineffective, because it was to flourish and spread out during the next few centuries.

The Widening Source Base

During the twelfth century the condemnation recorded by Burchard continued to be repeated in further codifications of canon law and penitentials.[14] Other clerical authors expanded the information available on the night rides. One was the Englishman John of Salisbury, writing in the 1150s: he had been educated in France and became a bishop there, and travelled to Italy as well, and drew on all three countries for information. He inveighed against the ability of the Devil to make people believe that they were doing things in actuality which they were only imagining, and took as an example the claim by some that:

a *nocticula* (female night-spirit) or Herodias or the 'mistress of the night' convokes nocturnal councils and assemblies at which they feast and revel; where some are punished and others are rewarded according to their merits. Moreover, infants are exposed to *lamiae* (child-killing demons) and some appear to be cut to pieces and greedily devoured, before by the mercy of the mistress, they are restored to their cribs . . . Indeed it is obvious from this that it is merely poor old women and the simpler kind of men who enter into these beliefs.[15]

In this account the night rides on animals seem to have been replaced by the holding of entertainments at a formal royal court, with the interpolation of a child-killing theme from the Roman tradition of the *strix*.

He was followed in the early thirteenth century by another French bishop, this time a native: Guillaume d'Auvergne, who held the see of Paris and a chair at its university. He introduces us (once again with a maddening lack of geographical specificity) to another kind of nocturnal female potentate:

the spirit who, in the shape of a woman, visits homes and storehouses at night. She is called Satia, from satiation, also Lady Abundia, because of the abundance she bestows on the said houses that she visits. She is the same kind of demon as those whom old women call 'the ladies' and in regard to whom they maintain this error, to which they alone give belief, in delusions and dreams. They say that these ladies consume the food and drink that they find in homes without devouring them completely, or even reducing their quantity, especially if the dishes holding food are left uncovered, and the containers holding drink are left unstoppered for the night. But, if they find these containers covered or closed or stoppered, they will not touch any of the contents, and that is the reason why the ladies abandon these houses to grief and bad luck without bestowing either satiety or abundance upon them.

He went on to claim that, although this belief was held by both sexes, it was mostly one of old women; after all, it was the females of the household who mostly maintained the home.[16]

A few decades later in the thirteenth century, a Franciscan friar, Bertold of Regensburg, whose preaching tours took him across most of German-speaking Europe, revealed the number of different activities in which nocturnal spirits were by then believed to engage. In one sermon he claimed that 'the foolish peasant women indeed believe that the ladies of the night and night-roaming spirits visit their homes, and they set a table for them'. In another he told his audience that 'you should not believe at all in the night-roamers (*nachtwaren*) and their fellows, no more than the *hulden* and the *unhulden*, in pixies (*pilwitzen*), in nightmares of both sexes (*maren, truten*) in the night-women (*nachtvrouwen*), in nocturnal spirits, or those who travel by riding this or that: they are all demons. Nor should you prepare the table anymore for the blessed ladies (*felices dominae*).'[17] So it looks as if the tradition of the rides was still extant as well as that of the house visits and, given Bertold's cultural range and use of vernacular terms, that both were found in the German lands. Also, one of the names given to the night rides by Burchard, Holde or Hulde, and one of names given to the alleged leader of them in a recension of his work, Unholde, had seemingly become attached to troops of benevolent and malevolent sprites, the *hulden* and *unhulden*.

In the second half of the thirteenth century, accounts multiply, in accordance with the better survival of sources. One such is the manual for fellow preachers written in the 1250s by the Dominican friar Etienne de Bourbon, who worked all over eastern and southern France. He told the story of a man in the southern mountain area of the Cevennes who claimed to spend nights with the benevolent women whom common people called 'the good things'. To convince his priest of their existence, he got him to rise from his bed and straddle a piece of wood, which transported him to a place where he saw many women singing by torchlight and candlelight, and tables covered in food. The man advised the priest not to make the sign of the cross. Naturally, this happened, and the ladies all vanished (so making Etienne's point, which was to emphasise their unholy nature).[18]

There is no mention here of a leader for the ladies, but she features prominently a couple of decades later in another French work which has been cited before: *Le Roman de la Rose* by Jean de Meun. This condemned the folly of old women who claimed to wander at night with 'Lady Habonde' (Abundance) and her 'good ladies', saying that this gift was granted to the third child in every family. These fortunate individuals journeyed with their mistress three times a week, leaving their bodies behind in bed and travelling in spirit, so that they could enter locked houses through chinks and holes to make merry there.[19] In 1280 the bishop of Couserans, in the French Pyrenees, renewed the canon 'Episcopi' in Burchard's form at a council of his clergy, but added Bensozia (possibly meaning 'the good companion') to Diana and Herodias as the name of the leader of the rides.[20] In the early years of the following century, one of the best known of the new breed of heresy-hunting inquisitors, the Dominican friar Bernard Gui, enquired after belief in the night-wandering fairy women called the 'good things'. Gui was from southern France and spent most of his career in different parts of it.[21] Jacques Fournier, another famous inquisitor of the same kind and the same period, working in the same mountains which contained Couserans, examined a folk magician who claimed to have gained his knowledge by travelling with 'the good ladies'.[22]

By the late thirteenth century, the tradition of the house-blessing female spirits was also becoming the subject of multiplying cautionary tales designed to warn people off the belief. A collection of saint's lives from the late thirteenth century, made in northern Italy but drawing material from far beyond, told of St Germanus that he had seen a friend lay a table at the end of an evening for 'the good women who enter at night'. The latter duly arrived, with males as well, and Germanus's host recognized neighbours among them – showing that it was believed that humans could join this company. The saint, however, used his powers to make the visitors confess that they were actually disguised demons.[23] A continuation of an encyclopaedia of information and advice told of how youths robbed a rich peasant by coming into his house dressed as the 'good women', dancing and informing him that they would restore a hundredfold all that they took away.[24]

There are some obvious problems and questions in all this material which do not admit of clear solutions and answers. One is how much these references are rooted in the areas in which the documents concerned were issued. We can be fairly (though not absolutely) certain that Bertold's night-wanderers were from the German-speaking area, and that Etienne's 'good things' were actually reported in the Cevennes. Was Bernard, however, talking about a Pyrenean belief, or just repeating Etienne, and did the bishop of Couserans hear of Bensozia in his diocese or elsewhere? Too much of the context is missing to suggest a confident reply. The same lack leaves researchers equally baffled when considering whether the ladies who visited houses, with or without a leader, were another version of those who rode out with Diana or Herodias (or whomever), or whether they had an entirely independent origin. It is equally possible that they did indeed represent different branches of a diverging and spreading tradition, or else converging belief systems from different areas which were associated in the minds of the often highly mobile, educated and supranational churchmen and literary figures who recorded them. The amount of information which is missing makes any further understanding of the beliefs concerned virtually impossible to achieve.[25]

Apogee and Contraction

In the course of the later Middle Ages and the early modern period, the tradition of night-roaming female spirits seems to have reached its furthest geographical extent and undergone a set of further developments. One was the appearance of a new character, known as Percht, Perchta, Berchte or Berchta. She was part of the Germanic linguistic zone, and first seems to appear in the thirteenth century, in a bare reference to 'Lady Perchten'.[26] She starts to come into focus, however, in a pair of texts from the mid-fourteenth century.[27] One is a handbook of piety, the name of which translates as *The Mirror of Souls*. The passage concerned can be read as 'they sin also who on the night of Epiphany leave food and drink on their table so that all shall go well with them in the coming year and they shall be fortunate in all things . . . Therefore sinners also are they who offer food to Percht and red shoes to the "shrieker" or to the nightmare.' She thus takes her place in a set of Germanic spirits to whom offerings were left out by householders, and the first example seems to associate these with the medieval Christian feast of Epiphany, Twelfth Night, the end of the Christmas holiday and a winter date seen by people as especially numinous. Another pious work from the same period seems to give her a menacing or comic character, terming her 'Berchten with the long nose'. This is sustained in a Tyrolese poem from the opening of the fifteenth century, which states that women from the region claimed to have ridden out at night in companies of at least twenty, on calves, goats, cows, pigs, stools and cabinets, in the entourage of Herodias, Diana or 'Percht with the iron nose'.[28] The old tradition of riding on animals had thus become both domesticated and associated with the relatively new character. One recent scholar has suggested on linguistic grounds that Percht was in fact a personification of the Epiphany festival, and as such fits into a general late medieval tendency to personify feasts as characters.[29]

This picture is filled out slightly by a fifteenth-century Austrian academic, Thomas Ebendorfer, who identified Percht, as the spirit active at nights around Epiphany, with two other figures whom we have already encountered as visiting human houses and expecting food and drink in exchange for blessings: 'Habundia' and Satia.[30] In the same century, editions of the sermons of the German Dominican preacher Johan Herolt, like the Tyrolese poet, brought Percht into the rides of the canon 'Episcopi'. One of 1474 stated that 'Diana, commonly called in the vernacular

Unholde, that is the beatific woman, goes about at night with her army, travelling across vast spaces'. It added that she did so specifically during the twelve days of Christmas. Four years later, another edition added 'Lady Berthe' to Diana and Unholde.[31] A medical textbook, *Thesaurus pauperum*, went into explicit detail about how 'Lady Percht' or 'Perchtum', like the ladies Abundia and Satia, was believed to visit homes with her retinue. Those who left out food and drink for them were expected to earn wealth for their households, and Percht was abroad on nights between Christmas and Epiphany. Acceptable dishes were bread, cheese, milk, eggs, wine and water, and crockery and cutlery were also expected, for polite dining.[32] The tropes of the night rides and house visits were being combined into a distinctive German seasonal tradition. Its association with midwinter was also found in northern Italy at this period: in 1423 the famous Franciscan preacher Bernardino of Siena inveighed at Padua against old women who worked as service magicians and said that they travelled 'in the ride of Herodias on the night of Epiphany'. This combined the canon 'Episcopi' tradition with the new seasonality of the German references.[33]

Another development of the late medieval period was a growing belief in, and fear of, devil-worshipping magicians who met together at night to pay homage to Satan or one of his minions, and feast and plan misdeeds. This was to flower from the 1420s into the stereotype of a satanic witch conspiracy which produced the notorious trials for witchcraft that were a feature of the late medieval and early modern ages. The now venerable belief system of the night rides and revels of female spirits could easily be transmuted into this far more menacing construct, which resulted in proportionately more savage punishment of those who claimed or were claimed to participate in the activities concerned. The western Alps and northern Italy formed the geographical crucible in which this lethal transmutation occurred, and a beneficial result of it for historians, though not for the actual people involved, is that it generated records of what the people who actually believed in the nocturnal spirits concerned testified about it. One of the earliest such cases is also now one of the most famous, a linked pair of trials at Milan in 1384 and 1390. They were of two women who stated that they had attended the 'society' or 'game' of 'Lady Oriente' weekly for many years and paid homage to her. They said that people did so in the form of humans, living or dead (including executed criminals, who appeared ashamed), and of every kind of animal except the donkey (who had carried Christ) and the fox. They feasted off livestock that were then restored to life, and visited tidy homes to eat and drink there and bless them. Oriente's act of restoring the animals consisted of striking their bones and skin with a wand or staff. She also instructed her human followers in the arts of herb lore, divination, healing, the removal of bewitchment and the finding of stolen goods: all this was the standard trade of the service magician, which the defendants practised. One of the women declared that Oriente 'would be like Christ, ruler of the world', the other that the name of the Christian God could never be uttered in the presence of the lady. In the changing mood of the times, this counted as heresy, and things were hardly helped when one of the women (perhaps under duress) confessed to taking a demon as her lover. Having been sentenced to penance at the first trial, after the second they were burned at the stake.[34]

The major and very dangerous alteration that occurred in the region and in the neighbouring Alps during the early fifteenth century was that such individual cases began to be regarded as parts of a much wider diabolical conspiracy to seduce wicked humans to follow Satan and use them to blight good people. In 1438, 1456 and 1480 witch trials of this new style in the central Italian Alps involved references to the 'good society' or 'the lady of the revel'. In 1492 two preachers of the heretical Christian Waldensian sect, tried in a valley near the western end of the same mountains, were induced to confess to worshipping a list of diabolical entities including 'Sibilla and the fairies'. Ultimately, this 'Sibilla' was almost certainly the ancient Roman prophetess the Sibyl of Cumae. The nocturnal lady (under various names) and her travels, feasts and games were to continue to feature regularly in north Italian witch trials into the early sixteenth century, and sporadically thereafter into the seventeenth.[35] Sometimes the records furnish vivid detail of the sort found at Milan in 1390. Two old women tried in the Val de Fassa, in the Dolomite mountains of north-eastern Italy, in 1457 confessed to belonging to the society led by a 'the good mistress Richella'. She came to them by night, well dressed and riding in a cart, and, once they had renounced the Christian faith, led them to a gathering of people where they could feast, dance and make merry, and where (in apparent contradiction of the requirement to repudiate Christianity) hairy men ate those who had not been baptized. They claimed to have attended these for several years, during the Ember Days, which were three consecutive days which the Western Christian calendar set aside in each of the four seasons for fasting and prayer; they had acquired the reputation for being times at which spirits were especially active. The women made offerings to Richella and she stroked their cheeks with hands that were covered in hair; but they could not see her face because it was hidden by huge semi-circular and protruding ornaments in her ears. Their attendance at her parties was abruptly terminated, they explained, when they made the sign of the cross.[36]

Other images of the lady emerge from subsequent north Italian trials. At the city of Mantua on the Plain of Lombardy in 1489, a weaver operating as a service magician was accused of getting children to gaze into a vase of water and report what they saw. They saw first a crowd of people, some on foot, others on horses and some without hands, and then an isolated figure, 'the mistress of the game', dressed in black with her head deeply lowered. She said that she could teach 'the power of the herbs and the nature of animals'. At another of the cities of the region, Ferrara, in the early sixteenth century, women accused of witchcraft described how they had followed 'the wise Sibilla', but needed to avoid looking her in the face, which would have meant their death. In the Val di Fiemme in the eastern Italian Alps during the same period, a woman stated that 'the mistress of the good game' had a stone on each side of her eyes, which served to open or close them according to her will. Another said that the 'mistress' had a black band around her head from which hung patches to cover her eyes and ears so she could not see or hear, as everything she did see or hear 'she makes her own, if she can'. Another explained that the 'mistress' travelled through the air, and that patches on either side of her eyes kept her from seeing everything, lest her gaze harm it. The group was equally in accord concerning the rest of the lady's appearance. One described her as large and ugly, with a huge head; another as 'an ugly black woman with a black smock and a black kerchief, tied around her head in a strange way'; while a third spoke of her as 'an ugly brazen black woman, with a black kerchief wrapped around her head in a German manner'.[37] These members of the same community had clearly been trading ideas, or drawing on an existing fund in the neighbourhood.

It is hard to tell whether this widespread idea (within the northern Italian region) that the face of the superhuman mistress could not be seen was based on a sense that a being of such potency needed to be concealed from profane view or had a visage that would harm mere mortals, or was instead a means of escape from having to describe her more precisely. In general, the evaluation of the detail that actually is provided in such stray pieces of evidence suffers yet again from a crippling lack of known context. The crucial element of missing knowledge here is whether those details of the lady, her followers and activities were part of wider local traditions, or just generated by the particular individuals concerned, using their own imaginations (or dreams, or visions) to elaborate on a belief system which was only vaguely delineated in popular representation.[38]

It is clear also that other mythical elements could be imported and integrated into the concept of the lady and her following, even at the end of the Middle Ages. One example of this is the concept of the Venusberg, a mountain inhabited by the classical Roman goddess Venus. That deity had become a common figure in medieval romance literature, with a range of connotations relating to her ancient role as patroness of love, from the sleazy, worldly and carnal to the noble and virtuous. It was also an international trope, by the fourteenth century, to locate her court within a mountain. By the fifteenth century, German authors tended to demonize her as an embodiment of sensuality, tempting humans away from salvation, and her palace under the Venusberg as a sink of corrupting pleasures. In that century this theme became blended with the figure of the medieval poet Tannhäuser to produce one of the great German legends, of the poet's reception into her court, and his eventual repudiation of her and acceptance as fit for the Christian heaven.[39] The court of Venus and the entourage of the 'good mistress' had obvious similarities which set them on a convergence course.

One of these collisions was represented by the testimony of a service magician to judges in the Val de Fiemme at the opening of the sixteenth century that he had gone with a friar to the 'Sibilla's mountain' in the central Italian Apennine range, also known as the 'mountain of Venus where lived Lady Herodias', to be initiated as a witch. Arriving at a lake, they met 'a huge friar dressed in black, and he was a black', who demanded that they renounce the Christian faith before they crossed the water, and that they accept the Devil. They found the door into the mountain guarded by a serpent, but got in and were met by an old man, 'the faithful Ekhart', possibly referencing the famous German mystic of the early fourteenth century Meister Eckhart, who was tried for heresy at the end of his life. He warned them that if they stayed more than a year they would never return. In the mountain they met 'Lady Venus' and her court, which included an old sleeping man, 'the Tonhauser'. They then accompanied Venus to a witches' sabbath, where they also found 'the woman of the good game'. Subsequently, they went with Venus and her company on a Thursday night of the Ember Days of winter, riding black horses through the air, and circled the entire world in five hours.[40] The range of international cultural reference points in this narrative is considerable.

A different kind of melange, made from the same starting point, was provided by a Tyrolese woman, tried in 1525, who said that, on an Ember Day two years before, a woman had appeared to her leading a host of followers. She had declared herself to be Lady Selga, sister of Lady Venus, and ordered the woman to accompany her in the processions of human souls from purgatory and hell which she led in the parish. She added that the people to whom this invitation was made were those who lived virtuous lives, and that refusal meant death. The woman discovered that in the Ember Days this host would gaze into a basin and see those who would die in the parish in the next year. Lady Selga also claimed to know places where treasure was buried, which could be revealed to the devout.[41] Where ordinary people like these could achieve it, there is no surprise that more learned individuals could make similar ventures of syncretism. In 1508 in Strasbourg cathedral in the Rhine valley, a famous German preacher asked in a sermon just after the spring Ember Days if his audience believed in women who travelled at night to 'Lady Venusberg'. Into his portrait of this he mixed the rides of the canon 'Episcopi', the 'furious army' of the 'Unholden' (which here he seemed to take to mean the untimely human dead) and the legend of St Germanus, recounted earlier.[42]

This richer source material also allows a better sense of the developing geographical range of traditions surrounding the night-roving lady or ladies. As shown, for the first few centuries in which one is recorded, it is found in the Frankish lands north of the Alps, represented by what became subsequently France and Germany, with an apparent epicentre, at least for accounts of it, in the Rhine valley. By the thirteenth century, this is still the location of the references, stretching from seemingly deep into Germany across southern France to the Pyrenees. By the fourteenth century, the belief system seemingly had a grip on northern Italy which reached into popular culture. In 1354 a Tuscan Dominican friar delivered a sermon in which he asserted that:

> demons taking on the likeness of men and women who are alive, and of horses and beasts of burden, go by night in company through certain regions, where they are seen by the people, who mistake them for those persons whose likenesses they bear; and in some countries [i.e. regions] this is called the *tregenda* . . . There are some people, especially women, who say that they go at night in company with such a *tregenda*, and name many men and women in their company; and they say that the mistresses of the throng, who lead the other, are Herodias, who had St John the Baptist killed, and the ancient Diana, goddess of the Greeks.[43]

The final part of this passage is framed in the familiar terms of the canon 'Episcopi', but the use of an Italian vernacular term, and the additional detail, indicates that the tradition had put down popular roots in the peninsula.

Thereafter, as seen, it became very widespread and well established in at least the northern third of the modern country, both in the mountains and on the plain. How much further south it spread on the Italian mainland is less certain: the Terra d'Otranto, the heel of the peninsula, has good records for early modern local belief which have been well studied and show no sign of the lady.[44] On the other hand, there is a reference in a sixteenth-century work of theology to women in an unspecified part of the south who believed in spirits called *fatae* (usually translated as fairies) for whom they prepared banquets and kept clean houses, in the hope that they would visit and bless the children.[45] Moreover, there is abundant evidence of an equivalent folklore further south still, in the island of Sicily. There a set of inquisitorial records kept between 1579 and 1651 testifies to a major belief in the 'ladies from outside', small groups of beautiful fairy-like women dressed in black or white, often with animal hands or feet, who had a leader variously known as 'the queen of the fairies', 'the mistress', 'the teacher', 'the Greek lady' (Greeks being exotic to the Sicilians), 'the graceful lady', 'Lady Inguanta', 'Lady Zabella' or 'the Wise Sibyl': there seems to have been no standard local name for her. Sometimes she had a male consort, or a male musician played lute or guitar as the ladies danced. Knowledge of them was claimed by the local service magicians, usually female (again), some of whom said that they went forth at night in spirit to join these companies and learned skills from them. The chief of those skills, logically enough, was to cure ailments caused by offended fairies. Sometimes one of these informants said that she had been elected queen for the night herself. At times the ladies visited houses to bless them, and at others held feasts or dances, or both. All those who claimed acquaintance with them were commoners, often poor and/or old.

Some of the testimonies were vivid, such as that of a service magician at Alcamo in 1627 who said that her local company was 'the wise Sibyl's people who came from a cave that was in the tower of Babylon and that the Sibyl was King Solomon's sister' and also the educator of the Blessed

Virgin Mary who had wanted to be Queen of Heaven instead of her pupil. This woman had told people that she toured her town three nights a week with them, led by 'the Matron' who carried a torch which members alone could see. They had fine clothes and entered every house, danced and made music there, and blessed it with prosperity. An eleven-year-old girl reported that she had been visited six or seven times by apparitions of seven women in beautiful red and white clothes and Greek-style head-dresses who came in dancing to a tambourine. One told the girl that she was Gracia, sister of the Queen of the Fairies, and her followers were called 'the Company of Palermo' (the island's capital) and gave people riches. Sometimes both sexes were said to travel with these spirits, and also to be represented among them. One Palermo woman said that the 'ladies' went around 'like a wind', dressed up in the best clothes they found in chests in the houses they entered and made sweet music. She added that her son went out with them too and was locally popular as a result, as her late husband's father had been. The ladies had beaten her for being unwilling to go with them herself and left her with an injured arm. She estimated that the group consisted of twelve women and eighteen men, and said that they were invisible to the occupants of the houses they invaded. This belief system was already present in the island by the late Middle Ages, which we know because the offence of claiming to travel with the 'ladies' was mentioned in a penitential written there in the late fifteenth century.[46]

As said earlier, similar traditions were recorded in the thirteenth and fourteenth centuries in the heart of the Pyrenees, and it would be strange if they had not extended across the southern side of those mountains into Spain. Indeed, there is a reference from late medieval Catalonia to 'good ladies' who visited houses and with whom women were sometimes said to go.[47] During the late Middle Ages, however, less is heard of this sort of belief in France, where it was attested so well earlier, and by the sixteenth century it seems to have more or less vanished from it. In Germany, by contrast, it was still flourishing then, though seemingly dividing into distinctive regional traditions that focused on different figures as its leader. One was Percht, who features in texts which, when they can be geographically localized, can be found to derive from southern Germany and Austria. The other was Holda, now emerging as a much more fully realized character than before. Indeed, she seems by the early sixteenth century to have become a figure who appeared in folk rituals, probably seasonal, to judge by references left by two figures of the early German Reformation. One was the poet Erasmus Alberus, who spoke of 'Lady Hulda' leading her company with a sickle in her hand, and the other Martin Luther himself, who described 'Lady Hulda with the snout' as entering dressed in straw and rags to the music of a fiddle.[48] This last portrait suggests that, like Percht, Hulda had come to assume a comic-menacing aspect, with a particular costume and appearance including a long nose. What seems to be the case is that, in sharp contrast to what was being described in Italy at the same time, neither lady was now thought to include living humans in her entourage, but only to visit them or their homes. This would explain why neither seems to have featured in the exceptionally numerous and intense German witch hunts of the early modern period.[49]

On the other hand, living people were definitely swept up by the benign night-roaming spirits in the German-speaking Alpine region, and these experiences did sometimes feature in the trials there – not least because, as before and elsewhere, they were believed in some places especially to favour and instruct service magicians. By the sixteenth century their bands were thought to be of different kinds, even in the same district, some benevolent to humans and some frightening and menacing. These 'night companies', however, do not seem to have had a leader, save in those parts of Tyrol, as described, which bordered on the Italian-speaking region.[50] What had seemed to be a fairly homogenous cluster of customs in the thirteenth and fourteenth centuries, which had spread across the Alps and Pyrenees from its Frankish homeland and from the south-western edge of the French-speaking lands to a large part of the German-speaking region, was thus contracting and fragmenting into three regional variations: a German one in which the spirits travelled with a leader and visited but did not sweep up humans; a German Alpine one in which they apparently lacked a leader but incorporated humans in their travels as well as visiting them;

and an Italian one in which they did both things with humans and usually possessed a leader.

They do not seem to have ever reached northern France, the Netherlands, northern Germany, Scandinavia or the British Isles. In the British case, that apparent absence can be obscured by two different factors. One is that erudite and cosmopolitan early modern British scholars quoted the work of their medieval and contemporary Continental counterparts, and sometimes referred to the night-roaming lady in the process. Thus, the seventeenth-century Oxford don Robert Burton, author of the *Anatomy of Melancholy*, named Habundia as queen of the fairies as one of a list of spirits in which humans had believed or still believed.[51] Since the Middle Ages, English authors had repeated the canon 'Episcopi' as an authority on popular belief, and assimilated it to native ideas: thus, *Fasciculus Morum*, a preacher's manual from the early fourteenth century, had combined the nocturnal rides following Diana, in that text, with the indigenous tradition of beautiful elves who danced at night in wild places and carried heroes off to Avalon.[52] James VI and I made a similar combination, by referring to 'the wandering court of she whom the Pagans call Diana, among us called the Phairie or our good neighbours'.[53] Sometimes a British writer would repeat Continental texts without any attempt to mix in insular material, such as the author of the early fifteenth-century English moralizing tract *Dives and Pauper*, which condemned 'observances in the new moon or in the new year, as setting of meat and drink by night on the bench to feed All-holde', and then quoted the canon 'Episcopi'.[54]

The other factor that can obscure the absence of the 'lady' of the night travels from Britain is that in early modern Lowland Scotland the fairies were sometimes said to hold nocturnal rides of a similar kind. At the court of the young James VI, the poet Alexander Montgomerie provided a vivid portrait of them doing just that, with their king and queen, at Halloween.[55] This was not, however, a stock feature of British fairies, and it was even rarer for them to take humans along with them when they rode out: an exception was (allegedly) the magical healer Alison Peirson, who was satirized as being taken by the fairy queen in her entourage on its wild career across the eastern

Highlands at Halloween.[56] The real relevance of the British queen of the fairies, in this context, seems rather that she made the importation of the Continental lady of the night journeys unnecessary. She provided just the sort of benevolent patroness, offering instruction, companionship and (sometimes) access to feasts and revels, personified by the lady on the Continent.[57] Her point of origin, as described, seems, however, to have been entirely different.

Origins

Until the present time, reasonably enough, those who have studied the medieval European night-riding tradition have assumed that it must have come down from pagan antiquity, and that the female leader must have once been a goddess.[58] There has, however, been little systematic attempt made by any to find one, or a set of them, honoured across a great expanse of western and central Europe in ancient times who could have retained the loyalty of enough people to generate the medieval myth.[59] The candidature of Diana has already been considered above, and the difficulties with it pointed out. Another classical Mediterranean goddess proposed for the role has been the Greek Hecate or Hekate, who was certainly well known to Roman authors and associated with the night, magic and the dead.[60] She suffers, however, from both of the factors which limited the candidature of Diana as a progenitor of the medieval figure(s): that she seems to have had no widespread and popular cult in the western half of the Roman Empire, and that she was never credited with visiting homes or including living humans in her entourage.

What Hecate did was guide the souls of the recently deceased down to the land of the dead and, conversely, those of new-born babies into bodily life. This being so, she could also find and gather lost and exiled souls and protect the living from them – or else inflict the living with them. She did not so much wander this world as between worlds, and as such was also a guardian of highways, gates and doorways, and the attendant and guide to Persephone, or Kore, as that goddess journeyed between the terrestrial realm and Hades at the change of the seasons. There seems to be no iconographic evidence of her leading a retinue of earthbound spirits (as opposed to a pack of dogs). Nor does she hold revels or ride. She is portrayed as a young woman running with torches in her hands or having serpentine hair crowned with oak leaves, or else with her back to a pillar and three faces, looking different ways to signal her special quality as a deity of crossroads and to symbolize the three realms of heaven, earth and underworld between which she travels. At times Hecate was regarded as an illuminatrix of darkness and finder of lost things and in a late antique mystery tradition she became a saviour figure, manifesting as a formless speaking fire to devotees. Cakes were offered to her at the full moon.[61] None of these associations match the medieval construct, which, as shown, also rarely involves the dead (though there was a separate major medieval tradition of penitential nocturnal processions of deceased sinners and those who had died violently or before natural time, which lacked a female leader). Only two ancient references do at first sight have any similarity, and these have alternative readings. The late antique *Orphic Hymn* to Hecate hails her as 'mystery-raving with the souls of the dead', which seems to indicate her role of leading them to the underworld.[62] A fragment of much older Greek tragedy has the line 'if a night-time vision should frighten you, or you have received a visit from chthonic [underworld] Hecate's troop'.[63] This seems to have been a joking reference to ghosts in general, and to mean that the person to whom it is addressed may be in danger of suffering nightmares or hauntings.

Logically, the most likely origin point for the medieval lady or ladies would be in ancient goddesses worshipped widely in their early heartland of what became the Frankish cultural province, in the Alps and north of them east and west of the Rhine. Here there are two, at first sight very promising, possibilities.[64] One was Epona, a deity found in virtually every part of the Roman Empire but especially popular across most of the provinces north of the Alps, from France to Hungary in modern terms. The epicentre of her cult was in the Rhineland and adjacent parts of what are now France and Germany. It was spread largely by the cavalry units of the armies stationed along the northern frontier, for she was essentially a

goddess of horses, and so patroness of their welfare, breeding and performance and guardian of stables. She was linked to a range of classical gods,
including Hercules and Silvanus. She may in addition have had some
wider associations with fertility or prosperity, because her icons sometimes
show her holding a dish of corn or carrying ears of it, and more rarely fruit
or a horn of plenty, but these may have been intended simply as fodder for
the horses which she is almost always shown riding, or beside which she
stands or sits. Likewise, she is sometimes shown in company with fertility
goddesses, which may be further evidence for such a wider function, or just
to refer to horse-breeding. Sometimes on horseback she carries a bird,
perhaps a hawk, or she is shown with dogs. Given her connection with
riding, and the location of her ancient popularity, there are obvious links
with the medieval lady – but also clear discrepancies. Epona is never
portrayed with a company of followers, and the medieval rides were initially
not on horses but on wild beasts, with which she was never associated, and
later with a variety of domestic animals, never having any special equine
character.[65]

The other superficially attractive candidate for an origin point is a set of
goddesses known as the Matres or Matronae, the 'Mothers' or 'Ladies', who
were even more popular in the Western Roman Empire than Epona, while
having their centre of veneration in just the same area as hers, of eastern
France and the Rhineland. They are known only from images and inscriptions. The former take a standard pattern, of a trio of stately women, usually
identical and standing or (more usually) seated in a row. They often hold
dishes or baskets of food, or bread, fruit or flowers: emblems of fertility and
prosperity. Sometimes one of them, in the same form, appears alone. Like
Epona, they were especially venerated by soldiers, who accounted for most
of their cult, and for whom, perhaps, they represented general protectresses
and bringers of luck. It is not clear that the same three goddesses were being
represented, as the inscriptions to them often refer to them specifically as
the Mothers of particular provinces, military units or institutions (such
as the parade ground or the household). As apparent givers of blessings,
of abundance and prosperity, they would make good originals for the

superhuman ladies who came to bless medieval homes – save for the fact that, again, there are discrepancies. The Matres and Matronae were never shown in motion or with a retinue; indeed their only, occasional, association with other figures is with an enigmatic trio of hooded human-like beings wearing distinctive hooded cloaks. These are referred to in inscriptions as the *genii cuculati*, the hooded spirits, and seem to function as guardians for the goddesses when they are portrayed with these: mostly they appear by themselves, or singly, and attract a cult of their own, apparently as protective spirits. There are no equivalents to them in the medieval myth, and the medieval ladies did not travel in trios, while the ancient figures were not associated with animals, and are never shown riding.

No other deities or spirits in the abundant evidence for religious belief in the Roman Empire make any better fit with the ladies of the night journeys and visits.[66] There remains a possibility that the latter were somehow inspired by equivalent figures from the pagan Germanic lands outside it. Here, however, we hit a major problem of evidence: that the ancient Germans had no writing and made no images of their deities in durable materials, and so we have an almost complete lack of knowledge of their goddesses. For reasons given above, neither of the German names of the medieval lady – Holda and Percht – seem clearly to have an ancient religious origin. There were, indeed, no names at all attributed to her which can be shown to have any linguistic derivation from ancient Germanic languages; and this would make a fit with the distribution of the medieval night-riding mythology. This was located overwhelmingly within the former bounds of the Roman Empire, and in those Germanic lands closest to it. The northern and eastern areas of the Germanic linguistic zone, those least affected by Romanization, were also those in which the tradition of the rides does not seem to feature.

There is, however, another body of source material on which scholars have regularly drawn in an attempt to fill the void of ancient evidence when reconstructing a picture of Germanic and Scandinavian paganism, and that consists of medieval Nordic literature, almost all of it Icelandic, which deals with pagan times and deities.[67] That literature does have a tradition of women who ride around at night, on enchanted physical objects or animals, sometimes clearly in spirit form, while their bodies remain behind asleep. The favourite object is a staff, followed by a hurdle, fence or roof, and the favourite animal a wolf.[68] Those who did so, however, tended to go alone, or in pairs, not in companies or with a recognized leader. The single association made between them and a deity in a medieval text is adversarial: the chief Norse god, Oðinn, boasts contemptuously of his ability to see such people 'play frenzied in the air' and thwart them by rendering them incapable of finding their 'home shapes', 'true homes' or 'own skins' again.[69] There are some references in this literature to nocturnal assemblies, for revels, but these are not of humans, but of trolls – the human-like and often malevolent creatures famously thought to haunt wild places in Scandinavian mythology, often with homes underground – or similar beings. In *Ketil's Saga*, the hero meets a female troll hurrying on her way to meet others of her kind on an island. The narrator comments that 'there was no lack of *gandr* rides in that place that night': the term could refer to a kind of spirit or an enchanted object used as a steed, such as a staff or hurdle.[70] In one of the *Tales of Thorstein*, that hero follows a boy from the native Sámi (Lapp) people in a ride upon a staff to an underworld, to join a festival of its non-human inhabitants.[71] Night riders, human or not, could be dangerous: in *Eyrbyggja Saga* a woman is accused of injuring a boy in her community on his head and shoulders by abducting him as he walked home after dark and using him as her steed.[72] There is therefore some overlap with the tradition of the lady, but only in the broad sense of humans able to go by night to join the revels of non-human beings, which is a very common and widespread mythological trope.

A different sort of superhuman rider, this time clearly female and traversing great distances, is found in the same literature: the Valkyries, warrior maidens who in some accounts attended Oðinn and brought slain warriors from battlefields to function as recruits to his personal army. They are sometimes described in Old Norse poetry as winged, but more often as riding on supernatural horses which could cross sea and sky. There are also the Disir, described in one (late and most unusual) text as horse troops of superhuman female warriors clad in white or black, who seek the favour of human fighters and sometimes destroy them.[73] None of these beings, however, progress at night in companies behind a leader, or invite selected humans to join them; Oðinn may be served by the Valkyries but does not, apparently, accompany them. His own mythology, by contrast, is of a solitary traveller.

There is thus no known pagan goddess who can be identified as an obvious ancestress of the medieval lady or ladies. It remains entirely possible that elements of the ancient personae of Diana, Hera, Hecate, Epona, the Matres, the Valkyries or the Disir were employed to construct the concept of the latter. This is not, however, susceptible of any proof, and such a construction would still be a medieval one, in a form which has no precise or even close correspondence to what is known of ancient cultic belief and practice. It is equally possible that the medieval concept was generated as a new one in the centuries between the conversion of the regions concerned to Christianity and the composition of the canon 'Episcopi'. Between the fifth and ninth centuries churchmen made many denunciations of popular beliefs, individually and in councils, and none contain any apparent references to night rides with the lady. Instead, the existing evidence suggests a very dynamic and successful popular belief system, which appears to history in the ninth century, spreads or incorporates related traditions through the rest of the Middle Ages, and then disappears from some regions and in others fractures into distinctive local variations. Its success was clearly related to the needs which it served among many medieval commoners, especially women, in enabling them to cope with established social and economic structures that worked to their disadvantage and give them some pride, reputation and imagined or envisioned wish fulfilment.

Aftermath

In the regions in which it still existed by the end of the Middle Ages, and in those distinctive forms, the tradition put down deep popular roots. Holda (also known as Hulda, Holle, Hulle or Holl) survived into modern times as a major figure in central German folklore, especially well known in Hesse and Thuringia but also found in southern Saxony and Franconia. She was essentially benevolent, bringing fertility to the land and blessing spinners: at times she appeared in the guise of a spinning wife. Her realm was mostly the sky and the air, and she was especially associated with winter, snowflakes being said to be feathers from her bed. Between Christmas and Twelfth Night she travelled about in a wagon to bless the fields, and she was also believed to bathe in lakes and fountains. However, there was also a darker aspect to her, for she could ride the winds clothed in terror, inflict ill fortune on untidy houses, appear as old and hideous, and lead a host which included malevolent spirits, witches and the souls of unbaptized babies.[74] In her more kindly aspect she is still a figure in German popular culture today, and so known to an international audience.

Much the same is true of Percht (also Perchta or Berchte) in her more southerly range, which in the nineteenth century comprised parts of Alsace, Swabia, Switzerland, Bavaria and Austria. Like Holda, she was abroad during the twelve days of Christmas, and was a patroness of neat homes and spinners. She was also, however, much more clearly and regularly menacing, punishing bad children and social transgressors, usually by cutting open their bellies. Sometimes she travelled with a company, often of children.[75] In Bavaria and Austria, at least, she remains a well-known folk figure. Likewise, between 1840 and 1940 roving nocturnal companies of spirits without an established leader were still a feature of the popular imagination in most of German-speaking Switzerland and had the same varied character as before: some were black-clad figures who processed through villages to warn of impending mortality, others were violent spirit armies or hunts, dead humans, flights of witches or human-like figures of unearthly beauty who danced and feasted and welcomed human observers.[76] Likewise, in Italy the medieval and early modern lady of the 'good game' probably gave rise to the popular figure of Befana, who had appeared by the early nineteenth century as an old woman who flew around on the eve of the feast of Epiphany giving presents to children: her name is often thought to derive, as that of Percht may have done, from a local name for the festival itself. Her identity with the earlier being is strongly suggested by the fact that some Italians in the earlier records called her Herod's daughter, according to the medieval legend that mistook Herodias for that, rather than, as in the Bible, his wife.[77]

Herodias was, moreover, to have some more surprising modern after-lives. One was in Romania, a distant eastern outlier to her European range, where she is fairly clearly the 'Irodeasa' who is known in the twentieth century as queen of the local fairies. Those appeared usually as beautiful white-clad maidens who could either heal or (more usually) blight humans, and who were especially powerful at the early summer feast of Pentecost – Whitsun, in English. They were linked in a close relationship, both imitative and adversarial, with the *călus*, a small closed group of men who went from door to door in villages at that season, presenting dances and plays that were supposed to protect the fertility of the local farmlands, and sometimes to cure individuals with mysterious ailments. As such, they were the opponents of the fairies – who were a principal source of the danger to crops and the human ailments – but they were also said by some to have learned the dances from them, while in the region of Transylvania the performers were formerly said to have taken Irodeasa as their patron.[78] The other unexpected reappearance of the Herodias of the rides was in a unique text (cited earlier) published by the American folklorist Charles Godfrey Leland in 1899. He represented it as being the 'gospel' of a pagan witch-religion in central Italy which had survived there in secret since the Middle Ages. He claimed to have been given it by an Italian service magician, who had found the information in a mountain valley near Siena and copied it into a single book for him; it was not made clear whether she had taken it from a comparable single written source, verbatim, or collected it from several different sources, including oral testimony.

It was prefaced by a creation myth found nowhere else which brought together the Diana and Herodias of the Burchard version of the canon 'Episcopi' with a form of the Christian Devil in a family relationship. Thus, it had Diana, goddess of darkness, mate with her brother Lucifer, god of light, after his expulsion from heaven, so engendering a daughter,

'Aradia' (an Italian form of Herodias). When the latter was grown, Diana sent her to teach witchcraft and poisoning to humans who had taken to the mountains as bandits to resist the oppression of their feudal lords. Aradia duly did so, and instructed her pupils to meet naked in a wild place each full moon to adore Diana, as goddess of witches. They were to hold a sexual orgy and share crescent-shaped cakes baked and consecrated in the names of Diana and Cain. The secret witch cult thus formed was instructed by Aradia to endure until the last of the upper-class oppressors was dead; and then she returned to her mother, who thereafter granted magical powers to those who worshipped her as her daughter had urged. An appendix to this myth described how Diana had been the first created being, and divided into two to produce Lucifer. The rest of the book consisted of magical invocations and spells calling on the powers given by Diana, to which Leland had added other spells from different sources, and further traditions concerning Diana and other nocturnal spirits.[79] The portrait thus created is that of the nocturnal revels of the 'lady' and her followers, as diabolized in the early modern Italian witch trials, combined with outright class warfare. Leland himself noted its similarity to the medieval rebel witch religion created out of the imagination of the politically radical French historian Jules Michelet almost forty years before (which Leland took as historical). He shared Michelet's political attitudes and suggested that the document given to him was either one holy text of that religion or the main one. Nothing like it has ever been discovered elsewhere, and no actual trace has been found of the Italian witch religion that it portrays. It therefore remains an enigma, but one which has played an important role in the development of the viable and successful modern pagan witch religion of Wicca.[80]

Looking back at the figures of the night-roaming lady or ladies over the centuries, the most striking common feature of most of them is her or their essential *goodness*. There is no sense here that formulae like 'the good women' or 'the good game' are equivalent to the circumlocutory references to fairies, elves and similar beings as 'the good neighbours', attempts to propitiate and ward off potentially dangerous entities. The names that common people themselves gave the lady of the night overwhelmingly have connotations of abundance, satiation, wisdom, exotic opulence and benevolence. She was above all a generous and gracious patroness who provided for the needs of poor, malnourished and marginalized people. She was also extremely transgressive, roaming around at night when respectable people slept and frightening and threatening entities were abroad, riding on wild animals with her entourage, making her way uninvited into people's homes and slaughtering the livestock of farmers to feed her followers before restoring it to life, even as she and her fellow spirits removed the traces of their depredations in cellars and larders. As part of this, she was utterly un-Christian, never being assimilated to female saints even in the most beneficent of her activities and never apparently rendering homage to the Christian God (and, in some later accounts, asking her new recruits actually to forsake Christianity). She effectively ignored established structures of politics and religion, and her very identity as a female leader with no apparent superior was in itself a violation of their norms. If the name taken for her from a Biblical villainess, Herodias, was indeed assimilated by commoners even while the character was given a redeeming new story, this would make a good fit with a personality who managed to be quite shockingly rebellious without also – most of the time – having any negative qualities. As such, she is one of the great counter-cultural figures of the human record.

CHAPTER 5

•

THE CAILLEACH

The fourth figure to be considered in this book is also one from popular culture, being apparently unknown to members of the cultural elite until folklorists began to record the beliefs, stories and customs of ordinary people in modern times. For that reason, she is herself seemingly unrecorded until then, and so is in that sense the most recent of the sample to be considered yet; though, as will be seen, she has some medieval, and probably some ancient, components of identity. The discussion of her which follows is the most tentative and speculative of all those in the present book. She comes from the Gaelic world of the British Isles: native Ireland, the Isle of Man and the Highlands and Western Isles of Scotland. Her name is the Cailleach or Cailliach, signifying the Old Woman or Hag.[1] She is a mighty, giant female figure of immense age, associated with mountains, hills and other wild places, and in some areas with the winter season.

The Folklore

The late-nineteenth- and early-twentieth-century records of the Cailleach show both a remarkable ubiquity across most of the Gaelic world and an impressive homogeneity of some characteristics. One is her considerable age. One tale from County Kerry, in the far south-west of Ireland, collected in the early twentieth century, portrays her as roaming for centuries across Ireland with her large herd of cows and goats. In County Mayo on the west coast, a man asks her about a piece of remote history, believing she may have lived through it, and it is stated that only certain animals are older than she. Another story from Kerry made her live on a mountain top through the ages, amassing great wealth and killing a thief who comes to her house. In another western Irish folktale, she had lived almost two hundred years before a young man outwitted her and got her killed in a storm; but in Connemara it was told that she survived for millennia until St Patrick made her disappear in a flash of light. On the Blasket Islands, off the west coast of Ireland, she was given an origin myth by the 1930s as being a once-beautiful woman who was doomed never to die until a certain friar blessed her, which took an immense time. Another Connemara tale asserted that her death would come, after many centuries, when her name was called three times.[2] The same theme was found in Scottish Gaeldom. On the Hebridean island of Mull, it was told how she had existed since the time of Adam and Eve, living on a headland of the isle. At the opening of each century she renewed her youth by bathing at dawn in a lake, before a bird called or a dog barked, or the sun rose (according to the version of the story); but there came a century when one of those things occurred before she had bathed, and she died.[3] At various places in Scotland it was said that she had obtained immortality from drinking the water of a particular well, which had held miraculous, life-giving water. A tale from Tiree had her sing of her immense age.[4]

In both nations, too, she was often portrayed as a giantess who shaped the landscape. In the Beara peninsula of Ireland's western County Cork, a large cairn was said to consist of rocks which she had piled up as ammunition to pelt and overcome another of her kind. In County Mayo she tucked a male visitor under her arm to leap across a river. In the western province of Connacht it was said that the round towers which are a distinctive type of Irish medieval building were constructed by her in a bid to reach heaven.[5]

Various Irish landmarks are associated with her. The large cairns of the Neolithic passage tombs of Loughcrew, on the summit of Sliabh na Caillighe, the Hill of the Hag, were said to have been constructed by her using rocks dropped from her apron.[6] Another enormous Irish megalithic tomb, this time in County Cork, bears the name Labbacallee, the Hag's Grave or Bed, and a mountain in County Galway is called simply An Chailleach, the Hag. In Scotland she was represented as able to wade through deep lochs and stretches of sea. Most of the hills of the northern county of Ross were said to have been built by her with stones and earth from her pannier, and a prominent cairn in the West Highland region of Morvern was reputed to have been made in the same way. Lochs in Argyll and Mull (where she was reputed to have been the last of the native race of giants) were allegedly formed when she left the cover off her well and flooded a valley. She is associated with mountains in the south-west Highland region of Argyll and the western isles of Tiree and Skye, while a dangerous rounded rock on the coast near Inverness is called Bogha na Caillich, the Bow of the Old Woman.[7]

Her character was rarely portrayed as benevolent to humans. A northern Irish story had her slain by the famed band of medieval Irish heroes led by Finn mac Cumail and a worm creep from one of her bones that itself grew into a dangerous monster.[8] A western Irish tradition held that children born crippled were cursed by an action of hers far in the past. A tradition collected near Athlone on the eastern edge of Connacht in the late nineteenth century credited her with sending cattle plagues until a hero killed her. Another western Irish story made her kill a succession of young men by making them compete with her in work until they perished of exhaustion. Yet another credited St Caitiarn with turning her into a pillar-stone after she had enjoyed a long career of pillage and destruction in one district.[9] In her stories she is as often portrayed as a tragic or pathetic figure as she is as an ogress, but rarely if ever as a benefactress or protectress of people. Another quality which she has across both the Irish and Scottish Gaelic areas is her association with animals. To a great extent, this is hardly surprising, because the beasts with which she is usually concerned are livestock, cattle and goats, which she herds and lives off the produce. A pastoral economy was the mainstay of traditional Gaelic societies, and so in this respect she is merely adhering to a norm. Indeed, she covers a spectrum between savagery and domesticity in the Irish lore, from the wild and predatory being vanquished by St Caitiarn to one who lives with her daughter in a glen and runs a farm, or even one in Connemara who regularly attends mass at her parish church. The one from the Blasket Islands has a human name, Ana Ní Áine, and actually marries an Ulster gentleman; her only common trait with the others is that she lives to an inhumanly great age.[10]

In Scotland, the keeping of cows was still found in places as one of her activities.[11] In Mull she was even said to make cheeses, and a rock formation on the western mainland at Ardnamurchan was reputed to be her cattle byre. On three small Hebridean islands she was said to be especially fond of fish. Generally, however, the Scottish Cailleach was a wilder entity than the Irish one and more closely associated with the natural world. Hence, in the counties of Ross and Sutherland, in the northern part of the Highlands, she was said to herd and milk deer, something not found in Ireland.[12] In keeping with this partial persona as a nature-spirit, the Scottish Cailleach was often especially associated with the winter season. An epithet attached to her was 'the daughter of the pale winter sun'. In summer she was sometimes said to rest in the shape of a grey boulder, and in places she was visualized as carrying a rod or hammer in her right hand to strike the earth and call forth frost. Elsewhere she was thought to smite the autumn vegetation with a wand and so wither it, and to usher in the cold by washing her plaid in the Corryvrechan whirlpool, which lies between two Hebridean islands. Conversely, she was also represented as attempting to strike down the new spring greenery with a wand in the first week of April, until the warming sun made her cast it away and vanish in a cloud of passion. The last phase of winter was sometimes called *A' Chailleach*, the Old Woman, and 25 March *Latha na Caillich*, the Day of the Cailleach, marking her overthrow by spring. The spring gales were said to represent her last attempts to repel the returning warmth. In this seasonal guise she was sometimes visualized as having a blue or black face, one eye, red teeth and long tangled white hair, in a Highland garb of grey clothes and a dun-coloured plaid, with buskins on her feet, leaping from mountain to mountain and across arms of the sea.[13]

In the Isle of Man, also, she was known, or at least has been recorded, mainly as an indicator of changing seasons, although this was not quite in the same way as in Scotland. Thus, it was said that she went out on the first day of spring, 1 February, and if she could manage to gather sticks from a ditch the coming season would be one of bad weather, but if the ditch were flooded with water or snow it would be fine. This was a local version of a very widespread popular belief that good weather at the opening of spring was a bad omen for the rest of it. At times she was thought to take the form of a giant bird on 1 February, flying and carrying the sticks in its beak: the apparition of this creature was therefore a warning of a difficult season to come. In general, among the Manx, she had the uncomfortable reputation that she was given elsewhere, being known in the local language as *Caillagh ny Groamach*, the Sullen Old Woman, or *Caillagh ny Gueshagh*, the Old Woman of the Spells. She was said in the island to have been an Irish sorceress who was thrown into the sea to drown by her own people but made it to Man, where she took up residence on a particular mountain, Cronk yn Irree. As such, she was credited, uniquely in her range, with a gift for prophecy, and was said to have uttered a number of predictions which were cited as having come true in the isle.[14]

As part of her role in Scotland as a nature spirit, she shades into other characters which are similar to her in form and function. A marine being called the Muileartach or Muireartach has been classified as a version of her, being similarly powerful, aged and female. In her own element this being was devilishly dangerous, but at times went onto dry land in the shape of an old woman and sought hospitality at human homes. In one folk poem she calls on the hero Finn in this fashion, and when refused entry kicks down the door and seizes his 'cup of victory'. Finn and his war band pursue her and kill her and retrieve the object after a hard fight. An equivalent entity, the *Cailleach uisge*, Old Woman of the Water, inhabits the sea and flooding rivers and attempts to drown travellers. A third of this kind, the *Cailleach na h-Abhan*, the Old Woman of the River, haunts a dangerous ford on the river Orrin in Ross and Cromarty, and one ironically known as Gentle Annie occupies the equally perilous Heel of Ness, a promontory on the Cromarty Firth, and unleashes bad weather on vessels trying to round it.[15]

That, at any rate, summarizes the information provided by the folklorists who have collected it, in Scotland and Ireland, and this exercise has followed the practice of the more recent authors in using the definite article throughout: in other words, it has resolutely spoken of 'the' Cailleach, save in those cases, at the end, where apparently related entities with different names or specific and qualifying suffixes have been discussed. A closer look at the specific stories collected – where the secondary sources repeat them as individual pieces of work – does raise some doubts about this approach. Some of them refer to 'a' and not 'the' Cailleach, as though there could be more than one being of the same or similar type, and indeed the tale of the cairn in the Beara Peninsula depends on the simultaneous existence, and rivalry, of two of them. However, the attitude of those scholars who have most assiduously collected the information on her has been to assume that all or most of it refers to the same archetypal being, and those who have made the largest and most systematic of the compilations have stated that the being concerned was an ancient goddess – as will be discussed in more detail later. Even when the material itself is considered as an aggregation of different pieces of evidence, one specific character recurs in many of them, in both nations, who has a suffix to her name indicating her as a clearly marked individual: the Cailleach Bheara (or Bhéarrthach, Bhéarthach, Bhéarra, Bearra, Bhéarach or – in Scotland – Bheurr or Bheur).[16] It is time now to consider the earlier records for the Gaelic world, and see how far back this character, and references to 'the cailleach' or 'a cailleach' of the kind portrayed in the modern stories, can be traced. A steady descent of them through the ages would clearly substantiate the claim that they indeed represent memories of an ancient goddess, or a type of one.

The Older Records

An immediate location of the Cailleach Bheara can be made in medieval Irish records, in the form of a famous poem, 'Caillech Bérri Buí', commonly translated as 'The Lament of the Old Woman of Beare'. 'Bui' may in this context be her personal name, and it is probable that 'Bérri' signifies the Beara peninsula on the south-west coast of Ireland (especially as Bui is the name of an island off its end).[17] It is a highly literate and expertly composed piece of work, the language of which suggests a ninth- or tenth-century origin, putting it relatively early in the composition of medieval Irish literature; but there is no agreement on the date and no knowledge of the author. The problem from the point of view of the present exercise is that the character portrayed in it, who speaks in her own voice, is nothing like the one in the folklore, save for their common longevity. She is an aged human woman who was once beautiful and the consort of kings, and who has come to realize the futility of worldly pleasures and ambitions and to find her only true hope in Jesus. It may thus be read as a classic medieval Christian meditation on the vanity of earthly things, in comparison with those of heaven; it is certainly one on the woes of old age. The preface to one manuscript version names her as somebody called Digde, from the royal kindred of the Corcu Duibne, who became a nun and lived to over a hundred years of age.[18] This would make a good fit with the linguistic associations of the name Cailleach itself. It derives from the standard Old Irish term for a veil, *caille*, which was in turn borrowed from the Latin ecclesiastical one *pallium*, showing that it was introduced with Christianity. 'Cailleach' therefore originally meant not 'old woman' but 'veiled woman', and the term was used in early medieval Ireland of both faithful wives and adult women who had embraced celibacy, usually as nuns. Gradually the meaning shifted to signify older women, or older married women.[19]

The Cailleach whom we are tracking seemingly makes a further appearance in the medieval texts, and in the same persona as that of the poem. This is in a rollicking parody of conventional medieval Christian vision literature, *Aislinge meic Con Glinne* (The Vision of Mac Conglinne), which was written later than the poem, in the eleventh or twelfth century. Near its beginning, a list of notable individuals associated with the northern cathedral city of Armagh includes one usually translated as 'Dun Raven, white nun of Beare' (*cailleach Bérre bán*). No more information survives on why she has this name or what her connection was with Armagh, or indeed with the character who utters the lament in the poem. The audience was clearly expected to know these things, and we do not.[20] Those seem to be the only apparent traces of the Cailleach Bheara in the medieval literature, which is significant because the poetry and the prose tales of medieval Ireland are extraordinarily rich in references to legendary and mythological characters. In particular, there is no appearance of the immensely aged giantess, associated with landscape features, who is so prominent in the modern folklore. This is especially significant because the corpus of medieval Irish texts includes a particular genre, the *Dindshenchas*, which consists of explanations of the names of landscape features, and the stories attached to them. The modern Cailleach is completely missing from them.[21] The Corryvrechan whirlpool, to which a modern tradition of the Cailleach cited above is attached, is actually discussed in an Old Irish glossary, written around the year 900; but there is no mention of her in this account and a quite different legend is attached to the place.[22]

Could this be because the medieval authors who wrote the literature found her a distasteful character, too earthy and pagan for inclusion in it? That seems unlikely, because they did include, copiously, other supernatural females who would seem equally unpalatable to devout medieval Christians, such as the trio of bloodthirsty and troublemaking spirits associated with the fury and panic of battle – almost certainly former goddesses – the Morrigan, the Nemain and the Badb. Nor did they shirk the recording and copying of episodes of rampant earthy vulgarity, such as one concerning the grossest and most rumbustious of the male superhumans in the medieval tales, the Dagda, which appears in 'The Second Battle of Moytura'. It includes mockery for (temporary) impotence, a description of genitalia, overeating (of porridge) followed by copious defecation, and two episodes of outdoor copulation.[23] Could, then, the absence of the modern Cailleach from the medieval sources be explained if she were a favourite deity of the common people, and those sources were composed by a literary elite which had no regard for her? Again, this seems hardly credible, because, although medieval Ireland was certainly a very hierarchical society, it was also one

1. The rude virility of this hill figure, presumed for most of modern times to be an ancient representation of a pagan deity, was long a powerful prop of the case that an active paganism had long survived in Christian Britain.

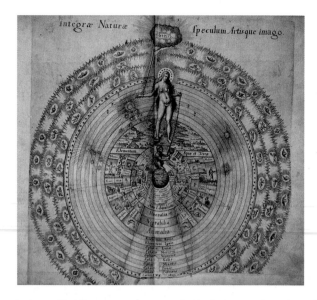

2. The frontispiece to Fludd's seventeenth-century book of science and occultism depicts the concept of a female world soul linking heaven and earth.

3. Here we have a classic late medieval illustration of a Wild Man, dressed in leaves, of a kind which could transmute easily into the figure of the Green Man in pageants.

4. This is an absolutely classic late medieval foliate head, of the kind which was the primary inspiration for the modern figure of the Green Man. The figure is unusual, however, in being armed.

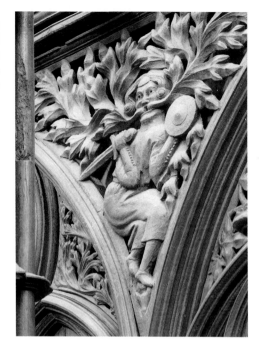

5. This fifteenth-century drawing testifies to the late medieval belief in Wild Women as well as Wild Men, and there may just be a faint echo in it of the belief in human women who rode at night in the entourage of a superhuman female.

6. The Green Knight, who features as the adversary and then friend of Sir Gawain in a famous fourteenth-century English poem, was often regarded in the twentieth century as a nature spirit also represented by the foliate heads in churches.

7. Morgan le Fay, originally Morgen, was the absolutely classic medieval 'fay', a human-like being possessed of magical powers, and is majestically represented in this late medieval illustration to an Arthurian romance.

8. The Arthurian wizard Merlin and the fairy queen of British literature and popular belief never met in story, but they do here in this painting, which is one of the best modern visual representations of the queen.

9. The Elizabethan author Spenser made one of the most successful and influential transmutations of the medieval romance tradition into early modern literature, and also one of the most famous literary personifications of the fairy monarch.

10. Fuseli's ghostly eighteenth-century art provided a very effective medium for the visual depiction of the fairy monarch of late medieval and early modern romance.

11. Blake's visionary artistic style created an especially memorable illustration of the fairy court of Shakespeare's *A Midsummer Night's Dream*.

12. Shakespeare's miniature fairy monarch, Queen Mab, is modernised into this sensual evocation of feminine beauty by Chalon in the early nineteenth century.

der heiligsten Weih- oder Mutternacht, um zwölf Tage lang bis zum heiligen Lichttag oder Obersttag zu währen. Noch erinnert der Name Zwölften oder Zwölfnächte, mit welchem man die Tage vom 25. Dezember bis zum 6. Januar bezeichnet, an die heilige Zeit.

Frau Holle (Perhta) mit dem wüthenden Heer.

Während ihr ruhte aller Streit und alle Waffen, keinerlei Arbeiten durften vorgenommen werden, und die Götter hielten ihre feierlichen Umzüge.

Zwölf Tage lang herrschte in den Wohnungen und auf den Straßen festlicher Jubel, wobei jeder Gast willkommen war; auf dem Herde brannte der Weihnachtskloß, den sich Jeder aus den Wäldern holen konnte, ohne als Holzfrevler bestraft zu werden, und in der mit Grün geschmückten

13. The German figure of Holle survived the Middle Ages to become one of the strongest modern aspects of the belief in a superhuman female being leading a nocturnal procession of spirts, and shown well in this nineteenth-century illustration.

14. Here Holle, under another of her popular names as Hulda, appears in a different guise, as a divine spinner. It is appropriately from an English version of the fairy tales collected by the Brothers Grimm, of whom Jacob was the one who combined different medieval and modern traditions into the composite concept of the Wild Hunt.

15. A fine representation of the Cailleach Bheara, as the mighty Scottish spirit of winter imagined in modern folklore.

16. This famous modern painting portrays the Gaelic folk tradition of seasonal cavalcades made up of the beings known as sidhe or sithean and equivalent to the Lowland Scottish and English fairies.

17. Harrison was a distinguished Cambridge classicist of the Edwardian period, who became one of the most influential early British promoters of the idea of the prehistoric veneration of a single great goddess.

18. Frazer, another leading Cambridge classicist of the very early twentieth century, produced a very influential theory that all ancient human religion had been focused at least partly on the cult of a dying and returning vegetation spirit.

19. Lady Raglan, a member of the British Folklore Society, was the originator of the name and concept of the Green Man as an ancient vegetation deity which linked the medieval foliate heads, the folk figure of the Jack-in-the-Green and the forester figure of pub signs.

20. This picture is an excellent early depiction of the entertainment provided by chimney sweeps in south-eastern English towns and cities, in which the foliage-covered Jack-in-the-Green featured with other costumed characters.

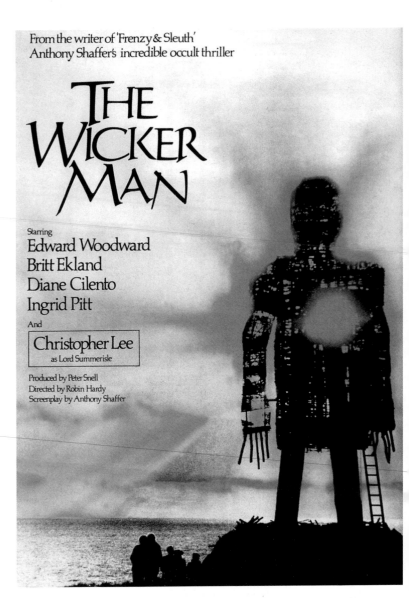

From the writer of 'Frenzy & Sleuth'
Anthony Shaffer's incredible occult thriller

THE WICKER MAN

Starring
Edward Woodward
Britt Ekland
Diane Cilento
Ingrid Pitt

And

Christopher Lee
as Lord Summerisle

Produced by Peter Snell
Directed by Robin Hardy
Screenplay by Anthony Shaffer

21. *The Wicker Man*, released by Lion Films, is the classic example of the folk horror cinematic genre, but also one version of a much older British fictional trope, of the dire consequences of reviving or preserving paganism in a modern community.

divided between hundreds of tiny kingdoms. Social and political units were therefore too small for a wide cultural gap to develop between different social orders. In striking contrast (for example) to the medieval French and English romances, the Irish stories do reflect situations – such as those just cited involving the Dagda – which could be appreciated by all social ranks.[24]

There are, however, figures in the medieval Irish literature that may well have contributed to the later figure of the Cailleach, and they consist of menacing and dangerous mature female beings who live outside of human society, or at least of settled and mainstream versions of it, and are designated by terms usually translated into English as 'hags' or 'witches'. Some feature as beings that dwell in wild places and are attracted by the din and violence of human battles, and indeed incite them, so functioning at once as lesser versions of war goddesses like the Morrigan and as spiritual equivalents to the carrion-eating birds and beasts which sought out human conflicts to feast on the slain. The twelfth-century historical saga called *The War of the Gaedhil with the Gaill* has 'battlefield spirits and goat-like battlefield spirits, and maniacs of the valleys, and destructive witches and shape-shifting supernatural beings and the ancient birds and the destroying demons of the air and the heavens, and the misfortune-giving demonic supernatural host' gather, eager for the great battle of Clontarf, which is the climax of the story.[25] In *Cath Finntrágha* (The Battle of Ventry), a tale of the hero Finn and his band from later in the medieval period, 'demonic females of the glen' join 'the hounds and the whelps and the crows' and 'the powers of the air, and the wolves of the forests' in 'howls from every quarter' to inspire warriors to kill each other.[26]

It is not clear how far, if at all, these battle-spirits are related to the murderous females who attack heroes with physical weapons in the Irish literature. In another story about Finn, *Bruidhean Chéise Corainn*, three such ogresses trap and bind him and some of his warriors by magic in a cave, and intend to kill them with swords. They are described as hideous, with coarse and dishevelled hair, red and bleary eyes, sharp and crooked teeth, very long arms and fingernails like the tips of the horns of cattle.

Their father is a non-human being from a parallel world who has been offended by Finn and sent them to take revenge; but they are thwarted when another of Finn's followers breaks in and kills two of them with his own sword before forcing the third to break the spell and release his comrades. In *Echtra Airt meic Cuinn* (The Adventure of Art, Son of Conn), seven similar horrors attack the hero, Art mac Cuinn, in a forest at night; again, they have been sent by an otherworld ruler, this time a queen, who has taken offence at him. He defeats them in hand-to-hand combat.[27] Fearsome women, or woman-like beings, using physical weapons with appalling strength, are also prominent in medieval Welsh literature. The Nine Hags of Gloucester, in the romance *Peredur fab Efrawg*, lay whole districts waste until they are killed by Arthur (the British national hero in some ways equivalent to Finn) and his band. Arthur and his men are pitted against one of the same kind of foe in another tale, *Culhwch ac Olwen*, a 'Very Black Hag' living in a cave, who fights and physically overcomes, wounds and throws them out one by one. Arthur himself eventually kills her by avoiding close combat and throwing a knife.[28] Such figures lingered in Welsh folklore as the *gwrach*, a hideous old female who haunts wild and lonely places and is a menace to travellers.[29]

The same sort of figure is found in Lowland Scotland as a character in comic or satirical verse written in the sixteenth century. Her most notable appearance there is as the 'gyre carling': 'gyre' probably meaning greedy or monstrous, and 'carling' a middle-aged or elderly woman or wife (dictionaries of Scots trace the latter term from the Old Norse *kerling*, an old woman, and not from *cailleach*). She crops up in passing in a number of poems between 1528 and 1581, but also gets a whole one to herself, which presumably tells the story to which the other works refer. This makes her a giantess dwelling in the Lothian district of Scotland in ancient times and living on human flesh, one of whose turds becomes North Berwick Law, a prominent hill in the region east of Edinburgh. She is eventually driven out of Scotland by the royal fairy host, escaping disguised as a sow to marry Mohammed and become queen of the Jews (as befitted a monster in the eyes of most Christians of the age).[30] Another creature of a similar kind is the wife of the legendary British giant Gog Magog, who is represented in another poem or ballad as creating Loch Lomond with a stream of her spittle and (in the scatological manner of these works) having bouts of wind that produce effects of thunder and lightning.[31]

It may thus be seen that component parts of the later composite figure of the Cailleach are clearly already present in the Middle Ages. The contest between Finn and his men and the hags in *Bruidhean Chéise Corainn* is very similar to that between the same heroes and the hags in the Hebridean poem and Ulster tale collected from the modern folklore. The Cailleach Bheara overcome by St Caitiarn and the one killed near Athlone are other medieval monsters of this kind surviving into modern popular tradition. In the gyre carling and Gog Magog's wife we see clear ancestresses of the giant Cailleach who creates lochs, builds hills and piles up large cairns in that tradition, again in both parts of the Gaelic world. The unifying figure that is represented by the folklorists, however, is missing in the earlier texts, and the Cailleach Bheara of the medieval literature does not provide it. Instead, she contributes other components of that later figure: her great age, the name which is most often given to her in the modern lore, and that element of pathos which hangs around the modern Cailleach in several of the folk tales about her. Indeed, in the case of the Cailleach Bheara we may well be encountering a similar phenomenon to that already suggested in the case of the fairy queen, of a figure with an origin in literary texts who became transplanted into popular culture and naturalized there, while being combined with aspects of older beliefs. So, there is still a problem to be solved here: of how this medley, of a literary character with those originally distinct beliefs and mythical beings, became the great nature-goddess of the modern folklore.[32]

A Goddess Emerges

Systematic folklore collection in the Gaelic cultural province, as elsewhere in Europe, commenced in the early nineteenth century and gathered pace through the Victorian period to reach an apogee between 1880 and 1930.

In the famous assemblages of native Irish and Highland Scottish and Hebridean lore made until 1900, the Cailleach is remarkable for her absence. This is the more striking in that the works concerned contain a great deal of information about fairy-like beings, nature spirits and other non-human entities which could take human form. Most make no apparent mention of her at all, and none do so as the great pan-Gaelic spirit of the later texts.[33] Instead, a few refer to individual legends of the kind which were subsequently to become part of the corpus assembled around her figure. Thus, in 1860 one important collection contained a story from Sutherland about the Cailliach Mhór Chlibhrich, represented as a 'great witch' or 'great hag' who cared for the deer in one district there and protected them from hunters (as long as the animals paid her respect).[34] By the 1830s the Neolithic cairns of Loughcrew were already ascribed to the efforts of the giant hag carrying stones in her apron, and this was a motif found on both sides of the Irish Sea, for a very similar large New Stone Age passage tomb, likewise covered by a huge cairn, on the coast of Anglesey bears the traditional name of Barclodiad y Gawres, the Apronful of the Giantess.[35]

One volume of a famous series on Argyllshire lore, which appeared in 1891, explained the name of Cailleach Point on the coast of Mull, which it translated as 'the Old Wife's Headland'. It claimed that an old woman had been trapped by the tide beneath it when gathering shellfish and had climbed the cliff to safety. Having reached the top, she exclaimed that she was now safe 'in spite of God', who promptly turned her to stone for impiety.[36] In 1900 Alexander Carmichael's celebrated collection of Hebridean songs, chants and stories, *Carmina Gadelica*, included two allegedly sung by the 'Carlin of Beinn Bhreac', who ranged the area around that double peak in the Cairngorm Mountains herding deer; they were included in a section on fairy women.[37] An Irish story described how a man had used trickery to frighten away a menacing hag, called a 'cailleach'.[38] What is striking about all these references is the apparent complete absence of any sense of a unifying or incorporating figure behind them: they are packaged in different contexts, with the female being at the centre of them variously represented as a witch, giantess, hag, human or fairy, and never as a mighty nature spirit, or goddess, whose domain spanned the whole of Gaelic Scotland or Ireland, let alone both.

That entity seems only to have been perceived in the twentieth century. In 1908 an author called E.C. Watson published an article about Highland mythology which on one page linked up the various references to wild hags and giantesses in Scottish Gaeldom and suggested that they all represented the same *form* (though not necessarily the same being) of malign supernatural female associated with wild places and winter which could be labelled 'Cailleach'.[39] It is possible that by then improved communications within the Highlands and Islands, and increased publication of their folk-lore, actually was causing the 'folk' themselves there to make such linkages as they told tales and portrayed local superhumans. At any rate, in 1915 a veteran folklore collector, John Gregorson Campbell, devoted a short article to the Scottish stories of the Cailleach Bheara, a name which he translated as 'Shrill or Cutting Old Wife' and suggested had referred to her sharp wits. He identified them as occurring along the whole western coast of Argyll and on the nearby islands of Mull and Iona, and as describing an immensely old giantess who herded cattle and goats. He shrewdly suggested that she might have been imported there from nearby Ireland.[40]

These two brief notices prepared the way for the dramatic developments between the world wars, commencing in 1927 when a respected scholar of Irish literature, Eleanor Hull, brought out a thirty-page essay in the main British folklore journal which dubbed the Cailleach Bheara an ancient goddess, belief in whom spanned the Gaelic world. Her knowledge of the medieval sources was good enough for her to puzzle over the apparent absence of such a character in them and wonder if the sense of her as a nature divinity had developed in relatively recent times.[41] As has been suggested, there is much to recommend this view, but her investment of the figure with a divine and pan-Gaelic status was to prove more influential than her concerns about the chronology. Five years later a veteran Highland folklorist, J.G. Mackay, put an equally substantial article into the same journal which proposed that the association between the local cailleach figures and deer in the region proved the existence of a cult of a deer goddess among the ancient Caledonians. He knew the material too well to fail to notice that there was no sense in it of a single being, as each district that had a mythology of a deer-protecting female linked her specifically to itself. However, he argued that they derived from the same cult, and he elevated the Cailleach Bheara into a universal great goddess, of the earth and the dead. If the influence of current scholarly fashion on this last interpretation is obvious (as outlined in the second chapter of this book) it is equally evident in his additional suggestion that the people regarded in former times as witches had actually been priestesses of the deer goddess(es).[42]

These pieces of work prepared the way for the breakthrough in 1935 when a Scottish journalist called Donald Alexander Mackenzie published a popular book on the folklore of his nation.[43] He was a keen amateur historian of religion whose ideas included some held by others in his time, such as that Neolithic society had been led by women and centred on goddess-worship, and had been overthrown by attacking patriarchal Bronze Age Indo-Europeans; and that all cultural change in prehistory had been due to successive invasions by different races. He also, however, propounded some which were truly his own, and wonderfully eccentric, such as the belief that the whole world, including Britain, had been colonized in prehistory by Buddhists. He now grouped together all the Scottish, and some Irish, traditions of hags and giantesses described above as memories of a single great ancient goddess, *the* Cailleach, who had been the Gaelic equivalent to the Greek Artemis as a deity of primeval nature. His view of her was the one that went into popular culture for the rest of the twentieth century and has been the most generally accepted one ever since; the characterization of her made at the beginning of this chapter is essentially his.[44] In making it, as in his views on Neolithic society and religion and on race and invasion as the motor of prehistoric change, he was very much of his age: this was after all the period in which interest in the survival of pagan ideas and figures into the Christian centuries, and in the concept of a great prehistoric goddess associated with the natural world (which had made an equally obvious impression on Mackay), was steadily strengthening.

As explained previously, both those ideas reached a climax and apogee in the mid-twentieth century, and they had reverberations that have lasted until the present. They aided the acceptance of the figure portrayed by Mackay among some Irish scholars from the 1960s onward who interpreted the poem 'Caillech Bérri Buí' as a Christianization of a pagan mother goddess or goddess representing the sovereignty of the land, a major figure in medieval Irish literature.[45] This acceptance culminated in the second notable book to propagate the concept of the Cailleach as a universal Gaelic great goddess, which appeared as recently as 2013. It was the work of a distinguished Irish folklorist, Gearóid Ó Crualaoich, who held a professorial chair at (the then) University College Cork, and was a study of the Cailleach mainly from the Irish folk material, with some from Scotland, so providing a counterpart to Mackenzie's now venerable book.[46] It was a joy and a gift for scholars to have the Irish stories concerning cailleach-like figures, mostly collected during the past hundred years, printed in such a convenient assemblage. He followed Mackenzie's model and treated them all as referring to the same ancient goddess, embodying the sovereignty of the land, who had been displaced by Christianity and patriarchy (we see here the influence of contemporary American radical feminist ideas) to the social and cultural margins. In his formulation she had descended in turn from the universal Neolithic Great Mother Goddess, whose paramountcy had been destroyed by Indo-European invaders. He gained these beliefs from the religious histories of the mid-twentieth century which had embodied the belief in the universal goddess as orthodoxy, refreshed in Ó Crualaoich's case by the writings of Marija Gimbutas. He was slightly aware of the criticisms made of them since the 1990s, but he absorbed these only to the extent of accepting that there may have been no single monolithic New Stone Age cult. He then disposed of this objection as a practical problem by recycling Erich Neumann's model of Jungian archetypes from the 1960s, in which the Great Mother Goddess had been the most important archetype for the primeval development of religion – so that the existence of an apparent plurality of ancient goddesses counted for nothing, as they were all really aspects of the same one. He then invested the Cailleach with an additional feminist significance by claiming that the stories of her underwrote and legitimized the power of women as healers and wisdom-keepers in human society. With his work, the modern development of her persona may have reached its climax.

It may therefore be suggested in conclusion that *the* Cailleach, as a great goddess of the ancient Gaels, is a creation of modern folklorists. This need not strip her of her current spiritual and symbolic significance, or indeed – depending on one's own concept of the origins of deities – of her possible objective existence. Moreover, the folklorists concerned were working with some very old materials, which probably do descend from pagan antiquity: local traditions of hags and giantesses, and spirits who protected the deer, which conform to types found more widely in societies that spoke Celtic languages, and beyond them. The bridge between these and the mighty deity of modern folklore was provided by the figure of the Cailleach Bheara, who seems on present evidence to have been a medieval Christian and literary creation. Like the British fairy queen, however, she made her way out of literature to spread very widely through popular culture, in her case through most of the Gaelic world by the end of the early modern period, if not before. Originally bonded by the theme of a female being of great age, provided by the Old Irish poem, the localized stories of her blended with and absorbed many of those older traditions to which reference has just been made. As in the case of Herodias, a character originally taken from Christian literature seems to have been relocated to a completely different social and cultural context. For those reasons, it may be proposed that she can take her place among the other figures that are the subject of this book.

EPILOGUE
The Green Man

The creation, discovery, development or contacting of apparently new forms of non-Christian superhuman beings – the choice of term accords with one's personal beliefs – did not cease with the coming of modernity. It has already been suggested that the Cailleach, as presented by some twentieth-century folklorists, was actually a product or perception of those same folklorists. This said, she was still a figure with a long preceding gestation which only culminated in the modern formulation. There is, however, one within the Anglophone world which seems to have appeared entirely in the late twentieth century, though composed of a medley of ancient, medieval and early modern components. It may also be a sign of changing times that, whereas all of the beings considered before have been manifestations of the divine feminine, this ultra-modern one is male, a belated counterpart to the Great Mother Goddess or Mother Earth figure who had long been a feature of European thought.

Lady Raglan's Construct

Julia Somerset, wife of the fourth Baron Raglan, was a British aristocrat by birth and lifestyle, daughter of a lord from a famous Scottish noble house and spouse of one from an equally eminent Anglo-Welsh one. Her husband, having retired from a career as a soldier and colonial administrator, developed interests in archaeology, architecture and folklore, eventually serving as president of the Folklore Society. She shared the latter enthusiasm, and in 1939 contributed an article to the society's journal which became her only notable publication.[1] Its subject was a particular kind of carved decoration found in medieval British churches and cathedrals, especially in England. It was both widespread and common, and consisted of variations on the theme of a human head, viewed full-face, that was associated with leaves. Sometimes it was simply set among them, gazing out, while at other times the foliage comprised its hair and/or beard, or gushed out of its mouth, mouth and ears, or cheeks and lips. She suggested that the figure which had inspired them was the same as that represented by the Jack-in-the-Green, a man who took part in English May Day celebrations wholly or almost wholly hidden within a frame covered in greenery and flowers. She went on to suggest that the English outlaw hero Robin Hood, who was traditionally dressed in green and associated with the forest, and had been another popular character in May Day celebrations, was another version of the same being: she proposed that his original name had been Robin of the Wood. She associated with all three the King of the May, who traditionally presided over these celebrations, and at one community, Castleton in Derbyshire, still rode through the town carrying a wooden frame woven with leaves and blooms. She suggested that the accidental fact that King Charles II had escaped capture in the English Civil Wars by hiding in an oak tree had resulted in his assimilation to the same kind of figure, resulting after his restoration in the emblem of the 'royal oak'.

All these were linked by her to characters found in folk celebrations of the coming of summer across central and northern Europe who likewise appeared covered in young foliage. She proposed that the same ancient pagan divinity lay behind every one of the English and Continental figures: a dying and reviving god who represented the natural world and its fertility, and who was represented in the ceremonies which brought in summer by a human male who was sacrificed in his honour to ensure the continuation of the annual renewal of the land. To this supranational entity she gave the name of 'the Green Man', taken from a popular pub sign which by her time (and long before) had conventionally shown a forester or gamekeeper, but which she held to have been taken originally from the central character in the primeval rite. She suggested that the regular appearance of the ancient god in medieval churches was yet another piece of evidence for the belief – which as shown above was something of a scholarly orthodoxy at this period – that an unofficial paganism persisted through the Middle Ages alongside the official Christian religion.

Her interpretation was based on previous publications, some very recent and others decades old. Lady Raglan had tested it in an address to the British Association for the Advancement of Science two years before, using slides of the medieval foliate heads made by C.J.P. Cave, a retired meteorologist with an interest and expertise in medieval roof bosses.[2] He had studied these in England, France and Germany, and in 1932 and 1934 he had published essays in provincial journals which made the connection between the foliate heads and the Jack-in-the-Green and suggested that they both represented the same pre-Christian deity.[3] The notion that medieval church carvings might represent a surviving attachment to pagan divinities was in the air at that time, because in 1934 another leading member of the Folklore Society, Margaret Murray, put an article into an anthropological journal which propounded it. Her interest was in the images of nude women depicted facing the observer with legs spread to emphasize their genitals, found on the interior or exterior walls of churches in Britain and Ireland. Scholars had come to give them the generic name, taken from Ireland, of sheela-na-gigs. She related these to similar figures from ancient Egypt and Babylonia, which were known to represent pagan goddesses or demi-goddesses, and suggested that the medieval examples also did, and that they may have been intended to stimulate the sexual desires of women. She proposed that churchmen had been forced to accept them in or on churches by popular demand.[4] In the previous year Murray had published the second in her series of books expounding the view that the people prosecuted as witches in medieval and early modern Western Europe had been practitioners of a surviving pagan religion. In that, she had suggested that Robin Hood had been the generic name for the god of nature worshipped by them.[5]

Lady Raglan was thus developing ideas very much current among the company she kept in that decade; but behind them stood a greater figure whose influence she explicitly acknowledged in her article: the Cambridge University classicist and anthropologist Sir James Frazer, author of *The Golden Bough*. This was the most popular and celebrated work of comparative anthropology ever published, having gone through three successive editions, in an ever-expanding number of volumes, between 1890 and 1915. It drew on an idea mooted among British scholars in the late nineteenth century and based on the then still new theory of evolution. This held that, as human bodies bore the same similarity across the planet, so human minds must do too, and that therefore basic notions had developed in the same way throughout the scattered branches of the human race. If this were accepted then it could be argued that different societies had passed through the same stages in the development of religion, although at different rates, worldwide. Frazer suggested that one of these stages had been rule by sacred kings, representing the spirit of vegetation on which farming depended. These were, according to him, ritually killed and replaced, either when their natural powers began to wane or after a fixed number of years. His starting point for the investigation which led to this conclusion was a unique ancient Roman custom, observed at one sacred grove near Rome, whereby its priest, dedicated to the goddess Diana, took office only by killing the previous man to hold the job.

One obscure Roman rite was, of course, not the real focus of Frazer's interest. Instead, he was gunning for Christianity, by suggesting that Jesus Christ had been one of those sacred kings and that the whole story of his crucifixion and resurrection had arisen from a misunderstanding of this bloodthirsty, ignorant and pointless ancient pagan tradition. He had no time for religion in general, and his whole view of human mental evolution was based on the premise that people would develop out of the need for it, to enter a superior world ruled by scientific rationalism. However, he never quite had the courage or folly to spell this out in his published work. Instead, he suggested it in the second edition of *The Golden Bough*, and then mitigated it by stating that devout Christians could still see the ancient tradition as instigated by their God, to prepare the minds of people for the coming of Christ. This did not shield him, either from outraged Christians or from academic colleagues who pointed out weaknesses in his argument. In the third edition, therefore, he cut it out and left readers to make the association between his ancient vegetation cult and the Christian story if they wished to do so; but he never missed an opportunity to snipe at Christianity by drawing comparisons between it and pagan and tribal religious beliefs until the end of his life. His dislike of it, however, did not do anything to reduce his greater contempt and loathing for paganism, which he regarded as an evolutionarily lower and so more ignorant and savage sort of religion. He made his reconstructed universal archetype of it a medley of bloodshed, sex and falsehood – very much the view taken in the Bible.[6]

Frazer's work initially gained considerable scholarly plaudits and influence, and he became the most heavily decorated anthropologist of all time. Ironically, however, by the time that writers like Julia Somerset and Margaret Murray embraced his ideas with such enthusiasm, they were already being rejected within his own discipline. When he died in 1941, the obituary notices in British academic journals mostly referred to them in negative terms, while the *American Anthropologist* did not even mention his passing. This was not entirely just. Some of his exercises in comparing data on a global scale still have merit, such as his perception of a worldwide tendency of humans to work magic in similar ways, especially by presumptions of sympathy (based on perceived connections between phenomena) and contagion (using objects which have been or are in physical contact with the target of the magic). More generally, the use of comparative data from across the globe has recently begun to revive among anthropologists after a long period in which close studies of individual societies were the disciplinary norm.[7] However, two of the foundations of Frazer's use of it were found to be defective. One was the assumption that human belief has evolved in the same manner all over the world just as human anatomy and language have done. In reality, beliefs seem to develop in much more independent, capricious, contingent and opportunistic ways. The other of Frazer's questionable foundational assumptions was that rural Europeans mindlessly acted out the same customs century after century. It is recognized now that illiterate people are often more willing and able to change ideas and habits than those who have preserved them in writing. His methods were also found often to be as faulty as his preconceptions. His three bodies of source material consisted of accounts of pagan practices made by ancient authors, those made of indigenous peoples in the extra-European world by travellers, missionaries and colonial officials, and folk rites and beliefs recorded in modern Europe. He approached all three with a disregard both for the possible unreliability of these records and for the proper context of each, and often made dizzyingly speculative leaps to link them together.[8]

As a result, his theory of a universal ancient pagan fertility cult based on the sacrifice of a human being representing the dying and returning vegetation god was generally rejected, at the time of his death, by most academic scholars and especially those concerned with history and prehistory. Moreover, one of his main theoretical tools, the assumption that folk customs recorded in Europe during medieval, early modern and modern times were living fossils left over from ancient religious rites, was abandoned altogether by the developing professional disciplines of history and anthropology. This had the unfortunate effect of preventing folklore studies from becoming established in British universities as an institutionalized field of enquiry in their own right. Instead, they were left to independent scholars such as Lady Raglan, who did not so much reject the reasons that compelled academics increasingly to abandon Frazer's theories and methods as remain unaware of them. *The Golden Bough* also made a tremendous impact on the general public, and on many novelists and poets including

W.B. Yeats, Robert Graves, John Synge, D.H. Lawrence, Wyndham Lewis, John Buchan, T.S. Eliot and Joseph Conrad: its concepts and arguments went into mainstream Western culture.[9] Its informing myth, however historically wrong, was a powerful one, and one of its enduring virtues is that it is a magnificent compendium of customs and rites of different kinds, however dubious the accuracy of some of it.

Lady Raglan's examples of central and eastern European folk customs centred on figures swathed in greenery, who featured in popular celebrations to bring in summer, were taken straight from Frazer, as was the interpretation that she placed on them as former rites of a vegetation god. He had found them recorded in accounts drawn from the period between the seventeenth and nineteenth centuries, though mostly from the final part of that, concerning Russian, Slovenian, Austrian, Romanian, Romanian gypsy, Swiss, French and German communities. The celebrations, like summer celebrations all over Europe, were usually provided by young people, and the leaf-clad figure was in most places one of them, decked out for the day. The custom occurred at a range of dates in April and May, especially on Easter Monday, St George's Day, May Day and Whit Monday – which were the principal feasts at which northern European communities have celebrated the coming of summer in the past millennium. The person swathed in foliage was variously called the Green George (on St George's Day), Little Leaf Man, Whitsuntide Lout, May King, Leaf King, Grass King or Wild Man. Frazer pointed out that the Jack-in-the-Green, on May Day, was the English equivalent to these.[10] Their appearance across such a large area of Europe and range of ethnic groups, in scattered communities separated by other groups in which the same kind of festival was marked by different customs, indeed suggests that this was one of the ways in which it naturally occurred to Europeans to mark the return of greenery – whatever specific ancient rites may have lain behind it.

Behind Frazer's treatment of it, in turn, lay another long development of ideas. Like so many of those that inspired the late Victorian British – including the great prehistoric goddess, witchcraft as a surviving pagan religion and the 'Wild Hunt' – it originated in Germany in the early nineteenth century. In this case the starting point was probably with the Brothers Grimm, who both encouraged European scholars to look to folk tradition in general as a trove of historical information and national identity and to treat modern popular beliefs and customs as timeless relics of ancient paganism.[11] This latter suggestion was taken a great deal further by one of the Grimms' most fervent disciples, the Prussian scholar Wilhelm Mannhardt, who carried out an impressive programme of systematic research among German peasant communities which he combined with the work of others. The results were published between 1860 and 1880, and the seasonal customs that played a prominent part in them were interpreted by him as survivals of ancient religion. As these customs were overwhelmingly concerned with the productivity of humans, livestock and crops – as was natural enough for farming people – Mannhardt tended to assume that the religion concerned was centred overwhelmingly on fertility rites. He provided Frazer not only with many of the actual examples of customs that the latter used as illustrations for his own ideas, but with the belief that the primeval rites from which they were supposed to derive were focused on an animating spirit of vegetation.[12] Frazer fully acknowledged the impact that Mannhardt had made upon him, declaring himself to be following in his footsteps and quoting him to make particular points.[13] Moreover, he was not the first British scholar to be swept away by the Prussian's arguments: a dozen years before the first edition of *The Golden Bough*, an article in a widely read literary and scientific journal had drawn attention to the importance of Mannhardt's work on customs concerning the bringing in of summer. This same author pointed to the Jack-in-the-Green as the English equivalent to those, so paving the way further for Frazer's utilization of the German's research and arguments.[14]

It is therefore clear that Lady Raglan's identification of the medieval foliate heads with the characters in folk customs from the greening of the year, as representations of the same ancient vegetation god, had a very long gestation within European scholarship. She had not been the first to associate the foliate heads with the Jack-in-the-Green or the Jack-in-the-Green with other figures from European early summer festivities, or to suggest that the latter all represented the primeval deity, or to propose that medieval English church carvings represented still-venerated pagan divinities, or that Robin Hood had been a god of the greenwood. She had not even been the first to take the pub-sign name 'the Green Man' and apply it to a universalized pagan nature deity.[15] Nonetheless, it was a novel step to bring them all together so comprehensively, under that charismatic and memorable name. The influence of her single short and sketchily researched, but clearly and boldly written, article was accordingly to be immense.

Lady Raglan's Followers

At first sight it may seem curious that she should have made an impact at a time when the ideas of Sir James Frazer – on which hers were so extensively and explicitly based – were becoming unfashionable, at least in mainstream historical and anthropological scholarship. There were two principal explanations for this. One was that she did not employ or endorse those aspects of Frazer's work that were incurring unpopularity: his reconstruction of a putative universal ancient religion and his piling up of evidence taken from a vast range of space and time. Instead, she appeared to provide a plausible explanation for a hitherto enigmatic medieval artistic motif. The second explanation was that, bereft of any competing explanation for it but also of any compelling proof of her suggestions, experts in medieval British religion reserved judgement, and so cleared the way for scholars and commentators in other fields to accept her construct if it seemed instinctually right to them. Given the still very widespread and respectable belief, during the mid-twentieth century, of the survival of paganism through and beyond the Middle Ages, it often fell on very fertile ground.

Within a single year it had been accepted by two respected scholars, one an expert in English medieval art and the other a Cambridge classicist who had been a member of the group which included Frazer.[16] In 1948 Lady Raglan's collaborator C.J.P. Cave at last published his book on medieval roof bosses, the product of decades of work, and naturally enough restated the belief that the foliate heads that often appeared on bosses were a pre-Christian fertility image.[17] In the 1950s the name Green Man was given very wide currency as that for the medieval carvings because of its adoption by the architectural historian Nikolaus Pevsner, in his county-by-county guides to the buildings of England. That decade also established another character in the cast of those swept under the umbrella of the Frazerian vegetation god: the Green Knight, a man laid under an enchantment who appears with flesh, hair, beard, clothing and horse all of green, and carrying a holly bush, in the famous fourteenth-century English poem *Sir Gawain and the Green Knight*. He had been long identified with Frazer's putative deity by scholars persuaded by Sir James's arguments,[18] but it was the work of a leading expert in medieval English literature from Exeter University, John Speirs, which gave widespread credit to this idea. Especially influential was his textbook, published in 1957, which declared of the Green Knight that he was 'surely a descendant of the Vegetation or Nature God of almost universal and immemorial tradition . . . whose death and resurrection are the myth-and-ritual counterpart of the annual death and rebirth of nature'.[19]

Lady Raglan's construct entered the 1960s with the endorsement of an eminent retired professor of the history and philosophy of religion and former president of the Folklore Society, Edwin Oliver James. He had always been deeply influenced by Frazer, and published a study of seasonal festivals in 1961 in which he linked together the foliate heads (called 'the Green Man') Robin Hood and the Jack-in-the-Green to represent Sir James's annually reborn vegetation spirit.[20] Something of the currency which the figure was enjoying in British culture in general may be illustrated by three very different works of creative fiction published in the second half of that decade. One was a novel by Henry Treece, a successful and prolific author of popular fiction, set in fifth-century Britain and Scandinavia and entitled *The Green Man*.[21] It portrayed European paganism in Frazerian fashion as a barbarous religion carried on by humans who seem to know no love, fidelity or compassion. This religion – which the author makes clear was once carried on universally throughout the continent – is centred on a divine couple, the Green Man and the Earth Mother (who is the deity discussed in the second chapter of the present book), the union of whom makes the crops grow. The second work was a novel by a yet more famous writer, Kingsley Amis (later Sir Kingsley), with the same title. Amis's satirical humour did not lend itself, however, to grandiose vistas of Treece's (or Frazer's) kind, and confined itself to contemporary settings. He makes the vegetation spirit of Lady Raglan's vision rematerialize at a modern pub of the same name, as a mischievous and destructive entity which haunts the place until banished again.[22] Finally, another future knight, and cultural leader, the composer Harrison Birtwistle, provided as one of his first major works an opera based on the then current idea that the English Mummers' Play was a surviving prehistoric rite, centred on death and resurrection. To underscore this belief, he represented the character who carries out the act of resurrection as the green spirit of vegetation.[23]

Through all this, experts in medieval religious belief and practice continued to reserve their judgement on Lady Raglan's identification of the foliate heads, and the accompanying notion that such medieval carvings represented a continuing cult of pagan deities. They accordingly drew an indignant reproach in the mid-1970s from Anne Ross, the former pioneer of research into British Iron Age religion, who had now commenced her campaign to convince people of the persistence of that religion into modern times. She published a book in partnership with a photographer friend that was devoted to a range of decorative motifs in medieval churches that had no clear Christian relevance, including Green Men and sheela-na-gigs. She asserted that all of them were representations of pagan deities still dear to the common people which the Church was unable to eradicate and so allowed to subsist alongside the Christian Trinity and saints. Her evidence of this was analogy: with religious imagery in parts of South America that combined elements of Roman Catholicism with some from older native traditions. She accused specialists in medieval religious history of 'almost a conspiracy of silence' on the issue.[24] Her call made little apparent impression on either academics or the public, and what followed instead, in the 1980s, was the beginning of the integration of Lady Raglan's concept of the Green Man, represented visually by the medieval foliate heads, into the rapidly developing awareness of the global ecological crisis that was now in progress. It was adopted by some of the responses to that crisis as a label and symbol of the endangered natural world, with which humanity needed urgently to remake its relationship. This step seems to have been taken first by Common Ground, a London-based arts and environmental charity founded to celebrate the connection between people and place, and to empower the former to care for their local environment. In 1986 it started a project to raise awareness of the importance of trees, called 'Trees, Woods and the Green Man', the third of these being represented as the animating spirit of the first two and linked to Robin Hood and the Green Knight. It concluded in 1989, when the Green Man was made the central motif of a national celebration held by the charity.[25]

In the following year the key work was published which turned the character and the motif (now standardized as a medieval foliate head) into a late modern environmental icon. It was a book simply entitled *Green Man*, by a London poet with a passion for medieval buildings, William Anderson, and was lavishly illustrated with photographs taken by a professional, Clive Hicks. It hailed Lady Raglan's construct – a deity personified in the foliate heads, Jack-in-the-Green, Green George and Green Knight – as our best symbol of the union of humanity and the vegetal world. It then set the construct in a much wider frame of reference by pointing out that many human cultures have had deities or spirits of the forest associated with foliage, and using the theories of Carl Jung to suggest that they all represented the same primal archetype. This archetype was, the book argued on the basis of ideas drawn from Frazer and James, and from Michael Dames and Marija Gimbutas (for whom see earlier in this book), that of a young vegetation deity born to the Sky God and the Earth Mother who is constantly sacrificed and reborn. It then asserted that faith in him, as the greatest source of living power on earth, had been too strong to be repressed by Christianity, which instead brought him into its churches and so under the sway of Christ.

Most of the book then consisted of a detailed account of the development of the motif of the foliate head through the Middle Ages, and through successive styles of architecture, in France, Germany and Britain. It suggested that a further source of influence for it had come from Islam, the figure of al-Khidr, the Green One, in Muslim literature, and that it had been subsequently assimilated to the Tree of Life of Christian allegory and the figure of the Creator. It therefore made the concept an instrument for the harmonization of pagan past and Christian present. William Anderson had too good a knowledge of medieval art and architecture to be unaware that there is no actual evidence of what medieval people themselves called the heads, or that any of them regarded them as images of a pagan deity. Here, however, his reliance on Jungian psychology came into its own, because in his formulation the churchmen who commissioned and housed the carvings did not need to realize their true nature: instead the power of the ancient archetype, working through the collective subconscious, was manifesting in them whether they knew it or not. Likewise, it did not matter if the same clerics thought that sheela-na-gigs were images of sinful desire, designed to deter lust: they were *really* proof that 'the archetype of the Great Mother was stirring in the dreams and thoughts of men' once more. So the Earth Mother and her green son had returned at the same time, and it was quite probable that the common people had never lost their pagan beliefs and turned to these figures for fertility and prosperity in the old way. Anderson went on to suggest that the medieval cult of the Virgin Mary, icons of whom were (occasionally) associated with foliate heads, had been another remanifestation of the Great Goddess.

He concluded his book with a clarion call to readers to recognize that both archetypes were resurgent once more in the present time, in the environmental and feminist movements. In his vision, the Green Man had returned, after being almost buried by the Industrial Revolution and the spirit of scientific rationalism, as the living face of the earth, offering a new understanding between humans and the universal, and as the mouthpiece of the inspiration of 'the Divine Imagination', calling on nature and humanity to become one once more. All in all, the considerable power of the book lay in the fact that it was essentially a religious text, illustrated with medieval art. Even its apparent anchoring in psychological theory was really a profession of faith, as there is no objective evidence for the existence of

Jung's archetypes or collective subconscious. Its impact was immediate and was signalled by a British Broadcasting Corporation television programme screened a few months after its publication to celebrate its message. Entitled *The Return of the Green Man*, it included contributions not just from Anderson himself but from Sir Kingsley Amis and Sir Harrison Birtwistle.[26] By the end of the decade the Green Man had become established among contemporary British Pagans as one name for the god of the natural world whom most of them venerated, partnered with a great goddess in the manner portrayed by Anderson.[27]

His book, and the interest in and passion for the figure that it embodied, also generated a literary genre of books which treated the Green Man broadly in his way and with his message.[28] Most of them likewise were profusely illustrated and included a guide to or gazetteer of examples of foliate heads. Most related those heads to the Jack-in-the-Green, Green George and other Continental festival characters, the Green Knight and Robin Hood, sometimes including King Arthur as another alleged example of a dying and (prospectively) returning hero associated with the prosperity of the land. Most were clearly dependent on Lady Raglan's construct and beyond it on the ideas of Sir James Frazer. All were attractively packaged and presented, to appeal to a general readership, and most adopted the popular (and very old) format of a quest romance, a personal journey by the author to discover the truth about the subject. Almost all the authors were British, with one American. They differed among themselves in size and erudition, in tone, in geographical range (comprising Britain, Europe and parts of the rest of the world as well) and in their knowledge of the possible limitations of their evidence and of possible counter-arguments to theirs (and in the degree of courtesy with which they attempted to see off those). Despite all these variations, they were very clearly further manifestations of Anderson's approach, source base and message: a distinctive subset of writing in the field of spiritual ecology, peaking around the year 2000 but continuing to the present. That article by the noble lady in 1939 had inspired a remarkable, and long-lasting, progeny. Moreover, it was one which was written distinctively in English: despite the almost universal recognition of the current ecological crisis, the traditional affection of many Continental Europeans for their forests and the prevalence of the medieval foliate heads and of foliate characters in folk festivals across most of Europe, there has been no comparable adoption of the Green Man figure outside of Britain and (to a much lesser extent) the wider Anglophone area.

Alternative Views: The Folk Figures

Readers of this book will have recognized the Raglan construct as part of a pattern of ideas considered in its first chapter: produced under the Victorians, developed and elaborated through the first half of the twentieth century and reaching an apex in the middle of it. In the case of this construct, its suitability for appropriation by the ecological awareness movement gave it a new lease of life at the end of the century. It might therefore be expected that it would also be vulnerable to the revisionist scholarship which commenced in the 1970s and 1980s; and that is exactly what occurred, setting up a countervailing stream of literature to that subsequently started by William Anderson. The contrast between them was emphatically not one between hard-headed professional scholars and starry-eyed amateurs. Some of those who wrote books in the Anderson tradition were themselves academics (though not historians or archaeologists).[29] Conversely, most of the key figures in the revisionist school were independent researchers. The division was, rather, between two different approaches to the role of the past, and of historical evidence, in late modernity.

A key work in the process of revisionism was the study of the Jack-in-the-Green, the wooden frame covered in flowers and greenery and carried in procession in English May Day celebrations, published in 1979.[30] It was written by a schoolteacher and local college lecturer called Roy Judge, and was one of the landmark products of the new wave of research by folklorists based on sustained scrutiny of historical records. Like most of the publications of late twentieth-century revisionists, across disciplines, it was not undertaken in a deliberate spirit of aggression or iconoclasm, but from a straightforward spirit of enquiry, to make a proper examination of the actual evidence for received ideas and see how well based they were.[31] In this case, the results came as a general surprise, as much to the author as others. The Jack, which had been taken as the supreme British example of a folk representation of an ancient vegetation deity, was essentially a nineteenth-century custom carried on by chimney sweeps in southern English towns to collect money against a summer season in which they would be largely unemployed. There was no certain record of it before the period between 1775 and 1800, when it had appeared in a similarly urban setting, apparently London.[32] Judge left open the possibility that it might have existed before then without being recorded, but he made clear that he thought this very unlikely; and subsequent research has reinforced this opinion.[33]

He also provided the backdrop to the development of the custom, which lay in a very old tradition, found across much of Europe, of celebrating the coming of summer in late April or May by carrying garlands of flowers through the streets and often setting them up on poles or frames, or in churches. In London, by the early to mid-seventeenth century, this had produced a distinctive local spin-off, in which bands of milkmaids danced in the streets on and around May Day, each with a pail decorated with flowers, to collect money from passers-by and customers. In the later seventeenth century the pail was replaced by a pyramid of (usually borrowed) silver objects, still called a 'garland', and during the eighteenth century other low-grade occupational groups in the city – the rag-pickers and chimney sweeps – began to put on similar shows in the street. The rag-pickers carried a similar 'garland' and staged a performance, and the chimney sweeps donned fancy dress and danced, sometimes with their own 'garland' of the same kind. During the last quarter of the century the sweeps replaced this with their distinctive construction of the Jack-in-the-Green.[34] Judge ended this summary of its origins with the declaration that 'one may conclude quite simply, that this name and this leafy structure appeared together at the end of the eighteenth century in a context of May-day begging. They make adequate sense within that context and there is no evidence for any earlier history or other interpretation'.[35] That was an absolutely plain, if oblique, refutation of the use made of them by Frazer and Raglan.

EPILOGUE

This book made Roy Judge a celebrity among folklorists, and he duly served as president of the Folklore Society in the 1990s. By that time he was becoming aware of the view of the Green Man launched by William Anderson and uncomfortable with it. In an address to a conference published in 1991, he pointed out that Anderson's approach rested directly on the work of Lady Raglan, which had produced a modern myth, a 'case study in the invention of tradition'.[36] In the second edition of his book on the Jack-in-the-Green, in 2000, he made an extended study of the development of the use made of the figure by Frazer, Lady Raglan and their successors, especially Anderson. He was too much a gentleman to deal roughly with it, commenting (correctly) in particular on the beauty of Anderson's book and the high quality of its illustrations. Nonetheless, his attitude was plain. He started by establishing that his latest research confirmed all the conclusions of the first edition and prefaced his discussion of the Frazerian tradition by stating flatly that Frazer had been wrong to use the Jack as evidence for vegetation spirit worship and regretting that *The Golden Bough* had dominated discussion of the subject ever since. He added that any interpretations of the Jack as being 'linked with a pagan and mythological past . . . had no evidence to support them other than intuition and poetic insight'.[37] He then noted that the concept of the Green Man, with the Jack as an important component part of it, now seemed stronger than ever, despite all the solid work that had been done to separate the two.[38]

Lady Raglan had made much of a second English folkloric figure in forming her construct: the Castleton Garland described earlier, which she had taken likewise to be a survival of ancient pagan ritual. In 1984 this was submitted to a proper historical study by another independent scholar and leading figure of the revisionist movement in folklore studies, Georgina Boyes, which was eventually published in 1993.[39] She proved from local records that it was no older than the Jack, having evolved in the late eighteenth and early nineteenth century. It had developed out of the older and widespread north-western English custom of rush-bearing, in which fresh rushes to cover the church floor were ceremonially gathered and taken by cart in a procession to the church in summer. At Castleton a garland had accompanied the cart, and this was retained during the nineteenth century when the cart was replaced by a morris dance, led by a man in ribbons and another dressed as a woman. In the 1890s the growing importance of the little town as a centre for tourism brought a desire to glamourize the event, and the morris was replaced by schoolgirls clad in white, while the two leaders were costumed as a king and queen; from 1933 the latter was represented by an actual woman. The 'king' rode and carried the garland.

The overall historic model for seasonal customs stated in the first chapter of the book holds good here: while specific forms of them change over the centuries, and most of those recorded by Victorian and Edwardian folklorists were relatively modern, the basic nature of a custom often remains constant. Thus, as said, processions carrying garlands at the opening of summer are recorded across Europe since records begin, and are therefore certainly older than history. They are one obvious way in which to celebrate the return of flowers and greenery and the warmth and long light that support them.[40] The Jack-in-the Green and the Castleton Garland, as wooden frameworks covered with foliage and blooms, are therefore quite accurate modern equivalents of those borne in medieval and early modern festivities, even if there is no continuity of tradition in their cases. The garland-carrying custom would almost certainly also have been associated with religious rites in ancient times, though it seems too widespread and diversely enacted to have been associated with one particular deity or cult, as Frazer would have had it. In that sense, it could legitimately be called a pagan survival, although only in the most generalized sense, and it could equally be called a timeless way of welcoming summer which could be combined with any religion. Likewise, it is quite possible that some, at least, of the greenery-covered characters who featured in the Continental spring and summer festivities collected by Mannhardt and Frazer are actually descended from ancient rites. They need detailed individual histories – if the records allow – of the sort now given to the English equivalents.

EPILOGUE

Alternative Views: The Literary Characters

Two characters from literary sources had become swept up into the concept of the Green Man by the mid-twentieth century, and continued to feature in it in some of the recent books on him inspired by William Anderson: Robin Hood and the Green Knight. Both likewise became the subject of revisionist scholarship in the latter part of the century – first Robin and then the Knight – but this time within the academy. The medieval outlaw and his legend were made the focus of a succession of works by distinguished professional historians and literary scholars.[41] The idea that he had originally been a supernatural being – a woodland fairy, spirit or deity – long preceded Margaret Murray, having been first popularized by the Victorian writer Thomas Wright. This was based largely on his undoubted popularity in English May celebrations during the late fifteenth and the sixteenth centuries, which seemed to assimilate him, along with his close association with the greenwood, to the foliate characters in Continental festivities at that time. It was a theory finally abandoned by professional scholars in the 1970s, because of new research.

That revealed that Robin Hood's legend long pre-dated his appearance in the May games, which is first recorded in 1474.[42] Plays in those which featured him, sometimes joined to processions and dances, then rapidly spread across southern England, especially to market towns, peaking in popularity in the early sixteenth century and declining in the second half of that century so that they had almost vanished by 1600. The plays did make a significant contribution to his legend, because it seems to have been in them that he met his female companion, Maid Marian, who had most probably arrived from France in a separate story performed in the games, as a shepherdess with a shepherd lover called Robin. The outlaw was originally made famous by ballads that celebrated him, and the earliest of those are now dated to the late fourteenth century, with material in them dateable to the 1320s, while Robin himself was already a well-known character by 1262. He did not, therefore, emerge from the May celebrations, but was added to them after enjoying an already long development as a character; and the ballads are the best evidence for his original identity.

Their tone is generally, and sometimes grimly and grittily, realistic. There are no mythological elements in them – no supernatural beings, impossible feats or magic – of the sort so abundant in medieval romances. There are indeed no real equivalent figures in actual pagan tradition or medieval folklore, across Europe, from whom he could have developed. His nearest equivalents in medieval literature are historic English outlaws such as Eustace the Monk, Fulke Fitzwarren and Hereward the Wake; and there is a good chance that Robin was a real person himself, an outlaw recorded as operating in the Yorkshire district of Barnsdale in the 1220s. He is certainly presented as a woodlander, but as a real human being, a yeoman, the most prosperous and independent sort of medieval peasant. He and his band are hostile to specific rich and corrupt churchmen, especially greedy Benedictine abbots, but they themselves manifest a fervent Christian piety, with an especial devotion to the Virgin Mary of a kind both common and conventional in the later Middle Ages. The early stories of him are deeply socially and politically subversive: Robin belongs to the woods which were on the edge of the medieval civilized and literate world, rejects royal service in order to return home to them and consistently violates the social distance that separated medieval commoners from the upper classes and deals with the latter on his own terms. They therefore carry a genuinely radical message – but not a pagan one.

The Green Knight waited longer for revisionist attention, until 1994, when a specialist in English literature from Southampton University, Bella Millett, posed the question of how green he actually was. She noted that he was not explicitly linked to nature, but to the world of knightly chivalry, and that green was a hue of enchantment, transgression and wildness in medieval culture. His colouring is compared in the poem to enamel rather than vegetation. He is also handsome and dressed in courtly fashion, and has well-tended hair and a richly decorated weapon; and King Arthur accordingly treats him as a knight and not a monster. Observers link him with the supernatural and not the natural – a phantom, fairy or elf – and he indeed turns out not to be a forest spirit but a gentleman under a spell. The natural world itself is treated as an adventure playground or an unpleasant wilderness, and the knight's (initial) colour is just part of his ability to shock. The tone of the whole poem, as of other work by the same poet, is both very courtly and very Christian. Such, at any rate were Millett's conclusions, and her article does not seem to have been answered; and, since its publication, acceptance of the Green Knight as manifestation of a vegetation spirit seems to have quietly disappeared from studies of the poem.[43]

Alternative Views: 'Real' Green Men

In much of the excitement over the Green Man in the second half of the twentieth century, sight was almost lost of the fact that the actual name had been taken from a pub sign. In 1997, however, an American academic epidemiologist, Brandon Centerwall, drew attention back to that.[44] He dismissed Lady Raglan's article with the comment that it displayed 'what was then a fashionably Frazerian Catholicity (or, as we should say today, lack of discrimination)', and with it any pagan context for the foliate heads. Nonetheless, he also argued that, effectively by accident, she had actually got the name for them right. He did so by tracing back the pub sign to its origins in the seventeenth century, when it first appeared. The green-clad figure on it seems to have been taken from the distilling industry, where it was used commonly from 1630 until the eighteenth century to advertise and symbolize alcoholic spirits. What the motif showed then was a man with a club, a body covered with leaves and leafy hair and beard, also called a wood man or wild man.[45] A commentator at that time suggested that this was because strong alcohol made men into wild savages, but there is an old and very widespread association between alcohol and greenery, perhaps because wine comes from vines. A leafy bough has been used in different parts of Europe as a sign of drink for sale, a fact immortalized in Shakespeare's saying 'good wine needs no bush'.[46] This was itself a translation of the ancient Roman tag *Vino vendibili hedera non opus* (in which the bush is specifically of ivy, the plant associated with the wine-god Dionysus), which has been rendered into modern French parlance as *Au vin qui vend bien, il ne faut pas de lierre.*[47] The 'wild man' figure on the Green Man sign was subsequently replaced by a forester, gamekeeper or (in the nineteenth century) Robin Hood.

Centerwall, however, spotted the precise origin point for the figure used by the distillers and then the publicans: in characters fairly common in Tudor and Stuart English urban pageants and entertainments. These were known as green men, wild men or savages, and worked in teams to clear back crowds to the edge of streets so that the processions and parades could pass down them. They were costumed like the figure on the distillers' sign, with leaves stitched onto their garments, shaggy hair and clubs, though they tended to use fireworks rather than the clubs to get people out of the way. The stereotype to which they relate is also quite apparent: that of the medieval Wild Man, a human entirely covered with hair, or sometimes leaves, carrying a club and living like an animal in the wilderness. Occasionally he was given a female mate and offspring, and he sometimes featured in groups. He featured in both literary texts and works of art, where he functioned as a repulsive and menacing antithesis to civilization, representing a humanity bereft of education, religion, morals and manners: a nightmare to a medieval and early modern world obsessed with religious and social order. He reached his apogee of popularity as a subject in the late Middle Ages but began to vanish during the sixteenth century, as growing European confidence and expansion made the noble savage seem a more attractive expression of primitive humanity. Although a distinctive medieval Christian creation, he drew on long and ancient roots, combining the beastly habits which Greek and Roman writers (such as Herodotus and Pliny) attributed to barbarian tribes and those associated by those writers with the amoral woodland beings called satyrs.[48]

Centerwall has performed a great service by reminding scholars of these figures, who after all bore the actual name 'green men'. He went further, however, by trying to tie them to the foliate heads, using three pieces of visual evidence. One was a bench end at Crowcombe church, Somerset, carved in 1534, which showed two figures waving clubs and with bare torsos and apparently leafy skirts exploding from the top of a standard foliate head. The second was an engraving by the Master of the Nuremberg

Passion, from Germany in the middle of the fifteenth century, depicting a figure wielding a club while carrying a shield apparently emblazoned with a foliate head. The third was a fourteenth-century carving in Winchester Cathedral of a foliate head with a body clad in normal clothing and holding a sword and shield. Centerwall proposed that, taken together, they reveal the evolution of the figure from a church carving of a head to a pageant character, retaining its name of the Green Man. This is fresh and valuable research, but the chain of evidence assembled may be illusory. For one thing, such a small number of very different images, spanning such a large amount of time and space, is a very slight basis on which to erect a large theory. Each may represent a one-off, of an artist combining different forms in an individual and experimental manner. For another, they can be read in other ways. It is not clear that the device on the shield of the German engraving actually is a foliate head, while the club-waving men erupting from the foliate head at Crowcombe could have scaly tails and not leafy skirts.[49] Centerwall's proposal is therefore possibly correct, but it remains unsubstantiated, and perhaps unlikely.

What he did demonstrate, on the other hand, was that the green men of the pageants were closely identified with the Wild Man by the end of the Middle Ages. An engraving from the 1460s by the German Master of the Housebook shows a nude Wild Woman riding a stag, with children, and opposite her a leaf-covered figure with a leaf crown riding a unicorn. A silver ewer probably made at Nuremberg around 1500 is surmounted by a Wild Man riding a dragon, with brown beard and hair and a rich green body. Further into the sixteenth century, Pieter Brueghel's painting *The Struggle of Carnival and Lent* shows a troupe of actors performing a play which includes a green Wild Man. Centerwall took these as showing that the figures of the Green Man and the Wild Man converged towards the end of the medieval period, but another interpretation could be equally well advanced on the same evidence: that the pageant green men actually evolved out of the Wild Man, as leaves began more often to substitute for hair as a body covering for the latter. This would leave the foliate heads as before, a separate and apparently nameless motif.

It may be proposed, therefore, that the pageant green men are really just wild men with a change of colour and texture. This would explain why they have much the same associations in their pageant duties, as figures at once comical and forbidding. A convergence by them, in turn, with the old association of foliage and alcohol would carry them onto the inn sign and so provide a history of this motif, and the original name 'The Green Man', from the Middle Ages to the present. There is also a link to the foliate festival characters from central and eastern Europe, because it may be remembered that 'the Wild Man' was the name for some of these in particular areas (namely in German-speaking communities in Saxony, Thuringia and the Erzgebirge mountains on the Bohemian frontier). After Frazer's time it became known that in other communities in Thuringia the same sort of figure was actually called 'The Green Man' as an alternative, reflecting the way in which the two had been versions of each other in late medieval and early modern northern Europe.[50] While the central contention of Centerwall's article may therefore be doubtful, it has done much to untangle other aspects of Lady Raglan's construct.

Alternative Views: The Foliate Heads

Sustained research into the history and nature of the foliate heads themselves began in 1978 with the publication of the landmark study of them by a botanist and geneticist at Manchester University, Kathleen Basford, for which she adopted the now familiar name for the heads as the title: *The Green Man*.[51] That was the only respect in which she followed the Raglan construct, instead devoting decades of patient research of her own to them which spanned much of Europe and supplied a large number of splendid illustrations. She pointed out that they were probably the most common decorative motif of medieval sculpture, found on roof bosses, capitals, corbels, fonts, tombs, tympana, screens and different parts of seats, benches and stalls. She traced the origins of this motif to pagan antiquity, where leaf masks appeared on carved faces in Roman art during the first century and spread during the second, being found throughout the empire in temples of many different deities. Especial associations were with the sea god Okeanos, who had hair and beard of seaweed, and the wine god Bacchus, who was commonly rigged out in vines. The leaf mask remained a popular ornament on secular buildings in the eastern, or Byzantine, part of the empire after its conversion to Christianity. None of these ancient versions had the widespread later medieval motif of foliage disgorging from the mouth, but a head on a fourth- or fifth-century Christian tomb at Poitiers, France, had leaves gushing from the nostrils.

However, Basford noted a problem for any theory of a direct chain of transmission from antiquity to the Middle Ages: that the Poitiers carving seemed a completely isolated example of that motif, and when foliate heads became common in medieval art, in manuscripts and churches between the tenth and twelfth centuries, they bore little resemblance to the ancient leaf masks. Instead, they appeared demonic, and she thought that this made a neat fit with a textual source, written by the eighth-century Christian scholar Rabanus Maurus, who equated leaves with the sins of the flesh. The twelfth century saw the specific image of foliage running from the mouth and nose become widespread: Basford matched this to a Biblical text (Ezekiel 8:17), which said of idolators 'see how they hold the branches to the nose'. She therefore suggested that an ancient artistic motif had been re-employed and redeveloped by Christian artists to deliver a new and hostile message. In the thirteenth century, France became the centre for further developments, as the style of head divided into two traditions: the leaf mask, now revived from ancient examples, and the disgorging head, which remained mostly demonic in appearance. These reached a peak of popularity in England and Germany during the later Middle Ages, the leaves associated with the figures becoming more naturalistic, and identifiable with particular species, during this period. From the sixteenth century, it became a popular ornament in a range of secular contexts.[52]

Basford concluded, therefore, that an ancient pagan artistic motif had become part of the symbolic language of the Western Church and evolved within it, serving a number of different messages: it might, for example, be used to symbolize resurrection, but equally well the transience and decay of all flesh. Like Roy Judge, she was too genteel to mount a direct attack on the idea that the heads represented a still-beloved pagan god, but, for those prepared to read her with care, her rejection of this idea was plain enough. Her early declarations that there was no one meaning to the heads, that many seemed to suggest death and ruin, not life and resurrection, and that a vegetation spirit would make no sense in a monastery church – the location of many examples – signalled her view of the Raglan construct. Later in the book she conceded that it was possible that some of the faces might allude to a May King or springtime foliage, but added that more often they seemed evil or anguished. She concluded that they conveyed an uneasy or hostile relationship between human and plant, and that the church Green Man was more likely to stand for 'the darkness of unredeemed nature as opposed to the shimmering light of Christian revelation'. Conversely, she thought it 'unlikely that he was revered as a symbol of the renewal of life in springtime'.[53] The same mixture of caution, courtesy and readiness to question the Raglan construct characterized her review of Anderson's book in 1991, where she compared him to Lady Raglan for his readiness to make 'intuitive leaps' which had immediate popular appeal. She pointed out that his interpretation ignored all of the darker aspects of the motif, and suggested that the Biblical view of the human relationship with nature, as one of responsibility for life on earth in enactment of the stewardship of Adam, might make a better one than Anderson's to encourage an effective response to the current ecological crisis.[54]

Kathleen Basford's book became the indispensable starting point for all future research into the medieval carvings, and as such she was honoured as a forerunner not only by William Anderson himself but by some of the authors whom he inspired, who dealt variously with her lack of enthusiasm for their standpoint by failing to notice it, by explaining it away or by believing that Anderson had answered her. She also, however, acted as an inspiration for a new generation of authors who rejected Anderson's approach to the subject and were galvanized partly by the outpouring of works on it that did follow his tradition. It was a new generation indeed, because by 2001 Basford, Anderson and Judge were all dead and four other independent British scholars had come forth to tackle the question of the meaning of the foliate heads, most producing their work in formats, like those of the Anderson school, designed to reach a wide popular audience. The first was Rita Wood, who published an article in a history magazine in 2000 which examined more fully the possible Christian meanings of the motifs. It suggested that foliage had enjoyed a much wider and more various span of connotations among pious and orthodox medieval people than the association with fleshly sins expounded by Rabanus Maurus. The vine was a symbol of self-sacrificing love, sometimes identified with Christ, and the Tree of Life from the garden of Eden represented another potent and enduring Biblical motif which was identified with the Cross and also with the heavenly paradise. Leaves were used in all sorts of ways to illustrate themes of death and resurrection, and of both life on earth and eternal life. She allowed that the rare cases of disorderly foliage might represent sin, but thought this exceptional.[55]

The second was a museum curator who became a leading figure in the Folklore Society and notable author on history and folklore, Jeremy Harte, who in 2001 brought out a booklet on the heads in the Pitkin Guide series – beautifully illustrated short introductions to historical and archaeological subjects sold commonly in British tourist shops. He emphasized the amazing range of apparent moods covered by the heads and repeated Basford's suggestion of multiple meanings, concluding that 'there is no single, archetypal meaning to which Green Men have to conform'. This struck in itself at the Anderson hypothesis, and he went on to note that spring blossoms were never depicted in the foliage of the heads but fruit often was, so they were associated more often with autumn than May.[56] The hairstyles were those of young men of the time, making the carvings unlikely to represent spirits of the wild. Harte stated directly that 'it would be a mistake to think of carvings like this as the work of some underground movement of mystics or pagans. All church sculpture, grotesque or not, was commissioned by good Christians.' He also noted that none of the many medieval pictures of Maytime revellers showed any wearing a framework of leaves, and pronounced Lady Raglan's theory 'almost certainly untrue'. On the other hand, he found that it was difficult to give the heads a clear Christian allegorical interpretation either, stressing again that they would have carried a range of meanings. He took notice of the Anderson school of literature on the subject, commenting that it had created 'a composite god, who had never existed'. He concluded that 'the Green Man began as a grotesque: it is we who have made him into a god'. Harte is however too genial a personality to regard this process with any hostility, opining that the modern world needed a symbol for the boundless vitality of nature, and that the medieval motif provided it and saved the modern world the effort of inventing one. He pronounced it to be now the instantly recognizable symbol of 'a new green religion'.[57]

Two years later the first major advance in knowledge of the motif since Basford's work was made by Mercia MacDermott, in a short book in the 'Explore' series published for a popular market (though to a high standard of scholarship) by the Heart of Albion Press. She and her photographer (who produced more abundant and high-quality illustrations) had themselves been friends of Basford's. Her work provided a more comprehensive coverage than before of the evolution of the foliate head through the whole medieval and early modern period, and across Europe. She was directly dismissive of the Raglan construct, stating that 'we have to reject the popular but anachronistic idea that the Green Man was smuggled into churches by recalcitrant, underground pagans'. She noted that nobody before the twentieth century seems to have thought the motif to be pagan, or even very significant. Instead, she emphasized that the locations in which it occurred indicate that it 'entered the Christian world with the blessing of the Church'. She cited a range of further Biblical texts, to join that from Ezekiel, that provided associations for leaves of fruitfulness and success, and persisting life, or else of transience and decay. By contrast, she pointed out, although most ancient religions venerated trees and other forms of greenery, and all early civilizations of Asia Minor and the eastern Mediterranean had gods representing vegetation or crops, there was no evidence that the medieval heads were related to them. Nor was there any involvement of the heads in May or any other seasonal festivities. Al-Khidr, the 'Green One' of Islamic tradition, only wore green robes and had no connection to foliage.

EPILOGUE

Surveying the heads surviving from their Gothic heyday of popularity, between 1150 and 1500, she found no uniformity of design even for a similar purpose such as a tomb, and no single unifying theological concept for them. Going back into the Romanesque period, from 900 to 1150, she found the heads fewer and more uniform – of the kind disgorging foliage – and more limited in their positioning in churches, and most were not human but feline.[58] They were also more likely to be found in other locations, such as manuscripts and ornaments. Before 900, foliate heads were very rare, and represented by Basford's ancient Roman and Byzantine leaf masks, mostly associated with Okeanus and Bacchus. There was no Roman god who equated to the vegetation deity imagined by Frazer and so Raglan. MacDermott, in fact, found only one ancient image that provided the kind of disgorging foliate head, feline or human, which appeared in the Romanesque churches, and that came from India. A few authors in the post-Anderson tradition had noted the occurrence in south and south-east Asia of heads of similar kind to the European, and made this a prop of the Anderson idea of a universal archetype. MacDermott had a simpler explanation: that the Indian design, related to legends of Shiva and Vishnu, travelled to Europe through the Arab world and was adopted into European art from the tenth century onwards, as Christian and Islamic communities mingled and exchanged ideas in places such as Spain and Sicily. The earliest known occurrence of it in Europe was indeed in a Spanish manuscript from around the year 900.[59] It is a suggestion which makes perfect sense and fits the known evidence. She concluded by agreeing with Basford and Harte that the medieval foliate head was primarily a decorative element, employed when required to deliver a range of messages (though none of these apparently pagan).

The fourth author was a heritage consultant, Richard Hayman, who published in popular history and archaeology magazines in the late 2000s, before bringing out a short book in the 'Shire' series of guides to different subjects, sold like the Pitkin set in tourist shops.[60] His own research was conducted principally in England. He summarized the knowledge of the foliate heads to date, with a direct attack on the idea that they had any pagan associations in the Middle Ages. He also made a heavier emphasis on the fact that they had featured earlier, most often in 'elite' churches such as colleges, cathedrals and monasteries, and become most popular in parishes in the fifteenth and sixteenth centuries. He was inclined to stress the more negative apparent connotations of the motif, arguing that foliage was often depicted in medieval art and literature as a snare and entanglement, and that the heads mostly represented sin, death and decay. He also emphasized that they appeared first in manuscripts, produced in a monastic context, and so had no discernible connection with popular culture. He pointed out that the relevance of the foliate heads in ancient pagan art to the medieval kind was not securely proved, and ascribed the popularity of the motif in contemporary counter-cultural circles to the fact that it was a simple, vivid image attractive to the branding mentality of modern consumerism.

It may therefore be suggested that by the 2010s any member of the public interested in the subject had access to a wide range of possible reading on it, in very accessible forms and with excellent visual illustrations, and representing a polarity of viewpoints. It seems likely (and conforms to the present author's ad hoc experience) that those already inclined to an environmental activist and counter-cultural set of attitudes would be both more likely to encounter and more likely to favour the books (and spin-off internet web sites) of the Anderson tradition. Those interested in churches and historic monuments in general have been more likely to come across and credit the works of those rejecting that tradition. In no case had the running been made in either stream of publishing by academic historians and archaeologists: the development of both had been powered by authors outside those disciplines, and generally outside of academia altogether.[61] Neutral observers might readily conclude that in the last analysis nothing has been proved or concluded, and that the foliate heads remain a mystery, susceptible to differing interpretations.[62]

To some extent this would make a fit with the suggestion made by Kathleen Basford, Jeremy Harte and Mercia MacDermott that the foliate head was always a decoration which had no single meaning but could be made to carry a range. Thus, to different medieval artists, churchmen and congregations they could have represented fresh hope, eternal life, resurrection, salvation or abundance, or else sin, entrapment, menace or damnation. One might add another possibility here: that the old association between foliage and alcohol could have made the heads an effective symbol of the twinned pleasures and evils of intoxication. However, all these possibilities run up against the problem that there is no evidence that medieval people actually attributed any of these meanings to the motif. This is really very odd, because those people were very fond both of giving figures and symbols stock allegorical meanings, and of expounding these. We are sure, for example, of the standard associations that they allotted to Wild Men, unicorns, mermaids, panthers and many other species and designs. However, all the considerable work that has now been put into medieval sermons, conduct manuals, pastoral handbooks, conciliar and episcopal directives and ecclesiastical court records all over Europe has not turned up a single reference to the heads. When, uniquely, a surviving record describes them, being an illustrated architectural notebook by a thirteenth-century master mason, Villard de Honnecourt, it provides four different examples and sums up all simply as *têtes de feuilles*: leafy heads.[63]

This complete objectivity, a technical professionalism drained of all signifying content, may actually be the truth of the matter – and the agreement of Basford, Harte and MacDermott, that the foliate head was essentially just a decorative motif, is at the heart of it. It could be that it is a sphinx without a riddle, a figure used simply for its artistic and structural potential which had not only no fixed, common or agreed meaning, but actually no meaning at all. That would explain the silence in the medieval records with respect to its attributions, its popularity during the period, as a harmlessly decorative, entertaining and neutral figure, imported from outside Christian Europe or disinterred from classical ruins (according to the style), and the readiness with which it has been pressed into service by modern concerns.

Summary

The Green Man therefore seems to provide a very close, if much belated, modern counterpart to Mother Earth or the Great Mother Goddess, discussed in the second chapter of the present book. Like her, he seems to have been conceived originally as a literary figure, treated in the abstract, though the literature concerned was that of academics and folklorists rather than of philosophers and poets. He then took on life of his own as a religious figure, responding to modern needs just as the goddess did, and coming in some contexts to feature very much as her male opposite number and consort. It is perhaps telling that it was necessary to wait until late modernity, and the progress of feminism in actual human society, before a male entity of this kind was envisaged: until then the beings considered in this book have been female, the significance of which will be considered further in its conclusion. For now, it may be helpful to consider the implications of this story, if correctly assembled, for our view of history and of scholarship. The accumulation of research since the late 1970s strongly suggests that Lady Raglan's construct was simply wrong: the foliate heads are not evidence of persisting belief in pagan deities through the Middle Ages and have nothing to do with the Jack-in-the-Green, Robin Hood or foliate figures from Continental European folk festivities to welcome summer. For that matter, neither the Jack nor Robin can be associated with surviving paganism either, and there seems to be no connection between them or of either with the continental figures. Nor can William Anderson's use of Jungian archetypes do anything to alter this situation, because belief in them is a matter of faith and not a scholarly methodology.

On the other hand, it is perfectly legitimate to pick foliate or woodland figures from all over European and Near Eastern art, folklore and literature, across the ages, or indeed from all over the planet, and group them together now as expressions of the human relationship with green and fertile nature. Such figures are indeed found in many different religions and ethnicities, and there is no reason why the foliate heads in churches, the Jack-in-the-Green, Robin Hood and the Green Knight should not be included among them. It is also justifiable to regard this collection of characters, motifs and images as infused with a common spirit, the animating one of the vegetation of the world, and especially of that which dies or is harvested and then renews itself. In the Western context there is no reason why the name The

Green Man should not be retained for such a being. There is no evidence that it was used of the foliate heads before 1939, but it was applied to figures representing wild nature, found in art, literature, pageants and folk customs. There should also be no reasonable objection if people then make this belief system the basis for, or a component of, a religion and/or a symbolism with which to approach the current global ecological emergency. As we know so little about how the divine operates – if it operates at all – it may well be that those who adopt or have adopted such a religion (or, in less structured form, a spirituality) are actually creating, empowering or contacting 'real' entities.

The trouble only starts if those who embrace such beliefs back-project them upon the past and declare that they are revealing an ancient mystery, or an eternal and universal archetype which once underpinned a global – or even just continent-wide – belief system, or else the truth about ancient or medieval religion. In many ways the story of the Green Man makes a parallel with that of other Victorian and Edwardian scholarly hypotheses which gathered support and momentum in the Anglophone world during the first half of the twentieth century, as that world thought and acted within cultural, social and economic parameters largely laid down during the nineteenth. Examples of those others considered earlier were the persistence of paganism through the Christian centuries, especially among witches, and the veneration of a universal prehistoric Mother Goddess. When those parameters shifted dramatically from the middle of the century, two very different responses were formulated to those hypotheses. One, concentrated among those concerned with sustained research into the past, was to examine and deconstruct them, and reject them if they were not found to match up to the apparent evidence. The other, concentrated among those concerned with responses to the problems of late modernity, and especially with those associated with counter-cultures, has been to appropriate the figures and beliefs embodied in those hypotheses and to remodel them for a new set of causes. Both have their value as reactions to a changing world, and it would be a very positive achievement if they could be diverted from clashing with each other.

The relationship between the two is not, however, the subject of this book, though it has been a recurrent theme in parts of it. What a history of the construct of the Green Man contributes to the main interest of the present work is a detailed, well-documented and recent example of the way in which new deities or spiritual forces can be perceived and established in the Western human mind which are neither straightforward survivals from ancient paganism nor anything directly to do with Christianity. There may be trace elements of both in the modern Green Man, the pagan because leaf masks were known as an architectural decoration in the ancient world, especially on temples, and the Christian because of Frazer's project of undermining belief in Christ by assimilating him to a universal ancient cult of a dying and returning god. In essence, however, he belongs to neither, but is an effective enough representation of a divinity-like being who has appeared in response to modern needs and within a post-Christian society.

CONCLUSION

In her groundbreaking book published in 2003, entitled *God and the Goddesses*,[1] Barbara Newman considered a number of figures whom she termed 'allegorical goddesses' who personified virtues and institutions in medieval literature. Among these were Wisdom, Philosophy, Lady Reason, Lady Poverty, Holy Lady Church, Lady Right, Lady Love and Lady Justice. They proliferated from the twelfth century and were all distinctive creations of the Christian imagination. The authors who wrote of them explicitly awarded them divine status, calling them goddesses or daughters of God, and Newman was quite certain that they were neither 'pagan survivals' nor versions of a 'Great Goddess'. Instead, she regarded them as a third order of superhuman being in medieval Christian thought, along with saints and classical pagan goddesses, with both of which they to some extent overlapped. In her opinion, they substantially transformed and deepened Latin Christianity's concept of the divine and represented a second Christian pantheon, generated after the saints. Their function in texts was to assist the authors in a spiritual project, and they were treated as being as real as angels or devils, as deserving of love and reverence and as being on intimate terms with the Christian God. As allegories, they could mediate religious experience not easily accommodated within scholastic doctrine, and formed an important part of an 'imaginative theology': the pursuit of serious religious thought through the techniques of imaginative literature. As divine figures who were the subordinates of God and the personifications of some of his attributes, they posed no danger to orthodoxy and provided a safe space within which to explore the Christian faith. So, it seems that it is possible to have Christian goddesses, and that the term is not an oxymoron.

Nonetheless, the beings discussed here are not equivalent to those who were the subject of Barbara Newman's study, with the partial exception of Nature; and she stands out from the rest of those considered by Newman. She did share with them the attributes of being put for a time under the umbrella of Christian cosmology and made into a lieutenant and agent of its God; and like them she could be treated as an allegory. On the other hand, she was not an abstraction as the others were, and represented something far more solid and dynamic, and on a much larger scale. She was simply more important, and more enduring as a literary character. She was also the only one of Newman's goddess figures to have clear antecedents in ancient philosophy and poetry, the only one to be invoked in spells, and the only one with enough independence and stature to survive the Middle Ages and cut loose from Christian theology again to become a part of modern culture. The other figures considered in this book seem even more like pagan goddesses than she does, but none of them can definitely be identified as such, in the sense of known deities once venerated in antiquity. They do not fit readily either into any of Newman's other categories of superhuman beings identified by medieval authors: they are not angels, devils or saints. In fact, they do not seem to fit anywhere at all.

Nonetheless, they all had considerable emotional traction, and inspired beliefs that covered large areas of space and time. To some extent, human relationships with them overlapped the categories of those usually associated with nature-spirits. The fairy queen (obviously), the lady of the night rides and the Cailleach all had some similarity to that class of beings variously called in English fairies or elves. In that sense, they have connections to the 'small gods' of peoples across the globe who have had their indigenous religions officially replaced by major religious systems such as Christianity or Islam, that whole panoply of spirits and human-like beings who live parallel lives to humans, often in wild places or underground, and interact with them, but have none of the grandeur of deities. Worldwide, they tend to linger as a belief system among ordinary people when the major goddesses and gods have disappeared from their mental universes.[2] The difference in the figures considered here, however, is that none of them seem particularly 'small': on the contrary, they do seem at times to operate on the scale of deities. Two of them had definite connections with the natural world in a broader sense. Mother Earth or Mother Nature, whether envisaged by early medieval farmers seeking fertility for their land, early medieval herbalists seeking plant remedies, high medieval scholars, medieval or Victorian poets or modern intellectuals constructing ideas about primitive religion, generally represented its more wholesome, nurturing and providing aspects. By contrast, the Cailleach, to ordinary Gaelic folk, personified or wielded the more menacing ones: winter, wild and hostile environments, the threat of predators and the inescapability of ageing and dying. Both therefore embody mental consequences of the human experience of living in environments which seem to have their own independent, animating powers.

To some extent, the same could be said of the fairy queen and the lady of the night rides, but neither of those personifies natural forces and neither indeed seems to live much closer to nature than the humans of the time. The fairy queen has a court, with royal or noble trappings, and the night-roving lady holds revels and games for her retinue and enjoys visiting houses to feast. Their social importance is that of friends and patronesses, especially to socially disempowered or marginalized humans. In this respect, they resemble Christian saints, and both they and the saints draw on the genuine human experience, in a pre-modern society, of the need to obtain the favour of the wealthy and powerful in one's social and political world. Neither, however, is in the least saintly. Both apparently exist outside of Christian structures of authority, human and divine, and of the bounds of civilized and ordered society: they come out of hollow hills, or the uncultivated countryside, or the night. They teach magic, a group of practices repeatedly condemned by orthodox Christianity, and the names first given to the lady of the rides reflect bogey-figures of New Testament tradition, Diana and Herodias. They are profoundly counter-cultural.

Every one of the figures considered in the body of this book is transgressive in another sense as well: all are female. They are females with power, agency and authority, in a medieval and early modern world in which both heaven and earth were theoretically placed firmly under masculine control. Even in the single case in which one was brought safely and respectably into Christian cosmology – that of Nature – the responsibility allotted to her was still considerable, with much day-to-day freedom of action. Even Nature, moreover, resides in the terrestrial world and is not part of the company of heaven, nor a messenger from it.[3] In their gendering, the beings considered here have more in common with Barbara Newman's 'allegorical goddesses', who are likewise female, as part of the medieval view of woman as a dichotomized Other to formal and normal structures of power. Their role, however, is, as has been said, very different and far more of a direct challenge to those structures.

They also offer a direct challenge to current structures of academic debate, as outlined in the first chapter of this book. They suggest that Christian Europe, both in the Middle Ages and after, was capable of developing new superhuman figures which operated outside of Christian cosmology. These did not do so in direct opposition to Christianity and were not associated with a particular sect or faction, although they were often thought to favour and teach service magicians. They were part of the thought-world of people who were otherwise orthodox Christians for their place and time. It seems wrong to refer to such figures as 'pagan survivals'. Though they may have drawn on ancient ideas and motifs, they appear to have been products of the Christian period and to have gone on being produced – if the characterization of the Cailleach made here is correct – in the late medieval and early modern periods. On the other hand, to describe them as Christian, unproblematically and straightforwardly, is to

CONCLUSION

miss the point of how completely they functioned outside of, and along-side, the Christian world picture. It may be that we need to find a new labelling system for such entities, to fit an increasingly post-Christian society in which more of their kind, such as the Green Man, are arising, and for which the old polarizing terminology of Christian and pagan is no longer suitable.

NOTES

Chapter One: What is a Pagan Survival?

1. G.L. Gomme, 'Opening Address', *Folk-Lore*, 3 (1892), 4–12. The name of the journal changed in the mid-twentieth century from *Folk-Lore* to *Folklore*, in conformity with general usage, and I have followed that change in the references.
2. G.C. Coulton, *Five Centuries of Religion: Volume One*, Cambridge, 1925, 179–83.
3. Richard Bernheimer, *Wild Men in the Middle Ages*, Cambridge, MA, 1952, 78.
4. Jacquetta Hawkes, *A Guide to the Prehistoric and Roman Monuments in England and Wales*, London, 2nd edn, 1954, 125–7.
5. E. Sidney Hartland, 'Peeping Tom and Lady Godiva', *Folk-Lore*, 2 (1891), 5–11.
6. For general overviews of this ideology among British folklorists, see especially the work of Georgina Boyes, 'Cultural Survivals Theory and Traditional Customs', *Folk Life*, 26 (1987–8), 1–15; and Gillian Bennett, 'Geologists and Folklorists: Cultural Evolution and the Science of Folklore', *Folklore*, 105 (1994), 25–37.
7. T.F. Ordish, 'Folk Drama', *Folk-Lore*, 2 (1891), 253–71; R.J.E. Tiddy, *The Mummers' Play*, Oxford, 1923; E.K. Chambers, *The English Folk-Play*, Oxford, 1933 (quotation from p. 225).
8. E.K. Chambers, *The Medieval Stage*, Oxford, 1933, vol. 1, 195–201; Cecil Sharp and Herbert C. Macilwaine, *The Morris Book: Parts One and Two*, 2nd edn, London, 1912–19; Maud Karpeles, 'English Folk Dances', *Folk-Lore*, 43 (1932), 123–43.
9. This started with Sidney Addy, 'Guising and Mumming in Derbyshire', *Journal of the Derbyshire Archaeological and Natural History Society*, 29 (1907), 31–44, and was generalized by Violet Alford, 'Some Hobby Horses of Great Britain', *Journal of the English Folk Dance and Song Society*, 3/4 (1939), 221–407.
10. Mabel Peacock, 'The Hood Game at Haxey, Lincolnshire', *Folk-Lore*, 7 (1896), 330–50.
11. Violet Alford, 'The Abbots Bromley Horn Dance', *Antiquity*, 7 (1933), 206–7.
12. S.H. Hooke, 'Time and Custom', *Folk-Lore*, 48 (1937), 17–24.
13. The most notorious case here was the upbraiding of one of the performers in the Padstow May Day hobby horse procession by Mary Macleod Banks in 1931 for 'spoiling the rite' by wearing an altered costume: see her note in *Folk-Lore*, 49 (1938), 392–4. Violet Alford had

the mummers' play at Marshfield, Gloucestershire, changed to make it seem more solemn and religious: Simon Lichman, 'The Gardener's Story and What Came Next: A Contextual Analysis of the Marshfield Paper Boys' Mumming Play' (Pennsylvania University PhD thesis, 1981), 1–2, 213–15. The distinguished anthropologist R.R. Marett informed the English Folk Dance and Song Society that such 'relics of bygone rituals and sacraments' should be restored to a more 'mystic' form and rescued from their current 'boorish' reduction to 'merry-making pure and simple': 'Survival and Revival', *Journal of the English Folk Dance and Song Society*, 1/2 (1933), 74.

14. E.g. Christina Hole, *English Custom and Usage*, London, 1941; Violet Alford, *An Introduction to English Folklore*, London, 1952; and F. Marian McNeill, *The Silver Bough*, Glasgow, 3 vols, 1957–68. The journal articles restating the theory of pagan survivals also continued, throughout the whole period: cf. Theo Brown, 'Tertullian and Horse-Cults in Britain', *Folk-Lore*, 61 (1950), 31–4; and E.O. James, 'Superstitions and Survivals', *Folklore*, 72 (1961), 289–99.

15. Violet Alford, *Sword Dance and Drama*, London, 1962, 13–28, 201–16.

16. Alford, *An Introduction to English Folklore*, 7.

17. Such as Iorwerth C. Peate, *Tradition and Folk Life: A Welsh View*, London, 1972; and Ralph Whitlock, *In Search of Lost Gods*, London, 1979.

18. Published by John Lane in a collection called *The Three Imposters*.

19. Lofts published the book under the pseudonym of Peter Curtis, with Macdonald. It was then republished by Pan in 1966 as *The Witches*, and subsequently filmed under that title.

20. Although the theme of a revival of ancient paganism was already firmly established by then, classically in the form of somebody discovering an ancient pagan shrine or ritual and deciding to reactivate it, either because of romantic personal inclination or because it takes them over. This was as old a literary tradition by the 1970s as that of paganism surviving secretly within a rural community, both Machen and Buchan having also treated it (the latter no fewer than three times). The message remains the same as in the other theme: the revival almost always has catastrophic consequences.

21. Luc Ricaut, 'Sacrifice, Society and Religion in *The Wicker Man*', in Benjamin Franks et al., eds, *The Quest for "The Wicker Man": History, Folklore and Pagan Perspectives*, Edinburgh, 2006, 57. The most famous actor in the film, Christopher Lee, had already starred in a more readily forgotten film of 1968, *The Curse of the Crimson Altar*, directed by Vernon Sewell, about a modern English village which hid an ancient cult with rites of human sacrifice.

22. The two key authors were Margaret Murray, 'Female Fertility Figures', *Journal of the Royal Anthropological Institute*, 64 (1934), 93–100; and Lady Raglan, 'The Green Man in Church Architecture', *Folk-Lore*, 50 (1939), 45–57. The history of this idea will be explored in detail in the last chapter of this book.

23. The great nineteenth-century edition was by T.O. Cockayne: *Leechdoms, Wortcunning and Starcraft of Early England*, Rolls Series, London, 3 vols, 1864–6. Famous further editions from the twentieth century were Godfrid Storms, *Anglo-Saxon Magic*, Halle, 1948; and J.H.G. Grattan and Charles Singer, *Anglo-Saxon Magic and Medicine*, Oxford, 1952. The last of these seems the most authoritative.

24. It is entry LXXX in the compilation called *Lacnunga*, found in the editions cited above. It is sometimes elided with the preceding entry, the so-called Nine Herbs Charm or Lay of the Nine Herbs.

25. Again, found variously translated in the editions above. It will be examined in detail in the next chapter of this book.

26. This is *Lacnunga* CXXXIV–V, again variously translated in the different editions.

27. Above all Grattan and Singer, in the much-cited edition entered above. Two other charms mention pagan deities. In one, Woden himself speaks, to cure wrenched body parts, and there is also mention of Baldur, the name of another god known from the Norse pantheon: it is analyzed by Bill Griffiths, *Aspects of Anglo-Saxon Magic*, Hockwold-cum-Wilton, 2003, 174. The other calls on Thor, another Norse god (the Anglo-Saxon equivalent is Thunor,

so this is a charm influenced by Viking settlers) to stop blood poisoning: see John Frankis, 'Sidelights on Post-Conquest Canterbury', *Nottingham Medieval Studies*, 22 (2000), 1–27.

28. Aelfric, *De Auguris*, lines 75–182, passim, in *Aelfric's Lives of Saints*, ed. Walter W. Skeat, Early English Text Society, 76, London, 1881, 364–83; and *The Sermones Catholici, or Homilies*, ed. Benjamin Thorpe, Aelfric Society, London, 1844, vol. 1, 476–7.

29. James Obelkevich, *Religion and Rural Society: South Lindsey 1825–1875*, Oxford, 1976: quotations on pp. 280–1, 287.

30. For a discussion of the sources for this, and its application to different national contexts, see Ronald Hutton, *The Triumph of the Moon: A History of Modern Pagan Witchcraft*, Oxford, 2nd edn, 2019, 137–40.

31. Karl Ernst Jarcke, 'Ein Hexenprozess', *Annalen der Deutschen und Auslandischen Criminal-Rechts-Pflege*, 1 (1828), 450; Franz Josef Mone, 'Uber das Hexenwesen', *Anzeiger für Kunde der Teutschen Vorzeit* (1839), 271–5, 444–5.

32. Matilda Joslyn Gage, *Women, Church and State*, Chicago, 1893.

33. I have dealt with the complex issues concerning Leland's work in *The Triumph of the Moon*, 147–54.

34. Charles Godfrey Leland, *Aradia, Gospel of the Witches*, London, 1899.

35. George Lawrence Gomme, *Ethnology in Europe*, London, 1892, 48–57.

36. Karl Pearson, *The Chances of Death and Other Studies in Evolution*, London, 1897, vol. 2, 1–50.

37. *The Witch Cult in Western Europe*, Oxford, 1921; and *The God of the Witches*, London, 1933.

38. See the review by R.W. Halliday in *Folk-Lore*, 33 (1922), 224–30; and the works of C.L. L'Estrange Ewen, especially *Witch Hunting and Witch Trials*, London, 1929; and *Witchcraft and Demonianism*, London, 1933.

39. Notably Coulton, cited above.

40. Such as Lewis Spence, The Witch Cult in Scotland', *Scots Magazine* (January 1930), 17–20; and 'Modern Theories about Witchcraft', *Occult Review*, 69 (1942), 89–93; Dion Fortune, 'The Brocken Tryst', *Occult Review*, 56 (1932), 23; Dolores Ashcroft-Nowicki, *The Forgotten Mage*, Wellingborough, 1985, 187–9; Ralph Shirley, 'Notes of the Month', *Occult Review*, 38 (1923), 193–205; and J.W. Brodie-Innes, 'The Cult of the Witch', *Occult Review*, 35 (1927), 150–63.

41. J.W. Wickwer, *Witchcraft and the Black Art*, London, 1925; Theda Kenyon, *Witches Still Live*, London, 1929.

42. C.N. Deedes, 'The Double-Headed God', and Violet Alford and Rodney Gallup, 'Traces of a Dianic Cult from Catalonia to Portugal', both in *Folk-Lore*, 46 (1935), 194–243 and 350–61.

43. G.N. Clark, *The Seventeenth Century*, Oxford, 1945, 245–8.

44. *Society and Puritanism in Pre-Revolutionary England*, London, 1964, 187 and 486 n. 4; *Reformation to Industrial Revolution*, London, 1967; review of Peter Laslett, *The World We Have Lost*, in *History and Theory*, 6 (1967), 121.

45. Elliot Rose, *A Razor for a Goat*, Toronto, 1962, 14–15.

46. *The Night Battles*, London, 1983, is the English translation of that book, with the comment from the 1966 preface preserved on p. xix.

47. In *Paysans de Languedoc*, Paris, 1966, 407–14.

48. In *Occultism, Witchcraft and Cultural Fashions*, Chicago, 1976, 57–8, 69–92.

49. R. Trevor Davies, *Four Centuries of Witch Beliefs*, London, 1947; Arne Runeberg, *Witches, Demons and Fertility Magic*, Helsingfors, 1947; Rose, *A Razor for a Goat*.

50. Hugh Ross Williamson, *The Arrow and the Sword*, London, 1947; Pennethorne Hughes, *Witchcraft*, London, 1952; Arkon Daraul, *Secret Societies*, London, 1961, 163–78; and *Witches and Sorcerers*, London, 1962; T.C. Lethbridge, *Witches*, London, 1962; Gillian Tindall, *A Handbook on Witches*, London, 1965; Ronald Seth, *Witches and their Craft*, London, 1967; Peter Haining, *Witchcraft and Black Magic*, London, 1971; Raymond Lamont Brown, *A Book of Witchcraft*, Newton Abbot, 1971; Clifford Lindsay Alderman, *A Cauldron of Witches*, Folkestone, 1973; Frank Donovan, *Never on a Broomstick*, 1973; Michael Harrison, *The Roots of Witchcraft*, London, 1973.

NOTES to pp. 13–16

51. George Ewart Evans and David Thomson, *The Leaping Hare*, London, 1972, 145. Evans, being also influenced by the ideas of the poet Robert Graves, was more inclined to think that the worship of the medieval pagans centred on an ancient Great Goddess than a god.

52. A classic example here is the one at Rydale in Yorkshire, which had some very good documents relating to nineteenth-century cunning folk, which were misinterpreted in harmony with Murray's ideas. The exhibits have long been given new labels, and the old interpretative scheme remains lodged in the 'Notes on Witchcraft in Ryedale' made by the curator in the 1960s and preserved at the museum.

53. It was directed by Malcolm Leigh.

54. For an example from the period between Buchan and Sutcliff, see Hugh Ross Williamson, *The Silver Bowl*, London, 1948.

55. Pp. 204–5 in the original, Oxford University Press, edition. She supplied an extended picture of a Lammas (beginning of autumn) festival in the period, led by a local king in honour of the horned god, in *Sword at Sunset*, London, 1963.

56. In chapter 8 of the original, Oxford University Press, edition.

57. Similarly, most of the huge number of novels about a historical King Arthur published since the 1950s have made Arthur's native Britain an ideological battlefield between Christianity and paganism, in contrast both with the medieval sources for the legend (where he is leader of a Christian people against heathen Saxon invaders) and the available historical evidence. These books are clearly exploring the anxieties and tensions of a multifaith modern society: see Ronald Hutton, 'The Post-Christian Arthur', *Arthurian Literature*, 26 (2009), 149–70.

58. E.g. Philippa Wiat's trilogy, *The Mistletoe Bough*, *Bride in Darkness* and *Wychwood*, published in London in 1982 (about a witch religion descended from the Druids and set in rural Oxfordshire in the 1560s); and Alan Massie, *The Hanging Tree*, London, 1990 (which is set up and down Britain across the mid-fifteenth century, with a witch religion linked to the fairies).

59. The books were *The Divine King in England*, London, 1954; *The Genesis of Religion*, London, 1963; and *My First Hundred Years*, London, 1963.

60. *Birmingham Gazette* (2 Sept. 1950), 1.

61. *Witchcraft Today*, London, 1954.

62. A sample of classic works by Pagan witches from this period, which embodied the idea of the surviving Old Religion, would include Doreen Valiente, *An ABC of Witchcraft Past and Present*, London, 1975; and *The Rebirth of Witchcraft*, Phoenix AZ, 1989; Starhawk, *The Spiral Dance*, San Francisco, 1979; Charles Bowness, *The Witches' Gospel*, London, 1979; Janet and Stewart Farrar, *Eight Sabbats for Witches*, London, 1981; and Rae Beth, *Hedge Witch*, London, 1990. The example of Wicca and its offshoots or cousins encouraged various spokespeople to come forward from the 1970s onward, identifying themselves as members of pagan traditions not related to witchcraft which had likewise survived the centuries in Britain. These were given much support and publicity by Ann Ross, who had pioneered the study of Romano-British and Romano-Gallic religious iconography in a marvellous book, *Pagan Celtic Britain*, London, 1967. Thereafter, however, she dropped out of the academic world and primary historical research to write popular books and help make television documentaries. As part of these, she accepted on face value the claims of such informants, without subjecting them to any critical scrutiny, and so did her utmost to perpetuate belief in the unbroken survival of ancient British paganism to the present, into the twenty-first century: see especially her documentary in the BBC Chronicle series, broadcast 31 Oct. 1977, and her book *The Folklore of Wales*, Stroud, 2001, 70–1, 103, 151–3.

63. Oscar A. Haac, *Jules Michelet*, Boston, 1982, 138.

64. Peter Burke (ed.), *A New Kind of History, from the Writings of Febvre*, London, 1973, 265.

65. *Aradia*, 103–6, and see his *Etruscan Roman Remains in Popular Tradition*, London, 1892, 209–10.

66. Pp. 130–1 in the Bodleian Library edition, which has a note attributing the work firmly to Wright. In most of these works, even Leland's, the design was more to undermine Christianity, or at least Catholicism, than to extol paganism itself, let alone recommend it for preservation or revival. Indeed, there was a genre of fiction which exploited the theme of surviving paganism to suggest that all religions could be equally abhorrent. One of the most famous writers to work in this was the American horror novelist H.P. Lovecraft, who in 1924 produced a short story, 'The Rats in the Walls', featuring a medieval English priory built on the site of a Neolithic stone circle. He adds of the prehistoric temple 'that indescribable rites had been celebrated there, few doubted, and there were unpleasant tales of the transference of these rites into the Cybele worship which the Romans had introduced . . . Tales added that the fall of the old religion did not end the orgies at the temple, but that the priests lived on in the new faith without real change' (pp. 22–3 in the *H.P. Lovecraft Omnibus 3* published by Panther in London in 1985. There may have been a specific strain of anti-Catholicism in Lovecraft's work here, as there certainly was in that of Michelet and Leland.

67. Richard Ellmann, *The Identity of Yeats*, London, 1954, 52, where the passage is reproduced from an unidentified article.

68. Their stories are told in Hutton, *The Triumph of the Moon*, 81–6, 157–76.

69. E. Clodd, 'Presidential Address', *Folk-Lore*, 7 (1896), 47–8.

70. Especially influential here was Walter Johnson, a medical doctor whose fanciful books still got published by university presses: see his *Folk Memory or the Continuity of British Archaeology*, Oxford, 1908; and *By-Ways in British Archaeology*, Cambridge, 1912.

71. See his *Wold Without End*, London, 1932, 205; and *Remembrance*, London, 1944, 95–6.

72. Some readers may be tempted to point out that the very names 'pagan' and 'heathen' originally signified country-dwellers, but, although this is often asserted, it is not proven to be so. The adoption of it as an orthodoxy during the period under discussion was itself a result, and not a cause, of the identification of the rural and the pagan in that period. See Hutton, *The Triumph of the Moon*, 4.

73. See Raymond Williams, *The Country and the City*, London, 1973; and Keith Thomas, *Man and the Natural World*, London, 1983, 243–4.

74. These passages are all in book 4, chapter 1.

75. Johnson, *Folk-Memory*, 19.

76. J.G. Frazer, *Balder the Beautiful*, London, 1913, vol. 1, viii–ix.

77. Williams, *The Country and the City*; and Thomas, *Man and the Natural World*, 244–61.

78. For this, see Williams, *The Country and the City*; W.J. Keith, *The Rural Tradition*, Toronto, 1975; Jan Marsh, *Back to the Land*, London, 1982; Alun Howkins, 'The Discovery of Rural England', in Robert Colls and Philip Dodds, eds, *Englishness: Politics and Culture 1880–1920*, London, 1986, 62–88; Martin Wiener, *English Culture and the Decline of the Industrial Spirit*, Cambridge, 1987, 42–64;

79. In *Hodge and His Masters*, London, 1880: quotation on p. 7.

80. In *Puck of Pook's Hill*, London, 1906, and *Rewards and Fairies*, London, 1910.

81. Gillian Bennett, 'Folklore Studies and the English Rural Myth', *Rural History*, 4 (1993), 89.

82. Sir Lawrence and Lady Gomme, *British Folk-Lore, Folk-Songs and Singing Games*, National Home-Reading Union Pamphlets Literature Studies 4, n.d., 10.

83. Joseph Jacobs, 'The Folk', *Folk-Lore*, 4 (1893), 234, 235–6.

84. In *Ask the Fellows Who Cut the Hay*, London, 1956, 13–14.

85. P. 390 of the Oxford University Press edition of 1990.

86. Though this message took a while to get through even to members of other scholarly disciplines, let alone the public. At the very end of the century Aubrey Burl, an acclaimed expert in British archaeology, could write that 'in spite of Christian teaching repugnant rites of sexuality and the worship of pagan deities continued at megalithic rings, chambered tombs and standing stones. The Church fulminated censoriously but impotently against the blasphemy . . . Paganism persisted and would persist even into modern times': *Great Stone Circles*, New Haven, 1999, 11.

87. Timothy Darvill et al., *The Cerne Giant*, Oxford, 1999.

88. A.E. Green, review of Alan Brody, *English Mummers*, in *English Dance and Song*, 34/3 (1972), 118–19; E.C. Cawte, ' "It's an Ancient Custom" – But How Ancient', in Theresa Buckland and Juliette Wood, eds, *Aspects of English Calendar Customs*, Sheffield, 1993, 41–4; Georgina Smith, 'Chapbooks and Traditional Plays', *Folklore*, 92 (1981), 208–17; Craig Fees, 'Towards Establishing the Study of Folk Drama as a Science', *Roomer*, 4/5 (1984), 41–51; Georgina Boyes, 'Excellent Examples: The Influence of Exemplar Texts on Traditional Drama Scholarship', *Traditional Drama Studies*, 1 (1985), 21–3.

89. R. Dommett, 'How It All Began', *Morris Matters*, 1/4 (Autumn 1978), 4–8; A.G. Barrand, 'ABCD Morris', *English Dance and Song*, 42/3 (1980), 11–13; Michael Heaney, 'Kingston to Kenilworth: Early Plebeian Morris', *Folklore*, 100 (1989), 88–104; John Forrest and Michael Heaney, 'Charting Early Morris', *Folk Music Journal*, 6/2 (1991), 169–86; John Forrest, *The History of Morris Dancing 1458–1750*, Cambridge, 1999.

90. E.C. Cawte, *Ritual Animal Disguise*, London, 1978.

91. Cawte, *Ritual Animal Disguise*, 79; Michael Heaney, 'New Evidence for the Abbots Bromley Hobby Horse', *Folk Music Journal*, 5/3 (1987), 359–60; Theresa Buckland, 'The Reindeer Antlers of the Abbots Bromley Horn Dance', *Lore and Language*, 3/2A (1980), 1–8.

92. Venetia Newall, 'Throwing the Hood at Haxey', *Folk Life*, 18 (1980), 7–24.

93. My book *The Rise and Fall of Merry England: The Ritual Year 1400–1700*, Oxford, 1994, covers this period and illustrates this point in detail.

94. Theresa Buckland, 'English Dance Scholarship', in Theresa Buckland, ed., *Traditional Dance*, Crewe, 1982, vol. 1, 3–18 (quotation on p. 4).

95. Georgina Smith, 'Social Bases of Tradition', in A.E. Green and J.D.A. Widdowson, eds, *Language, Culture and Tradition*, Sheffield, 1981, 77–87.

96. Boyes, 'Cultural Survivals Theory', 8. See also her full-length study of the 'myth' created by former folklorists, *The Imagined Village*, Manchester, 1993.

97. Bennett, 'Folklore Studies and the English Rural Myth', 89.

98. The full story of this with respect to foliate heads will be found in the last chapter of this book. The challenge to the straightforward pagan interpretation of sheela-na-gigs was mounted by Jörgen Andersen, *The Witch on the Wall*, Copenhagen, 1977; and Anthony Weir and James Jerman, *Images of Lust*, London, 1986. The debate over them continues, but the point here is to register the challenge to the previous reading of the figures made in this period, and, furthermore, there seems now to be general agreement among scholars that whether or not pagan or folk ideas were embodied in them – and this really seems a possibility confined to the Irish cases – they were fashioned and installed in a purely Christian context. See the overview in my *Pagan Britain*, London, 2017, 148–51.

99. Karen Jolly, 'Father God and Mother Earth', in Joyce E. Salisbury, ed., *The Medieval World of Nature*, New York, 1993, 235. Jolly's full-length study, *Popular Religion in Late Anglo-Saxon England*, is among other things a sustained polemic against the earlier emphasis on the pagan elements in the charms. Caution in handling the apparent references to pagan figures is also advised by Griffiths and Frankis, in n. 27 above.

100. This point was to be deployed by Carl Watkins as a polemical weapon in a debate to be considered below.

101. In the present book, following the practice established in a previous book of mine, *The Witch*, London, 2017, I have adopted the term 'service magician' for these people, to define a person who provides magical services to others at their request, usually for payment of some kind. It seems to sum up their role well, and can be applied worldwide, for English readers, avoiding the cultural and national specificity of traditional popular terms such as 'cunning folk' or 'wise folk'.

102. Research into popular service magic in England only really began in the 1990s, but there are now independent studies by three different people which accord remarkably in their conclusions: Owen Davies, *Witchcraft, Magic and Culture 1736–1951*, Manchester, 1999; *A People Bewitched*, Bruton, 1999; and *Cunning-Folk*, London, 2003; Hutton, *The Triumph of the Moon*, 87–115; and Jim Baker, *The Cunning Man's Handbook*, London, 2014.

103. The first local studies of the new kind, which provided solid evidence, were Alan Macfarlane, *Witchcraft in Tudor and Stuart England*, London, 1970 (a study of Essex); Erik Midelfort, *Witch-Hunting in South-Western Germany, 1562–1684*, Stanford, 1972; and William E. Monter, *Witchcraft in France and Switzerland*, Ithaca, 1976. Norman Cohn's work from 1975, which will be discussed below, represented the first attempt to construct an overall new model to replace that of a surviving pagan religion. The evolving general picture of the witch trials over the next forty years can be appreciated by comparing the three successive editions of Brian Levack, *The Witch-Hunt in Early Modern Europe*, published in London and Harlow between 1987 and 2006; Robin Briggs, *Witches and Neighbours*, London, 1996; Diane Purkiss, *The Witch in History*, London, 1996; Geoffrey Scarre and John Callow, *Witchcraft and Magic in Sixteenth- and Seventeenth-Century Europe*, Basingstoke, 2001; Wolfgang Behringer, *Witches and Witch-Hunts*, Cambridge, 2004; Malcolm Gaskill, *Witchcraft: A Very Short Introduction*, Oxford, 2010; Julian Goodare, *The European Witch-Hunt*, London, 2016; and Marion Gibson, *Witchcraft: The Basics*, London, 2018.

104. In his review of one of my own books, *The Restoration*, in the *London Review of Books*, 5 Sept. 1985, 22–3. Conrad once told me that in 1972 he had suddenly realized that in his own field, of early Stuart British history, he could believe that James I and Charles I had existed, with an accompanying cast of characters, but not anything else that he had been told about their reigns: it all had to be researched and rebuilt from scratch. That perfectly captures the mood of early revisionism and also that of a whole generation at that time: I think of the hippy slogan prevalent in it, 'Trust nobody over the age of thirty'.

105. Ronald Hutton, *The Pagan Religions of the Ancient British Isles*, Oxford, 1991, 284–341.

106. Leonard W. Moss and Stephen C. Cappannari, 'In Quest of the Black Virgin', in James J. Preston, ed., *Mother Worship*, Chapel Hill, 1982, 53–74.

107. Five years later these were expounded much more concisely and systematically in Ronald Hutton, 'The Roots of Modern Paganism', in Graham Harvey and Charlotte Hardman, eds, *Paganism Today*, London, 1995, 3–9.

108. Papyri Graecae Magicae VIII, 65–85; C.J.S. Thompson, *The Mysteries and Secrets of Magic*, London, 1927, 58; David Porreca, 'Divine Names: A Cross-Cultural Comparison', *Magic, Ritual and Witchcraft*, 5 (2010), 17–29; Joannis Marathakis, ed., *The Magical Treatise of Solomon*, Singapore, 2011, 56, 60, 64, 85, 159.

109. Ronald Hutton, *Witches, Druids and King Arthur*, London, 2003, 153–66, 176–89.

110. Ronald Hutton, *The Witch*, London, 2017, 99–119.

111. Hutton, *The Triumph of the Moon*, passim.

112. See sources at n. 102.

113. Ronald Hutton, *The Stations of the Sun: A History of the Ritual Year in Britain*, Oxford, 1996, 22–5, 116–17, 218–25, 311–21.

114. Kenneth Hurlstone Jackson, *A Celtic Miscellany*, London, 1951, 263–4.

115. They have been treated in that context by Michael Ostling, ed., *Fairies, Demons, and Nature Spirits*, London, 2018.

116. I have used the English translation, *Catholicism between Luther and Voltaire*, London, 1977: quotation on p. 165. The book initially made a great impact, but subsequently his apparent denial that medieval Catholicism actually was Christianity has found less favour, in the face of the view that it was just a different kind of Christianity from the Counter-Reformation sort.

117. Norman Cohn, *Europe's Inner Demons*, London, 1975.

118. His book was published in Italian, and translated into English as *Ecstasies*, London 1991. I use the 1992 Penguin edition, where the quotations are on pp. 8, 10, 112. It must be admitted that his theory has proved very controversial, and I differ from him in details, which I discussed at many different points of *The Witch*. Nonetheless, I would emphasize that I still think his approach fundamentally the right one, and endorse his brilliance (and personal charm) as a historian, which is why he was one of the three people to whom I dedicated that book (another being Norman Cohn).

119. Éva Pócs, 'The Popular Foundations of the Witches' Sabbath and the Devil's Pact in Central and Southern Europe', in Gábor Klaniczay and Éva Pócs, eds, *Witch Beliefs and Witch Hunting and Central and Southern Europe*, Budapest, 1992, 305–70 (remarks on previous historians on 305, 335); *Between the Living and the Dead*, Budapest, 1999; and her contribution to the round table discussion in Gábor Klaniczay and Éva Pócs, eds, *Witchcraft Mythologies and Persecutions*, Budapest, 2008, 37–42.

120. Edited by Ludo Milis and brought out in English at Woodbridge in 1998.

121. Ludo Milis, 'The Spooky Heritage of Ancient Paganism', in Carlos Steel, ed., *Paganism in the Middle Ages*, Leuven, 2012, 1–18.

122. The beginning of this tendency is sometimes credited to Eamon Duffy's justly celebrated and influential study of late medieval English religion, *The Stripping of the Altars*, New Haven, 1992, 293, where he proposed 'lay Christianity' as an alternative expression for 'paganism' with reference to popular practices. However, the practices concerned were healing and protective charms and incantations which employed phrases and concepts borrowed from the Christian liturgy, and objects – specifically 'sacramentals' such as consecrated candles, water and salt – also taken from orthodox worship. His aim was to rescue these from the earlier tendency, embodied above all for him by Jean Delumeau, to view such use of words and objects as pagan, and his argument is a plausible one: being taken directly from the regular usage of the established Church, those particular practices cannot be classed as 'pagan survivals' except in the most remote and attenuated sense, and their use should not be termed paganism.

123. Jolly, *Popular Religion in Late Saxon England*, 140.

124. Chris Wickham, *The Inheritance of Rome: Illuminating the Dark Ages 400–1000*, London, 2009, 176, 181.

125. Steven P. Marrone, *A History of Science, Magic and Belief from Medieval to Early Modern Europe*, London, 2015, 35.

126. C.S. Watkins, *History and the Supernatural in Medieval England*, Cambridge, 2007, 76–106: quotation on p. 103. I was, however, flattered to be placed in such company.

127. The central work here is Michael York, *Pagan Theology*, New York, 2003: quotations on pp. 66, 67, 74. I myself have never fared well in print at the hands of this author. On p. 6 of the book under discussion, he misattributes to me a view actually expressed by the Oxford classicist Robin Lane Fox, which I do not share, and then quotes against me one from the Frenchman Pierre Chuvin, which I have actually endorsed instead: compare p. 4 of Hutton, *The Triumph of the Moon*, in the first, 1999, edition which is the one he will have read. That said, I have some sympathy for his overall thesis, because there *are* family resemblances between ancient European and Near Eastern paganism, and the other religious traditions that he associates with it, and with some aspects of world religions such as Hinduism. Whether this justifies the use of the term pagan to cover all, however, is a politically loaded question and has earned the book criticism by other specialists in religious studies: see the reviews by Melissa Raphael in the *Journal for the Scientific Study of Religion*, 43/4 (2004), 556; and Mary Jo Neitz in *Sociology of Religion*, 65/3 (2004), 314; Michael Strmiska, 'Modern Paganism in World Cultures', in Strmiska, ed., *Modern Paganism in World Cultures*, Santa Barbara, CA, 2006, 11–13; Kaarina Aitamurto and Scott Simpson, 'Introduction', in Aitamurto and Simpson, eds, *Modern Pagan and Native Faith Movements in Central and Eastern Europe*, Durham, 2013, 2; and Ethan Doyle White, 'Theoretical, Terminological, and Taxonomic Trouble in the Academic Study of Contemporary Paganism', *The Pomegranate*, 18/1 (2016), 45–8.

Chapter Two: Mother Earth

1. Thorkild Jacobsen, *The Treasures of Darkness*, New Haven, 1976, passim.

2. Walter Burkert, *Greek Religion*, Cambridge, MA, 1985, 175. The lack of evidence for a popular cult of Gaia was stressed before Burkert by Peter Ucko, *Anthropomorphic Figurines of Predynastic Egypt and Neolithic Crete*, London, 1968, 410–11. Even in the late twentieth

century, however, popular survey works and encyclopaedias on Greek religion were still influenced by an Edwardian classicist, Lewis Richard Farnell, who argued that Gaia must have been a major deity before the beginning of history, as apparently evidenced by her prominence as a literary figure: *The Cults of the Greek States*, Oxford, 1907, vol. 3, 28. This reasoning, which has been abandoned by more recent experts (as has been seen) was driven by the belief of academics of Farnell's time in a universal prehistoric Great Mother Goddess, which will be described below.

3. Jennifer Larson, 'A Land Full of Gods', in Daniel Ogden, ed., *A Companion to Greek Religion*, Chichester, 2010, 67.

4. Mary Beard et al., *Religions of Rome*, Cambridge, 1998, vol. 1, 203, and vol. 2, 142.

5. H.J. Rose, *Ancient Roman Religion*, London, 1948, 25.

6. Apuleius, *Metamorphoses*, XI.5. The idea that Isis was a mighty creatrix who could be identified with other goddesses was found quite widely before Apuleius, but it is his particular identification of her with both the moon and the natural world which was to be especially influential.

7. Aristotle, *Metaphysics*, 1014B–15A.

8. Plato, *Timaeus*, 34C.

9. A process surveyed in George D. Economou, *The Goddess Natura in Medieval Literature*, Cambridge, MA, 1972, 4–40, which is the indispensable current starting point for the study of this figure in antiquity and the Middle Ages.

10. Ovid, *Metamorphoses*, I.23; Lucretius, *De rerum natura*, passim. Another poet of the early imperial era, Statius, called Natura both maker and ruler of the world: *Thebaid*, XI.465–7, XII.561–2, 642–8.

11. It is usually quoted in Thomas Taylor's luxuriant translation, *The Mystical Hymns of Orpheus*, of which I have used the London, 1896, edition, 29–33. The latest edition, by Apostolos N. Athanassakis and Benjamin M. Wolkow, Baltimore, 2013, dates the collection to the mid-third century. It is not apparent whether these hymns were purely literary productions or actually used in the cult practice of the mystery religion of Orpheus.

12. Claudian, *De raptu Proserpinae*, I.249, II.370–8, III.18–49; and *De consulate Stilichonis*, II.431–3.

13. Lynn Thorndike, *A History of Magic and Experimental Science*, vol. 2, London, 1923, 5–6.

14. In particular, Lactantius, Prudentius and Ambrose of Milan are important here, and their theology is examined in Economou, *The Goddess Natura*, 54–8.

15. J. Wright Duff and Arnold M. Duff, eds, *Minor Latin Poets*, Cambridge, MA, 1934, 339–50.

16. Source references in nn. 23 and 25 of chapter 1.

17. Caroline M. Batten and Mark Williams, 'Erce in the Old English *Aecerbot* Charm', *Notes and Queries* (2020): https://doi.org/10.1093/notesj/gjaa.005. I am grateful to Dr Williams for sending me this work in draft.

18. Bernard Sylvester or Bernardus Sylvestris, *De mundi universitate sive megacosmos et microcosmos*.

19. Alan of Lille or Alanus ab Insulis, *De planctu naturae*.

20. Alan of Lille, *Anticlaudianus*.

21. Jean de Hauteville or Johannes de Altavilla, *Architrenius*.

22. Jean de Meun, *Le Roman de la Rose*, esp. IV.16005–19436 and V.20027–31.

23. Geoffrey Chaucer, *The Parlement of Briddes, or The Assembly of Foules*, II.295 to end.

24. Guillaume de Deguileville or Diguileville, *Le Pèlerinage de la Vie Humaine*, translated into English as *The Pilgrimage of the Soul*. I have used the latter, where Nature appears or is addressed in lines 3344–448.

25. Évrart de Conty, *Les Échecs amoureux*, translated into English by John Lydgate as *Reson and Sensualltye*. Nature manifests in lines 720–82 of the latter.

26. Edmund Spenser, *the Faerie Queen*, Mutabilitie, VI.35 and VII.13–15.

27. Athanasius Kircher, *Oedipus Aegyptiacus*, Rome, 1652.
28. Robert Fludd, *Utriusque Cosmi Historia*, Oppenheim, 1617.
29. Simon Schama, *Citizens*, New York, 1989, 746–8.
30. What follows in the next two sections is an updated and extended version of data and suggestions first published in Ronald Hutton, 'The Discovery of the Modern Goddess', in Joanne Pearson et al., eds, *Nature Religion Today*, Edinburgh, 1998, 89–100; and 'The Neolithic Great Goddess', *Antiquity*, 71 (1997), 91–9.
31. Percy Bysshe Shelley, 'Song of Proserpine' (1820).
32. 'Sleep and Poetry' (1816).
33. John Keats, 'Endymion' (1818), IV.141–88. For another address by the poet to the moon, see 'I Stood Tip-Toe Upon A Little Hill', lines 116–22.
34. Charlotte Brontë, *Jane Eyre*, first published London, 1847, chapters 27 and 28.
35. 'Artemis Prologizes', in John Pettigrew and Thomas J. Collins, eds, *Robert Browning: The Poems*, New Haven, 1981, 365.
36. Algernon Charles Swinburne, 'Hertha' (1867), lines 1–15.
37. The citations are from 'Ode to the Spirit of Earth in Autumn' (1862), 'The Woods of Westermain' (1883) and 'Earth and Man' (1883). The verse quoted is in the original draft of the first of those, for which see *The Poetical Works of George Meredith*, London, 1912, 585–6.
38. George Russell or A.E., 'Dust' (1890s).
39. 'The Virgin Mother' (1910s).
40. The extracts above, and these reflections as a whole, are based on the collected works in *Selected Poems by A. E.*, London, 1935, especially at pp. 17, 18 and 85.
41. A.E., *The Candle of Vision*, London, 1918.
42. These are on pp. 365 and 516 of the Penguin edition.
43. P. 144 in the Penguin edition of *Lady Chatterley's Lover* (1928).
44. Pp. 224, 276–80 and 348 of the Penguin edition.
45. From 'Pan in America', in Edward D. Macdonald, ed., *The Posthumous Papers of D. H. Lawrence*, New York, 1936, 31.
46. Eduard Gerhard, *Über Metroen und Götter-Mütter*, Berlin, 1849.
47. Especially Francois Lenormant and M.J. Menant at Paris in the 1870s and 1880s and Ernst Kroker at Leipzig in the 1890s.
48. For this, see Ucko, *Anthropomorphic Figurines*, 409–12, and sources cited there.
49. A.J. Evans, *Cretan Pictographs and Prae-Phoenician Script*, London, 1895; 'The Neolithic Settlement at Knossos and its Place in the History of Early Aegean Culture', *Man*, 1 (1901), 184–6.
50. A.J. Evans, 'The Palace of Knossos', *Annual of the British School at Athens*, 9 (1902–3), 74–94.
51. Sir Arthur Evans, *The Earlier Religion of Greece in the Light of Cretan Discoveries*, London, 1931, esp. 38–42. His ideas were then echoed at each stage by followers writing their own books on Minoan Crete, such as Charles Henry Hawkes and Harriet Boyd Hawkes, *Crete: The Forerunner of Greece*, London, 1909, 135–9; and J.D.S. Pendlebury, *The Archaeology of Crete*, London, 1939, 273.
52. His classic work was *Das Mutterecht*, Stuttgart, 1861.
53. Jane Ellen Harrison, *Prolegomena to the Study of Greek Religion*, Cambridge, 1903, 257–322. See also the further development of her ideas in *Themis*, Cambridge, 1912.
54. For this see especially Prudence Jones, 'A Goddess Arrives', *Culture and Cosmos*, 9.1 (2005), 45–71.
55. Gilbert Murray, *Four Stages of Greek Religion*, New York, 1912, 45–6; Arthur Bernard Cook, *Zeus*, Cambridge, 1914, vol. 1, 776–80; J.G. Frazer, *Adonis, Attis, Osiris*, London, 1914, vol. 1, 39–40; 161; Lewis Richard Farnell, *Outline History of Greek Religion*, London, 1920, 24.

56. E.K. Chambers, *The Medieval Stage*, Oxford, 1903, vol. 1, 264.

57. Albrecht Dieterich, *Mutter Erde*, Berlin, 1905.

58. For this see Samuel D. Gill, *Mother Earth: An American Story*, Chicago, 1987; and Tony Swain, 'The Mother Earth Conspiracy: An Australian Episode', *Numen*, 38 (1991), 3–26.

59. Joseph Dechelette, *Manual d'archaéologie préhistorique celtique et gallo-romaine*, Paris, 1908, 594–6.

60. Angelo Mosso, *La Prehistoria*, 1910, immediately translated into English as *The Dawn of Mediterranean Civilization*, London, 1911: passages on 173 and 401–17 of that edition.

61. G.D. Hornblower, 'Predynastic Figures of Women and Their Successors', *Journal of Egyptian Archaeology*, 15 (1929), 31.

62. John Arthur Goodchild, *The Light of the West*, London, 1898.

63. Harold Massingham, *Wold Without End*, London, 1932, passim: quotations on p. 171. The survey was that of O.G.S. Crawford, *Long Barrows of the Cotswolds*, Gloucester, 1925, with reflections on Neolithic religion on pp. 23–4.

64. Stuart Piggott, 'Ancient British Craftsmen', *Antiquity*, 60 (1986), 190; Gilliam Varndell, 'The Ritual Objects', in Ian Longworth et al., *Excavations at Grimes Graves, Norfolk, 1972–1976: Fascicule 3*, London, 1991, 103–6.

65. C.F.C. Hawkes, *The Prehistoric Foundations of Europe*, London, 1940, 84–9, 153, 180, 198; Jacquetta Hawkes, *Early Britain*, London, 1945, 16–18.

66. Jacquetta Hawkes, *A Land*, London, 1951, 158–61; *A Guide to the Prehistoric and Roman Monuments of England and Wales*, London, 1954, 20–1, 198, 243–4; *Man on Earth*, London, 1954, passim; *Man and the Sun*, London, 1962, 57–87; *UNESCO History of Mankind: Volume 1.1*, New York, 1963, 204–344; and *Dawn of the Gods*, London, 1968, passim.

67. V.G. Childe, *What Happened in History*, Harmondsworth, 1954, 64–5, 268; and *The Prehistory of European Society*, Harmondsworth, 1958, 21, 46, 58, 124–39; O.G.S. Crawford, *Said and Done*, London, 301–2; and *The Eye Goddess*, London, 1957; Stuart Piggott, *The Neolithic Cultures of the British Isles*, Cambridge, 1954, 46 and plate IV; Glyn Daniel, *The Megalith Builders of Western Europe*, London, 1958, 74. Another leading figure in British archaeology accepted the universality of the Neolithic goddess slightly earlier: Grahame Clark, *From Savagery to Civilisation*, London, 1946, 101.

68. Which were given great publicity by Frazer in *Adonis, Attis, Osiris*, vol. 1.

69. His original excavation reports were published in *Anatolian Studies* between 1962 and 1966. His textbooks were *Earliest Civilizations of the Near East*, London, 1965; *Catal Huyuk*, London, 1967; and *The Neolithic of the Near East*, London, 1975. In all of these, veneration of the Goddess is assumed to be normative of the whole period and region. His preoccupation with her was a feature of the 1960s, being absent from his earlier excavation reports of the 1950s, as visible in his series on the site at Hacilar, in *Anatolian Studies* between 1958 and 1961.

70. Mellaart, 'Excavations at Catal Huyuk, 1962', *Anatolian Studies*, 13 (1963), 49.

71. Robert Briffault, *The Mothers*, London, 1927. His contribution to the development of the triple goddess was especially noted by Jones, 'A Goddess Arrives'.

72. For the development of the book and its place in Graves's own life and work, see Martin Seymour-Smith, *Robert Graves*, London, 1982; Richard Perceval Graves, *Robert Graves: The Assault Heroic*, London, 1986; *Robert Graves: The Years with Laura*, London, 1995; *and Robert Graves and the White Goddess*, London, 1995; Ian Firla and Grevel Lindop, *Graves and the Goddess*, Selinsgrove, 2003; and S.J. Penicka-Smith, 'Reinventing Robert' (University of Sydney PhD thesis, 2010).

73. George Ewart Evans, *The Pattern under the Plough*, London, 1966, 62–3, 101, 192; and George Ewart Evans and David Thomson, *The Leaping Hare*, London, 1972, 107.

74. Mellaart, *Earliest Civilizations of the Near East*, 92–3.

75. See the midwinter invocation printed in Gerald Gardner, *Witchcraft Today*, London, 1954, 21.

76. W.J. Gruffydd, *Rhiannon*, Cardiff, 1953.

77. Gertrude Rachel Levy, *The Gate of Horn*, London, 1948; E.O. James, *The Cult of the Mother-Goddess*, London, 1959; Johannes Maringer, *The Gods of Prehistoric Man*, London, 1960.

78. Carl Jung, *Collected Works: Volume Nine, Part One: The Archetypes and the Collective Unconscious*, London, 1959, 75–102.

79. Erich Neumann, *The Great Mother*, Princeton, 1963; quotations on pp. 1–2, 336.

80. Jacquetta Hawkes, 'The Proper Study of Mankind', *Antiquity*, 42 (1968), 255–62.

81. This was especially true of Martin P. Nilsson, who was a, and perhaps then, dominant figure among Continental classicists between 1920 and 1950: his critique of Evans was first published in 1921 and translated into English as *A History of Greek Religion*, Oxford, 1925, 18–33.

82. J.D. Evans, *Malta*, London, 1959, 136–67.

83. Ucko, *Anthropomorphic Figurines*; Andrew Fleming, 'The Myth of the Mother Goddess', *World Archaeology*, 1 (1969), 247–61.

84. Hawkes, 'The Proper Study of Mankind'.

85. In the second edition of *A Land*, published in London in 1978, p. ix.

86. Gill, *Mother Earth*; and Swain, 'The Mother Earth Conspiracy'. I am not aware of any attempted refutations of these works by colleagues; but it is not my own field, which is the only reason why I characterize their arguments as assertions.

87. Shirley Ardener (ed.), *Perceiving Women*, London, 1975, xviii.

88. S.J. Peacock, *Jane Ellen Harrison*, New Haven, 1988; T.W. Africa, 'Aunt Glegg amongst the Dons', in W.M. Calder (ed.), *The Cambridge Ritualists Reconsidered*, Atlanta, 1991, 21–35.

89. Harold Massingham, *Remembrance*, London, 1944, 49.

90. Massingham, *Wold Without End: The Tree of Life*, London, 1943.

91. Sources at n. 71.

92. See especially *A Land*, 143, 198, 200–1; 'The Proper Study of Mankind', 260; *Man and the Sun*, 240–1; *Man on Earth*, chapter 8.

93. See especially the critique of his work in Rosemary Radford Ruether, *New Woman, New Earth*, New York, 1975, 154–7.

94. For these changes of thought with respect to Britain, see Ronald Hutton, *Pagan Britain*, London, 2013, 126–34.

95. *The Silbury Treasure*, London, 1976; and *The Avebury Cycle*, London, 1977.

96. Marija Gimbutas, *The Prehistory of Eastern Europe*, Cambridge, MA, 1956; *The Balts*, London, 1963; *The Slavs*, London, 1971; 'The Beginning of the Bronze Age in Europe and the Indo-Europeans', *Journal of Indo-European Studies*, 1 (1973), 1–20, 163–218; *The Gods and Goddesses of Old Europe*, London, 1974.

97. Key texts in its development include Mary Daly, *Beyond God the Father*, Boston, 1973; Merlin Stone, *When God was a Woman*, New York, 1976; and Zsuzsanna Budapest, *The Holy Book of Women's Mysteries*, Oakland, CA, 1980. A good overview of the movement is provided by Cynthia Eller, *Living in the Lap of the Goddess*, Boston, 1993.

98. The progress of her ideas can be tracked through 'The First Wave of Eurasian Steppe Pastoralists into Copper Age Europe', *Journal of Indo-European Studies*, 5 (1977), 271–338; 'The Kurgan Wave No. 2', *Journal of Indo-European Studies*, 8 (1980), 272–315; *The Goddesses and Gods of Old Europe*, London, 1982; *The Language of the Goddess*, London, 1989; 'The Collision of Two Ideologies', in T.L. Makey and A.C. Greppin, eds, *When Worlds Collide*, Ann Arbor, MI, 1990; *The Civilization of the Goddess*, San Francisco, 1991.

99. Her knowledge of Western Europe was shakier, and especially of the British Isles, where (for example) she identified the Linkardstown culture of fourth-millennium Ireland as belonging to the later, patriarchal takeover of prehistory, and the third-millennium British superhenges as belonging to the earlier, matriarchal phase. That was, however, in her final and most wide-ranging and populist book, when she was working against the timescale of a lethal and debilitating illness.

100. Gimbutas, *Language of the Goddess*, xiii–xxi; *Civilization of the Goddess*, vii.

101. Pioneers of this approach, with a critical eye on Gimbutas's work, included Ruth Tringham, in her review of *The Civilization of the Goddess* in *American Anthropologist*, 95 (1993), 196–7; and her joint essay with Margaret Conkey, 'Archaeologists and the Goddess', in Donna C. Stanton and Abigail J. Stewart, eds, *Feminisms in the Academy*, Ann Arbor, MI, 1995, 199–247; and Lynn Meskell, 'Goddesses, Gimbutas and the New Age', *Antiquity*, 69 (1995), 74–86. I would not presume to state myself what a 'true' feminist archaeology should be, but (self-evidently from my work) I wholeheartedly support the concept of plural, and differing, interpretations of the same archaeological evidence which have equal status as speculations.

102. For a reinterpretation of the site by the team leader, see Ian Hodder, *Çatalhöyük*, London, 2006. For a study of the feminist tourism to it, and the problem of interaction between the team and the visitors, see Kathryn Rountree, 'Archaeologists and Goddess Feminists at Çatalhöyük', *Journal of Feminist Studies in Religion*, 23/2 (2007), 7–26.

103. I supplied a selection of the main such publications, amounting to forty titles, on pp. 410–12 of my book *Pagan Britain*. It may be worth emphasizing here that to interpret that material as evidence for the worship of a single great goddess is still possible, as one reading of it among many.

104. I would say myself that it is a wholly justifiable and feasible one. Apart from the point made above about the legitimacy of the subjective and personal reading of the prehistoric evidence in this way, I would repeat a statement that I have made a number of times before (in 'The Discovery of the Modern Goddess', 99; and in both editions of *The Triumph of the Moon*, p. 51 in the 1999 one and p. 44 of the 2019 one): that such a deity may actually exist. It could well be that divine figures are all projections of the human heart and mind, but equally so that human belief gives them real life, or else that they have always existed but are perceived at particular times when humans have need of them. It may be necessary to state this a fourth time because some of the Goddess's modern adherents have seemed capable of reading my work without apparently noticing it. Incidentally, a few readers may wonder why I have made no reference in the context of Mother Earth of the 'Gaia Hypothesis' of the biochemist James Lovelock, his theory that our planet in some respects exhibits the behaviour of a living creature: unveiled in a string of publications between 'The Quest for Gaia', *New Scientist*, 65 (1975), 304–6, and *Gaia*, London, 1979. This is because he ultimately denied firmly that he had identified the earth as a goddess, instead characterizing it as 'a self-regulating system like the familiar thermostat of a domestic iron or oven' (*Gaia*, London, 1991, 6–11). However, he had earlier commented that 'the peaceful, artful, Goddess-orientated culture in Old Europe' had venerated the earth and been the better for it, a clear echo of Marija Gimbutas (*The Ages of Gaia*, London, 1988, 203–23). So there is some slight connection.

Chapter Three: The Fairy Queen

1. The first half of this chapter draws partly on material which was used for my article 'The Making of the Early Modern British Fairy Tradition', *Historical Journal*, 57 (2014), 1157–75.

2. Alaric Hall, *Elves in Anglo-Saxon England*, Woodbridge, 2007.

3. Gerald of Wales or Giraldus Cambrensis, *Itinerarium Kambriae*, 1.5–12; Ralph of Coggleshall, *Chronicon Anglicarum*, ff. 88–90; Gervase of Tilbury, *Otia Imperialia*, III.45, 60; Walter Map, *De nugis curialum*, II.11; William of Newburgh, *Historia rerum Anglicarum*, 1.27–8; Edmund Craster, ed., 'The Miracles of Farne', *Archaeologia Aeliana*, 4th series, 29 (1951), 101–3.

4. *Itinerarium Kambriae*, 1.12.

5. For this, see especially C.S. Lewis, *The Discarded Image*, Cambridge, 1964, 122–38; Robert Bartlett, *England under the Norman and Angevin Kings*, Oxford, 2000, 686–92; C.S. Watkins, *History and the Supernatural in Medieval England*, Cambridge, 2007, 62–5, 203–15; and Richard Firth Green, *Elf Queens and Holy Friars*, Philadelphia, 2016, 1–41.

NOTES to pp. 78–84

6. Augustine, *De Civitate Dei*, XV.23; Burchard, *Corrector*, section 152.
7. *Leechbook III*, ff. 123–5. Details of editions and translations of such texts are in chapter 1, n. 23.
8. Map, *De nugis curialum*, II.11.
9. British Library, MS Reg. 15C, vii, f. 74.
10. *Itinerarium Cambriae*, 1.5.
11. C. d'Evelyn and A.J. Mill, eds, *The South English Legendary*, Early English Texts Society, 1956–9, St Michael, Part 2, lines 238–58; W.A. Wright, ed., *The Metrical Chronicle of Robert of Gloucester*, Rolls Series, London, 1887, vol. 1, 196 (lines 2736–56).
12. For this see particularly Alfred Nutt, *The Fairy Mythology of Shakespeare*, London, 1900; Lucy Allen Paton, *Studies in the Fairy Mythology of Arthurian Romance*, New York, 1903; Roger Sherman Loomis, *Celtic Myth and Arthurian Romance*, New York, 1927.
13. Figures especially like the fays of French and English romance are found in the texts *Imram Brain maic Febail*; *Echtrae Chonnlai*; *Tochmarc Etaine*, *Euchtra Airt*, *Serglige Con Culainn*, *Eachtrae Laegari* and *Eachtrae Nerai*. The obvious equivalent in the Welsh literature is Rhiannon in *Pedeir Keinc y Mabinogi*.
14. For an excellent consideration of these beings in Irish literature, see Mark Williams, *Ireland's Immortals*, Princeton, 2016. My own essay, 'Medieval Welsh Literature and Pre-Christian Deities', *Cambrian Medieval Celtic Studies*, 61 (2011), 57–85, is an argument against the possibility of determining whether the characters of high medieval Welsh literature were once pagan goddesses and gods. Once again, this was an idea conceived in the late Victorian period which became dominant among scholars and was elaborated until the 1960s.
15. See Hall, *Elves in Anglo-Saxon England*, 167–75; and James Wade, *Fairies in Medieval Romance*, Basingstoke, 2011, 147–9. In 2016 Richard Firth Green could declare that the 'fashion associated in English scholarship particularly with Roger Sherman Loomis, for uncovering hidden Celtic motifs in medieval romance, has long passed' (*Elf Queens and Holy Friars*, 66). Indeed C.S. Lewis already termed the quest for Celtic roots to romance irrelevant to an understanding of the latter in 1962: see his *Selected Literary Essays*, ed. by Walter Hooper, Cambridge, 1969, 301–11. Even so, Celtic texts were still credited with great influence over the figure of the fay in Carolyne Larrington, 'The Fairy Mistress in Medieval Literary Fantasy', in Ceri Sullivan and Barbara White, eds, *Writing and Fantasy*, London, 1999, 32–47; and Corinne Saunders, *Magic and the Supernatural in Medieval English Romance*, Woodbridge, 2010, 179–206.
16. Especially memorable here are Larrington, 'The Fairy Mistress in Medieval Literary Fantasy'; and *King Arthur's Enchantresses*, London, 2006; Hall, *Elves in Anglo-Saxon England*, 157–75; Saunders, *Magic and the Supernatural in Medieval English Romance*; Wade, *Fairies in Medieval Romance*; and Piotr Spyra, *The Liminality of Fairies*, New York, 2019.
17. This was all worked out by Noel Williams, 'The Semantics of the Word "Fairy"', in Peter Narvaez, ed., *The Good People*, Lexington, 1987. See also Richard Firth Green, 'Changing Chaucer', *Studies in the Age of Chaucer*, 25 (2003), 27–30.
18. This episode is in stanza 74.
19. I have used the edition of Lord Berners' translation, with an accompanying history of the work, made by S.L. Lee for the Early English Text Society in 1882.
20. Geoffrey of Monmouth, *Vita Merlini*, lines 916–40.
21. See the discussion in Basil Clarke's edition of the *Vita*, published at Cardiff in 1973, on pp. 203–7; and Larrington, *King Arthur's Enchantresses*, 7–28.
22. Layamon, *Brut*, VII, lines 14277–82.
23. *Claris et Laris* also makes Morgana Arthur's sister, a not really logical or explicable addition to her persona first effected by Etienne de Rouen in *Draco Normannicus* in the middle of the twelfth century and adopted by the great French romance-writer Chretien de Troyes near its end (in his *Erec et Enide*). There she is still benevolent. As Arthur's sibling, however, she has to be a human woman who has learned magic deliberately, which was a step on

which medieval Christian culture generally frowned. *Claris et Laris* drives home the point that she did so for purely selfish reasons and is entirely human; but she is still called a 'fay' in the story.

24. All three versions of the romance were helpfully edited by A.J. Bliss for Oxford University Press in 1966.

25. One manifestation of this had been the growth in reports of nocturnal processions or cavalcades of these unfortunates, doomed to wander the earth after death. For the context, see Jean-Claude Schmitt, *Ghosts in the Middle Ages*, Chicago, 1994; for the nocturnal processions, Ronald Hutton, 'The Wild Hunt and the Witches' Sabbath', *Folklore*, 125/2 (2014), 161–78; and for the particular application to *Sir Orfeo*, Bruce Mitchell, 'The Fairy World of Sir Orfeo', *Neophilologus*, 48 (1964), 155–9; and Dorena Allen, 'Orpheus and Orfeo', *Medium Aevum*, 33 (1964), 103–11.

26. For this, see Williams, 'The Semantics of the Word "Fairy"', 470–8; and Jeremy Harte, *Explore Fairy Traditions*, Loughborough, 2004, 27.

27. I have used the English translation by Lord Berners, *The History of the Valiant Knight Arthur of Little Britain*, ed. by E.V. Utterson, London, 1814, lines 115–18, 297–300.

28. Siegfried Wenzel, ed., *Fasciculus Morum*, London, 1989, Part 5, lines 61–72.

29. In *The Wife of Bath's Tale*, lines 857–81.

30. *Sir Thopas*, lines 784–803.

31. *The Merchant's Tale*, lines 2225–318.

32. All three versions of the story were helpfully edited together by A.J. Bliss in London, 1960. The significance of the change of colour was noted by Diane Purkiss, *Troublesome Things*, London, 2000, 81–2.

33. Ralph Flenley, ed., *Six Town Chronicles*, Oxford, 1961, 127.

34. F.R.H. du Boulay, ed., *Documents Illustrative of Medieval Kentish Society*, Kent Archaeological Society, 1964, 254–5.

35. The best-known edition is probably that by James Murray for the Early English Text Society.

36. Especially in 'Y Dyllvan' and 'Y Niwl'.

37. Accessible versions are in Sabine Baring-Gould, *Lives of the Saints*, London, 1898, vol. 16, 223–4; and Elissa R. Henken, *Traditions of the Welsh Saints*, Cambridge, 1987, 221–6.

38. Richard Suggett, *A History of Magic and Witchcraft in Wales*, Stroud, 2008, passim; and *Welsh Witches*, n.loc., 2018, 123–33; Lisa Maria Tallis, 'The Conjuror, the Fairy, the Devil and the Preacher' (Swansea PhD thesis, 2007).

39. It is on pp. 132–53 of Denton Fox's edition of *The Poems of Robert Henryson*, Oxford, 1981.

40. It is found in the Bannatyne Manuscript, and is published in editions of that, sometimes catalogued under the first line, 'Sym of Lyntoun'. Other specimens of whimsy verse that feature the fairy king are 'Lichton's Dreme', in which the dreamer is taken prisoner by him and bound with ropes of sand, and 'The Gyre-Carling', about an ogress who is driven out by him and his host. There is an overall consideration of this 'eldrich' verse in Lizanne Henderson and Edward Cowan, *Scottish Fairy Belief*, East Linton, 2001, 152–3.

41. Lines 1254–5, 1536–74, 4188–9; on pp. 422–3, 440 and 532 of the Early English Text Society edition of 1865.

42. Lines 1132–5. In quotation from Scots verse I have modernized and anglicized the spelling, save for the versions of 'fairy' itself.

43. In 'Sir Thomas Norny', lines 4–6.

44. 'The Goldyn Targe', lines 125–6.

45. 'Ane Flytting or Invective be Capitaine Alexander Montgomerie against the Laird of Pollart', Book 2, lines 14–26.

46. James VI, *Daemonologie*, Edinburgh, 1597, 73–4.

47. *Philotus*, eventually printed in Edinburgh in 1603, stanza 132.

48. *Daemonologie*, 73–4.

49. National Records of Scotland, JC26/1/67.

50. Robert Pitcairn, ed., *Ancient Criminal Trials in Scotland*, Edinburgh, 1833, vol. 1, part 2, 51–8.
51. Pitcairn, *Ancient Criminal Trials*, vol. 1, part 2, 161–5.
52. James Cranstoun, ed., *Satirical Poems of the Time of the Reformation*, Scottish Text Society, 1891, 365.
53. John Stuart, ed., *The Miscellany of the Spalding Club*, Aberdeen, 1841, 117–25.
54. P. Hume Brown, ed., *The Register of the Privy Council of Scotland*, 2nd series, vol. 8, Edinburgh, 1908, 347.
55. David Masson, ed., *The Register of the Privy Council of Scotland: Volume XI*, Edinburgh, 1894, 366–7.
56. National Records of Scotland, CH2/467/1, pp. 76–83.
57. Pitcairn, *Ancient Criminal Trials*, vol. 3, part 2, 602–16.
58. This rethinking with respect to fairies in general is covered in my book *The Witch*, London, 2017, 237–42. See also, inter alia, Minor White Latham, *The Elizabethan Fairies*, New York, 1930; K.M. Briggs, *The Anatomy of Puck*, London, 1959; Diane Purkiss, *Troublesome Things*, London, 2000, 124–85; Mary Ellen Lamb, 'Taken by the Fairies', *Shakespeare Quarterly*, 51 (2000), 277–311; Marjorie Swann, 'The Politics of Fairylore in Early Modern English Literature', *Renaissance Quarterly*, 53 (2000), 449–73; Regina Buccola, *Fairies, Fractious Women, and the Old Faith*, Selinsgrove, 2006; and Peter Marshall, 'Protestants and Fairies in Early Modern England', in L. Scott Dixon, ed., *Living with Religious Diversity in Early Modern Europe*, Farnham, 2009, 139–61.
59. This is the work edited by S.L. Lee for the Early English Text Society in 1882.
60. Its Tudor publication history is considered by Cooper, *The English Romance in Time*, 176, 466.
61. This was *Dead Man's Fortune*, recorded in Walter W. Greg, *The Henslowe Papers*, London, 1907, 135.
62. Robert Greene, *The Scottish Historie of James IV*, London, printed in 1598.
63. A point noted by Purkiss, *Troublesome Things*, 176–7.
64. *Hamlet*, Act 1, Scene 1, line 162; *The Merry Wives of Windsor*, Act 4, Scene 4, lines 73–4 and Act 5, Scene 5, lines 43–108.
65. The anonymous *Lust's Dominion*, the surviving edition of which is from 1657, lines 1583–605.
66. Latham, *The Elizabethan Fairies*, 143–4, runs down a list of such events, most notably at Hengrove Hall, Apethorpe, Quarrendon and Woodstock. To these can be added the Elvetham one, below, and that at the Lee family seat at Ditchley in 1592.
67. Jean Wilson, *Entertainments for Elizabeth I*, Woodbridge, 1980, 99–118.
68. Printed in 1607.
69. For context here see especially Matthew Woodcock, *Fairy in "The Faerie Queene"*, Aldershot, 2004.
70. Ben Jonson, *The Entertainment at Althorp*, printed 1616.
71. Ben Jonson, *Oberon, the Fairy Prince*, printed 1616.
72. *Robin Goodfellow: His mad pranks and merry jests*, London, 1628; *The merry pranks of Robin Goodfellow*, n.d.; *The Pranks of Puck*, n.d., all reprinted in James Orchard Halliwell, *Illustrations of the Fairy Mythology of "A Midsummer Night's Dream"*, London, 1845, 120–70, 237–9. In the last of these to appear, *The Midnight's Watch*, London, 1643, Robin serves the queen instead.
73. *Tom Thumb, His Life and Death*, London, 1630.
74. A.H. Bullen, ed., *The Works of Dr Thomas Campion*, London, 1889, 21–2.
75. Such as Thomas Randolph's *The Jealous Lovers*, acted before Queen Henrietta Maria at Cambridge in 1632, Act 3, Scene 7.
76. *A Description of the King and Queene of Fayries*, London, 1635.
77. For an overview here, see Hutton, *The Witch*, 217–27.
78. East Sussex Record Office, RYE 13/1–8, 12–13, 19, 21; G. Slade Butler, 'Appearance of Spirits in Sussex', *Sussex Archaeological Collections*, 14 (1862), 25–34. The case has been well studied by Annabel Gregory, 'Witchcraft, Politics and "Good Neighbourhood" in Early Seventeenth-Century Rye', *Past and Present*, 133 (1991), 31–66; and *Rye Spirits*, London, 2013.

79. Durant Hotham, *The Life of Jacob Behmen*, London, 1654, C3; John Webster, *The Displaying of Supposed Witchcraft*, London, 1677, 301.

80. British Library, Sloane MS 3851, f. 115v; *Norfolk Archaeology* 1 (1847), 57–9; Bodleian Library, MS e. Mus 173, f. 72v; Owen Davies, *Grimoires: A History of Magical Books*, Oxford, 2009, 60–1.

81. Bodleian Library, Ashmole MS 1491, f. 1362v.

82. British Library, Sloane MS 1727, p. 28; Folger Library, Washington DC, MS V626, 80, 156. Cf. Barbara A. Mowat, 'Prospero's Book', *Shakespeare Quarterly*, 52 (2001), 12–19.

83. Peter Grund, 'Albertus Magnus and the Queen of the Elves', *Anglia*, 122 (2004), 640–62.

84. William Lilly, *History of His Life and Times*, London, 1715, 102–3.

85. Historical Manuscripts Commission, Hatfield House Manuscripts, vol. 5, 81–3.

86. *The Brideling, Sadling and Ryding, of a Rich Churle in Hampshire . . .*, London, 1595.

87. *The severall notorious and lewd Cousonages of John West, and Alice West . . .*, London, 1613.

88. C.J. Sisson, 'A Topical Reference in *The Alchemist*', in James G. McManaway et al., eds, *Joseph Quincey Adams Memorial Studies*, Washington, DC, 1948, 739–41.

89. Thomas Jackson, *A Treatise Containing the Originall of Unbeliefe, Misbeliefe and Mispersuasion*, London, 1625, 178–9.

90. Printed in 1616. These episodes are in Act 1, Scene 2, and Act 3, Scene 5.

91. It was eventually printed in 1663, the action concerned being in Act 2, Scene 5.

92. This is in British Library, Additional MSS 2006-7, and the whole affair has been fully and affectionately recounted by Frances Timbers, *The Magical Adventures of Mary Parish*, Kirksville, MO, 2016, who makes the most determined possible case that Mary was not a confidence trickster but a fantasist.

93. Act 1, Scene 3, lines 53–95.

94. *The Maydes Metamorphosis*, London, 1600, II.i.sigs C4, D1.

95. Gervase of Tilbury, *Otia imperiala*, book 3, c. 60.

96. Michael Drayton, 'Nymphidia', in *The Battaile of Agincourt*, London, 1627. Dryden went back to the same theme three years later, to dress up Mab in petals, feathers and lady bird wings to attend the wedding of a cricket who functions as one of her maids, in 'A Fairy Wedding', in *The Muses Elizium: The Eight Nimphall*, London, 1630. Both texts are in Halliwell, *Illustrations of the Fairy Mythology*, 195–225.

97. Thomas Randolph, *Amyntas*, London, 1638, in Halliwell, *Illustrations of the Fairy Mythology*, 237–52.

98. In Halliwell, *Illustrations of the Fairy Mythology*, 253–4, 258–62. See other poems of Herrick which deal with this conceit at pp. 254–8, 262–3. See also the songs about tiny fairies printed on pp. 268–71 and 269–71.

99. Inigo Jones, *The Masque of the Twelve Months*, in Peter Cunningham, *Inigo Jones*, London, 1848, 137; John Day, *The Parliament of Bees*, London, 1641; Sir Simon Steward, *Musarum Deliciae*, London, c. 1656.

100. For an overview of this and the associated scholarly literature, see Ronald Hutton, *The Triumph of the Moon*, Oxford, 2019, 87–115.

101. See, inter alia, Jeremy Maas et al., *Victorian Fairy Painting*, London, 1997; Christopher Wood, *Fairies in Victorian Art*, Woodbridge, 2000; Jack Zipes, *Victorian Fairy Tales*, New York, 1987; Carole G. Silver, *Strange and Secret Peoples: Fairies and Victorian Consciousness*, Oxford, 1999.

102. I used these collections comprehensively for their material on seasonal customs in *The Stations of the Sun: A History of the Ritual Year in Britain*, Oxford, 1996. For a digest of the information on fairies from them, see Katharine Briggs, *The Fairies in Tradition and Literature*, London, 1967; and Harte, *Explore Fairy Traditions*.

103. That revival was launched symbolically by the superb picture book by Brian Froud and Alan Lee, *Faeries*, London, 1978. For contemporary experiences of it, see Sabina Magliocco, '"Reconnecting to Everything": Fairies in Contemporary Paganism', in Michael Ostling, ed., *Fairies, Demons and Nature Spirits*, London, 2018, 325–48.

104. See her in a work by an English practitioner, for example, which assumes actual contacts between readers and fairies: Teresa Moorey, *The Fairy Bible*, London, 2008. Her Queen Mab (on pp. 72–3) retains Shakespeare's trait of giving dreams, but otherwise is described as 'one of the many manifestations of The Goddess, in her autumnal guise of wise-woman and lady of magic, and she is linked with ancient ideas of sovereignty – for the king drew his power from the land, and Mab presided'. This is a clear connection with Maeve, whom some scholars have thought to be a sovereignty goddess. In the 1997 Anglo-American television series *Merlin*, about the famous Arthurian wizard and starring Sam Neill, Mab was turned into a (rather heartless and domineering) pagan goddess of the land: again, her personality there is reminiscent of Maeve.

Chapter Four: The Lady of the Night

1. The edition that I know is that of Hermann Wasserschleben, *Regionis abbati Prumiensis libris duo*, Leipzig, 1840, 355. There are translations in Norman Cohn, *Europe's Inner Demons*, 2nd edn, London, 1993, 167; Carlo Ginzburg, *Ecstasies: Deciphering the Witches' Sabbath*, trans. by Raymond Rosenthal, London, 1992, 89–90; and Claude Lecouteux, *Phantom Armies of the Night*, trans. by John E. Graham, Rochester VT, 2011, 9.
2. This set of references was collected by Jacob Grimm, *Teutonic Mythology*, trans. by James Steven Stallybrass, 4th edn, London, 1882, vol. 1, 285–6, and repeated by Cohn, *Europe's Inner Demons*, 168. I have checked the sources and provided extra material from the *Vita Caesarii Episcopi Arelatensis* II.18–19, and Gregory of Tours, *Historiae Francorum*, VIII.14.
3. Ginzburg, *Ecstasies*, 91–3, 104. Carlo was one of three great historians from the academic world of my youth to whom I dedicated my book *The Witch* in 2017. One of its reviewer delivered the opinion that that book was possibly unique in making so many criticisms of the ideas of people who were its dedicatees. Mercifully, no other appraisal of the book made this point, but it still struck me to the heart, and so requires some elucidation as I deal with Carlo's theories again here. There are many points of detail on which we differ, and like several colleagues I cannot support his proposal that an ancient pan-European shamanic religious system ultimately underpinned the concept of the witches' sabbath. Nonetheless, I consider his basic approach to the origins of the sabbath, of looking for roots in folkloric as well as learned tradition, to be perfectly correct, and believe that his application of it achieved more exciting and inspirational results than that of anybody else. To say this is of course to neglect his immense contribution to our profession and discipline in other areas, such as his paramount contribution to the genre of microhistory. He is also the perfect model of a gentleman, in scholarship as in all other respects.
4. Burchard of Worms, *Decretum*, X.29 and XIX.5.70,90,170–1. I have used the edition in *Patrologia Latina* vol. 140.
5. Carlo Ginzburg made a valiant attempt to discard this association and find a pagan goddess behind the Herodias of the nocturnal cavalcades in *Ecstasies*, 104 and 116. He proposed that such a deity had been called Hera Diana, which could be garbled into the Biblical name. There is no such goddess in the historical or archaeological record, although Carlo finds dedications to the Greek goddess Hera in Switzerland and North Italy. He also cites a roof tile from a late Roman grave in Dauphiné, south-eastern France, scratched with a human-like figure riding on an animal or ship, and the words 'Fera Comhera', which may mean 'with Hera the savage'. The riding posture does link it to the lady of the medieval retinues, but the context of the find makes it look like a curse tablet, a common kind of artefact from this period. Hera would be a good fit with that, as a notoriously vengeful goddess and especially one who took a dim view of marital infidelity, and her steed in the carving could well be a peacock, her symbolic animal. More generally, it does seem unlikely that a hybrid would be produced by linking together a Roman goddess with a Greek one of very different character. Carlo also brings in a third tantalizing piece of evidence, a fifteenth-century reference to a belief by peasants in the Palatinate area of the central Rhineland that a being called Hera

roamed around at the Christmas season, bringing abundance. This does relate – as will be seen – to seasonal Germanic traditions from that period of superhuman females doing exactly that, but it is hard to see how a Greek name for an ancient goddess could have lingered for a thousand years in what had been a Latin and Gaulish speaking area of the Roman Empire and then became a German-speaking one. It seems more likely to me that a classically educated author was mishearing the real name, such as Holle, and transforming it into that of a famous ancient deity. For these reasons, I find his suggestion inconclusive, though interesting.

6. Ratherius, *Praeloquiorum libri*, I.10. I have used the edition in *Patrologia Latina*, vol. 136, column 157.

7. *Reinardus Vulpes*, Book 1, lines 1143–64, translated into French as *Le Roman de Renart* and *Le Roman de Ysengrin*: there are various modern editions. The story varies in details between the Latin and French versions, and here I have followed the former.

8. These were teased out by Aron Gurevitch, *Popular Culture: Problems of Belief and Perception*, trans. by János M. Bak and Paul A. Hollingsworth, Cambridge, 1988, 84, 238.

9. Grimm, *Teutonic Mythology*, vol. 1, 267.

10. These and related figures are considered in my book *The Witch*, London, 2017, 67–72.

11. For successive discussions and employments of the different versions, see Hermann Wasserschleben, *Die Bussordnungen der abenländischen Kirche nebst einer rechtsgeschichtlichen Einleitung*, Halle, 1851, 624–82; Hermann Joseph Schmitz, *Die Bussbücher und das Kanonische Bussverfahren*, Düsseldorf, 1898, 402–67; Paul Fournier, 'Études critiques sur le Décret de Burchard de Worms', *Nouvelle revue historique de droit francais et étranger*, 34 (1910), 31–112, 213–21, 289–331, 564–84; John T. McNeill and Helena M. Gamer (eds), *Medieval Handbooks of Penance*, New York, 1938, 321–45; and Greta Austin, *Shaping Church Law around the Year 1000: The 'Decretum' of Burchard of Worms*, Farnham, 2004.

12. Strabo's poem is in *Patrologia Latina*, vol. 114, column 1094. For Huldah, see 2 Kings 22:14–20 and 2 Chronicles 34:22–33.

13. Such a connection was suggested as long ago as by the great German reformer Martin Luther, as was noted by Jacob Grimm, only for him to dismiss it out of hand: *Teutonic Mythology*, vols. 1, 272, and 3, 1367.

14. It was given even wider currency in the mid-century by its inclusion in the very influential code, the *Decretum*, issued by the Italian jurist Gratian, and subsequently appeared in local penitentials such as that of Bartholomew Iscanus, bishop of Exeter between 1161 and 1182. For a summary of its propagation see C.S. Watkins, *History and the Supernatural in Medieval England*, Cambridge, 2007, 219.

15. John of Salisbury, *Policraticus*, II.17.

16. William of Auvergne, *De Universo*, II.2.94.

17. Quoted in Lecouteux, *Phantom Armies*, 15. I have translated some of the original terms slightly differently.

18. A. Lecoy de la Marche, *Anecdotes historiques, legends et prologues tires du recueil inédit d'Etienne de Boubon*, Paris, 1877, no. 97.

19. Lines 18622–91.

20. Charles de Fresne, sieur du Cange, *Glossarium*, Paris, 1733, vol. 1, column 1127.

21. Bernard Gui, *Interrogatoria ad sortilegos et divines et invocatories demonum*, ed. by G. Mollat, Paris, 1927, c.2.

22. Jean Duvernoy, ed., *La Registre d'inquisition de Jacques Fournier*, Paris, 1965, vol. 1, 137–9.

23. Jacobus de Voragine, *Legenda aurea*, c. 102.

24. This is the completion of Vincent of Beauvais's *Speculum morale*, described in Wolfgang Behringer, *Shaman of Oberstdorf*, translated by H.C. Erik Midelfort, Charlottesville, VA, 1998, 57–8.

25. In *The Witch*, I accepted them as facets of the same cultural construct, as scholars had mostly done before me, including those I have cited. I had already departed from them in insisting on distinguishing the tradition of the night-roaming lady from that of a different major one of night-roaming processions which appeared around 1100 and featured the

human dead, the Hellequin or 'wütende heer': Ronald Hutton, 'The Wild Hunt and the Witches' Sabbath', *Folklore*, 125.2 (2014), 161–78. This had been rolled in together with the female leader's retinue by Jacob Grimm, in his *Teutonic Mythology*, along with other folk traditions of nocturnal hunters, to form one huge conglomeration allegedly derived from ancient paganism which he labelled 'The Wild Hunt', a construct which proved hugely influential until recent years.

26. Marianne Rumpf, *Perchten*, Würzburg, 1991, 61.

27. Gathered by Grimm, *Teutonic Mythology*, vol. 1, 276–81, and one given more fully by Lecouteux, *Phantom Armies*, 15–16.

28. Jeffrey Burton Russell, *Witchcraft in the Middle Ages*, Ithaca, NY, 1972, 175.

29. John B. Smith, 'Perchta the Belly-Slitter and her Kin', *Folklore*, 115 (2004), 167–86.

30. From Thomas Ebendorfer of Haselbach, *Sermones de tempore*, reprinted in Anston E. Schonbach, 'Zeugnisse zur deutschen Volkskunde des Mittelalters', *Zeitschrift des Vereins fur Volkskunde*, 12 (1902), 5–6.

31. Ginzburg, *Ecstasies*, 101, spots the change in the editions. Grimm, *Teutonic Mythology*, vol. 3, 933, prints a fuller version of the 1474 one.

32. Lecouteux, *Phantom Armies*, 16–17.

33. Ginzburg, *Ecstasies*, 297.

34. These records were first published in 1899, and the original texts and a translation are in Behringer, *Shaman of Oberstdorf*, 54–5, 173–4.

35. Ginzburg, *Ecstasies*, 96, 108–9, 296–7, 302: Behringer, *Shaman of Oberstdorf*, 58–64; Carlo Ginzburg, *The Night Battles*, London, 1982, 16, 33–6, 99.

36. *Nicolai Cusae Cardinalis Opera*, Paris, 1514, vol. 2, fos. 170v–172.

37. Ginzburg, *Ecstasies*, 131–2.

38. This ignorance vitiates a convincing answer to questions such as whether such vivid details can help to prove continuities with ancient religion. Both ancient historical testimony such as that of Tacitus and archaeological evidence portray goddesses or goddess-like figures as riding in carts as Richella allegedly did, and Carlo Ginzburg has taken Richella's hairy hands as evidence that she was a surviving memory of an ancient bear goddess, and her ear ornaments as echoing ancient female hairstyles (*Ecstasies*, 129–33). Without this sense of context, however, how can we ever know?

39. J.M. Clifton-Everest, *The Tragedy of Knighthood: Origins of the Tannhäuser Legend*, Oxford, 1979; C.S. Lewis, *The Allegory of Love*, Oxford, 1936, 121.

40. Ginzburg, *Ecstasies*, 108–9.

41. I.V. Zingerle, 'Frau Selde', *Germania*, 2 (1857), 430–7.

42. Johann Geiler von Kaisersberg, *De Emeis*, reprinted in Joseph Hansen, *Quellen und Untersuchungen zur Geschichte des Hexenwahns und der Hexenverfolgung im Mittelalter*, Bonn, 1901, 284–6.

43. Cohn, *Europe's Inner Demons*, 171–2.

44. David Gentilcore, *From Bishop to Witch: The System of the Sacred in Early Modern Terra d'Otranto*, Manchester, 1992.

45. This is Giovanni Lorenzo Anania, quoted in Giuseppe Bonomo, *Caccia alle Streghe*, Palumbo, 1971, 30.

46. Gustav Henningsen, '"The Ladies from Outside": An Archaic Pattern of the Witches' Sabbath', in Bengt Ankarloo and Gustav Henningsen, eds, *Early Modern Witchcraft*, Oxford, 1990, 191–218.

47. It is provided in Pau Castell Granados, '"Wine Vat Witches Suffocate Children": The Mythical Components of the Iberian Witch', *EHumanista*, 26 (2014), 70–95. He does not, however, provide enough detail (and perhaps his source does not) to establish whether this was a genuine local tradition or a case of a Catalan churchman reporting something of which he had heard elsewhere in Europe.

48. Both reprinted in Grimm, *Teutonic Mythology*, vol. 1, 269. I am very grateful to two great scholars of German literature, my own colleague Robert Vilain and Henrike Laehnemann,

for sorting out a question of mine concerning a word in my first copy of Erasmus Alberus's text, which turned out to be garbled by an OCR error.

49. The single exception that is known to me was in Hesse (in Central Germany) in 1632, where a serious local witch hunt was started by the claim of a service magician from Calbach that in the Ember Days he would go to the Venusberg on the 'night journey' (*nachtfahr*) and there 'Lady Holt' would show him the dead and the punishments inflicted on them for their sins: Walter Niess, *Hexenprozesse in der Grafschaft Büdingen*, Büdingen, 1982, 153–82. This is another classic example of the syncretization of different cultural elements.

50. They are especially well studied and discussed in Behringer, *Shaman of Oberstdorf*. A vivid description of those believed to operate around the Swiss city of Luzern, written in the early seventeenth century, is provided in Renward Cysat's chronicle and printed in Karl Meisen, *Die Sagen vom Wütenden Herr* und Wilden Jäger, Münster, 1935, 111–20.

51. P. 185 in the 1989 Oxford University Press edition of *The Anatomy of Melancholy*, by Thomas C. Faulkner et al.

52. Siegried Wenzel, ed., *Fasciculus Morum*, Philadelphia, 1989, Part 5, lines 61–72.

53. James VI, *Daemonologie*, Edinburgh, 1597, 73–4. Another now celebrated British writer of the period to quote the canon 'Epscopi' in his work on spirits was Reginald Scot, in his *Discoverie of Witchcraft*.

54. Priscilla Heath Barnum, ed., *Dives and Pauper*, Early English Text Society, 1976, vol. 1, 157–8.

55. See chapter 3, note 45. Andro Man's fairy queen also went riding at times, as discussed in the same chapter.

56. As recounted also in chapter 3, with the source reference at note 51.

57. Carlo Ginzburg, *Ecstasies*, 96–7, with typical perception and ability to range between regions, noted the similarity and proposed that both derived from the same 'ancient stratum' of beliefs. This is one of the points of detail on which we differ, but is another of the many areas to which, without Carlo's suggestion, attention would not have been drawn.

58. This is equally true, among those cited above, of Grimm, Cohn, Ginzburg and Lecouteux, though none of them agreed with each other on the best candidate for such a goddess.

59. The main exception hitherto has been Carlo Ginzburg, as will be shown. In *The Witch*, 136–43, I made my own attempt and what follows here is a repetition of that with some updating.

60. She was Claude Lecouteux's candidate, in *Phantom Armies*, 25 and 33.

61. Stephen Ronan, ed., *The Goddess Hecate*, Hastings, 1992; Sara Iles Johnston, *Hekate Soteira*, Atlanta, GA, 1990; and *Restless Dead*, Berkeley, 1999, 203–49.

62. In line 13.

63. Bruno Snell, *Tragicorum Graecorum Fragmenta*, Gottingen, 1986 vol. 1, 115.

64. Both were identified by Carlo Ginzburg in *Ecstasies*, where there are many references to them.

65. The main catalogue of material relating to her is René Magnen and Émile Thenevot, *Épona*, Bordeaux, 1956, updated by Jan de Vries, *La Religion des Celtes*, Paris, 1963, 132–5; Katheryn M. Linduff, 'Epona', *Latomus*, 38 (1979), 817–37; and Claude Sterckx, *Élements de cosmogenie celtique*, Brussels, 1986, 9–54.

66. The basic study of them remains F. Haverfield, 'The Mother Goddesses', *Archaeologia Aeliana*, 15 (1892), 314–36; but see Miranda Green, *The Gods of the Celts*, London, 1986, chapter 3; and her *Celtic Goddesses*, London, 1995, 106–11; and De Vries, *La Religion des Celtes*, 124–32; Graham Webster, *The British Celts and their Gods under Rome*, London, 1986, 63–70; and Sylvia Barnard, 'The Matres of Roman Britain', *Archaeological Journal*, 142 (1985), 237–45.

67. As commentators on the medieval night rides have done from Jacob Grimm, who established the tradition of using medieval Norse myth and legend as a guide to ancient Germanic paganism, to Claude Lecouteux.

68. For this see Hutton, *The Witch*, 92–5.

69. *Havamal*, st. 155.

70. *Ketils saga haengs*, c. 3.

71. *Thorsteins thattr boejarmagns*, c. 2.

72. *Eyrbyggja saga*, c. 16.

73. *Volundarkvida*, verse 1 (this text only names the winged women as Valkyries in the intro-duction, a probable later gloss as they do not resemble Valkyries in general); and *Helgakvida Hundingsbana II*, in the Poetic Edda, verse 4, prose opening fits 2 and 4. Lecouteux, *Phantom Armies*, 20–1, prints the passage on the Disir from *Flateyarbók*. The latter is from the end of the fourteenth century, and is a highly Christianized and schematic, and so atypical, account which identifies the women as *fylgjur*, female or animal ancestral spirits who often appear at a death. It therefore cannot be taken as normative.

74. Grimm, *Teutonic Mythology*, vol. 1, 267–72.

75. Grimm, *Teutonic Mythology*, vol. 1, 272–82; Smith, 'Perchta the Belly-Slitter'; Rumpf, *Perchten*.

76. The evidence is summarized in Behringer, *Shaman of Oberstdorf*, 26–46.

77. Grimm, *Teutonic Mythology*, vol. 1, 282. The nineteenth-century folklore collected by Grimm also at times mixed thoroughly together the originally different medieval traditions of the roving nocturnal hosts led by the lady and the penitential processions of the human dead, so causing Grimm to believe that they had originally been one and derived from the same primeval religion focused on death and fertility: ibid., vol. 3, 934–41.

78. Gail Kligman, *Calus*, Bucharest, 1999.

79. Charles Godfrey Leland, *Aradia: Gospel of the Witches*, London, 1899.

80. My own consideration of it, and of Leland, is in Ronald Hutton, *The Triumph of the Moon*, Oxford, 2nd edn, 2019, 147–54.

Chapter Five: The Cailleach

1. Pronounced, according to region, 'Cah-lehh', 'Cah-liahh', 'Coilleahh' or 'Cal-yuhh'.

2. All these are collected in Gearóid Ó Crualaoich, *The Book of the Cailleach*, Cork, 2013.

3. Ó Crualaoich, *The Book of the Cailleach*, 113–4.

4. Donald A. Mackenzie, *Scottish Folk-Lore and Folk Life*, Glasgow, 1935, 162–3.

5. Ó Crualaoich, *The Book of the Cailleach*, 104–7, 148.

6. 'Loughcrew, County of Meath', *The Dublin Penny Journal*, 4.192 (1836), 28; Eugene A. Conwell, 'On Ancient Sepulchral Cairns on the Loughcrew Hills', *Proceedings of the Royal Irish Academy*, 9 (1864–66), 357–8.

7. Ó Crualaoich, *The Book of the Cailleach*, 115–18; Mackenzie, *Scottish Folk-Lore*, 161, 164–6; Eleanor Hull, 'Legends and Traditions of the Cailleach Bheara or Old Woman', *Folklore*, 38 (1927), 244–9.

8. Mackenzie, *Scottish Folk-Lore*, 150–1.

9. Ó Crualaoich, *The Book of the Cailleach*, 109, 120–3, 132–8, 146.

10. Ó Crualaoich, *The Book of the Cailleach*, 132–8, 146, 150–2, 163–5.

11. Ó Crualaoich, *The Book of the Cailleach*, 115–8;

12. Mackenzie, *Scottish Folk-Lore*, 151–4; John Francis Campbell, *Popular Tales of the West Highlands*, Edinburgh, 1860, vol. 2, 46.

13. Mackenzie, *Scottish Folk-Lore* 137–43; Katherine Whyte Grant, *Myth, Tradition and Story from Western Argyll*, Oban, 1925, 8; E.C. Watson, 'Highland Mythology', *Celtic Review*, 5/17 (1908), 65; Hull, 'Legends and Traditions of the Cailleach Bheara', 247–8.

14. W. Walter Gill, *A Manx Scrapbook*, London, 1929, 160; Cyril Ingram Paton, *Manx Calendar Customs*, London, 1942, 35–8.

15. Mackenzie, *Scottish Folk-Lore*, 156–61.

16. The second part of the name usually pronounced 'vay-ruh' or 'vur', depending on the spelling and place.

17. The most recent discussion seems to be in Mark Williams, *Ireland's Immortals*, Princeton, 2016, 28 (n.92).

18. There are various editions and translations: for those interested in the later folklore, the most accessible and convenient is in Ó Crualaoich, *The Book of the Cailleach*, 48–51. Another is appended to the classic study of the medieval text, Gerard Murphy, 'The Lament of the Old Woman of Beare', *Proceedings of the Royal Irish Academy*, 55 (1952–3), 83–109. See also John Carey, 'Transmutations and Immortality in the Lament of the Old Woman of Beare', *Celtica*, 23 (1999), 30–7; and Katia Ritari, 'Images of Ageing in the Early Irish Poem *Caillech Bérri*', *Studia Celtica Fennica*, 3 (2006), 57–70. Ritari makes the point that there is no apparent supernatural character to the speaker in the poem, while Kim McCone, *Pagan Past and Christian Present in Early Irish Literature*, Maynooth, 1990, 154, stresses the Biblical references in it.

19. All this is discussed, seemingly definitively, by Máirín Ní Dhonnchadha, 'Cailleach and Other Terms for Veiled Women in Medieval Irish Texts', *Éigse*, 28 (1994), 71–96.

20. I use the standard edition and translation by Kuno Meyer, published in London in 1892: the reference is on p. 6.

21. Edward J. Gwynn, ed., *The Metrical Dindshenchas*, 5 vols., London, 1903–35; Whitley Stokes, ed., 'The Prose Tales in the Rennes *Dindshenchas*', *Revue Celtique*, 15 (1894), 272–336, 418–84; Whitley Stokes, ed., 'The Bodleian Dinnshenchas', *Folklore*, 3 (1892), 467–567.

22. The source is *Sanas Cormaic*, and the entry under 'Coire Brecain': I have the 1862 edition by Whitley Stokes, *Three Irish Glossaries*, and the entry appears there on pp. 13–14.

23. It is wonderfully analyzed in Mark Williams, *Ireland's Immortals*, Princeton, 2016, 118–23.

24. The epic sequence now usually called the 'Cycles of the Kings' does contain a character called Mongfhind, daughter of Fidach and wife of the high king Muredach, of whom it is said that 'women and common folk' especially favoured her after her death and prayed to her at the feast of Samhain, which was when she died. This might argue for some social division in the veneration of deities, but it seems to be the only case, and Mongfhind's followers were still drawn from elite women as well as commoners – if the text can be read like this – and her story still features in this literary text. I have used the standard translation of the cycle by Myles Dillon, Oxford, 1946, 30–1.

25. I have followed Mark Williams's translation of this passage, put in a personal communication and resulting in a more nuanced version than the traditional one by J.H. Todd in the Rolls Series, London, 1867, 174–5. I am naturally very grateful to him for this assistance.

26. The Fenian tales, here and below, exist in good translations posted on the internet under their titles.

27. I have used the standard translation by R.I. Best in *Ériu*, 3 (1906), 149–73.

28. The Welsh terms translated here as 'hags' and 'very dark hag' are *gwidondot* in the first tale and *Gwidon Ordu* in the second. Similar ogresses are overcome by heroes in the poem 'Pa gur yv y porthaur' and the hagiographical *Life of Samson*.

29. For which see Richard Suggett, *A History of Witchcraft and Magic in Wales*, Stroud, 2008, 42–3.

30. The poem, commonly called 'The Gyre Carling' but usually listed in contents pages under its first line, 'In Tiberus tyme the trew Imperiour', is in the Bannatyne Manuscript, ff. 136v–7r. The manuscript is available in various editions, including the Scottish Text Society one (new series, vol. 23) and the facsimile one by D. Fox and W. Ringler published in London in 1980, and on the internet. The context is given in J.E.H. Williams, 'James V, David Lyndsay, and the Bannatyne Manuscript Poem of the Gyre Carling', *Studies in Scottish Literature*, 26/1 (1991), 164–75. Passing references to the gyre carling occur in Sir David Lyndsay's *Dreme*, line 45; John Rolland, *The Seuin Seages*, available in the Scottish Text Society 3rd series, vol. 3, on p. 337; and the 'Flytting' between Montgomerie and Pollart, referenced in n. 45 to chapter 3 of this book.

31. She appears in lines 45–6 of 'Ane littill Interlud of the droichis pairt of th[e play]', on f. 118r of the Bannatyne Manuscript.

32. I am uneasily aware here of a gap in my own knowledge, represented by Ireland's rich trove of literature, and the significant quantity of surviving Scottish Gaelic poetry, dating from between 1500 and 1800. Much less of this is available in translation than the texts in Old and Middle Irish, and I can only say that the amount which I have managed to locate does

not seem to mention the Cailleach Bheara or an equivalent Cailleach figure, though it is replete with stately or tragic goddess-like figures representing Ireland as a whole.

33. There seems to be nothing relevant to her, for example, in William Grant Stewart, *The Popular Superstitions and Festive Amusements of the Highlanders of Scotland*, Edinburgh, 1823; Thomas Crofton Croker, *Legends and Traditions of the South of Ireland*, London, 3 vols, 1825–8; Hugh Miller, *Scenes and Legends of the North of Scotland*, London, 1851; Jane Francesca Wilde, *Ancient Cures, Charms and Usages of Ireland*, London, 1890; and *Ancient Legends, Mystic Charms and Superstitions of Ireland*, London, 2nd edn, 1919; or John Gregorson Campbell, ed., *Superstitions of the Highlands and Islands of Scotland*, Glasgow, 1900. Nor does she seem to feature in the extensive collections of lore made by Thomas Westropp in County Clare and the coasts of Connacht and published in *Folklore* in 1910–1912 and 1918–1923.

34. John Francis Campbell, *Popular Tales of the West Highlands*, Edinburgh, 1860, vol. 2, 46.

35. For the early references to the Loughcrew origin myth, see the sources at n. 6.

36. Lord Archibald Campbell et al, eds, *Waifs and Strays of Celtic Tradition: Argyllshire Series*, London, 1891, vol. 5, 65–7.

37. I have used the 1994 Floris Books reprint where they occur on pp. 493–4.

38. William R. Wilde, *Irish Popular Superstitions*, London, 1852, 55.

39. E.C. Watson, 'Highland Mythology', *Celtic Review*, 5/17 (July 1908), 65.

40. J. Gregorson Campbell, 'The Sharp-Witted Wife', *Scottish Historical Review*, 12 (1915), 413–17.

41. Eleanor Hull, 'Legends and Traditions of the Cailleach Bheara or Old Woman (Hag) of Beare', *Folklore*, 38 (1927), 225–54.

42. J.G. Mackay, 'The Deer-Cult and the Deer-Goddess-Cult of the Ancient Caledonians', *Folklore*, 43 (1932), 144–74.

43. *Scottish Folklore and Folk Life*, Glasgow, 1935; the sections on the Cailleach are on pp. 136–70.

44. Upon trawling the internet on 17 November 2020, I immediately found it repeated on Wikipedia, Mythopedia and the sites of FolkloreThursday, Owlcation, Puffins and Pies, Spooky Scotland and The Irish Place.

45. See Proinsias McCana, *Celtic Mythology*, London, 1968, 92–3; Tomás Ó Cathasaigh, 'The Eponym *Cnogba*', *Éigse*, 23 (1989), 26–7; and Katharine Simms, 'The Poet as Chieftain's Widow', in Donnchadh ÓCorráin et al., eds, *Sages, Saints and Storytellers*, Maynooth, 1989, 400–11.

46. Referenced in n.2. He had been working towards this book since publishing 'Continuity and Adaptation in the Legends of Cailleach Bhérra', *Béaloiddeas*, 56 (1988), 153–78, as part of the flurry of interest among Irish scholars in the Cailleach as an ancient goddess during the late 1980s, evident in the note above. The book may therefore be read partly as an impressive late consequence of that interest.

Epilogue: The Green Man

1. 'The "Green Man" in Church Architecture', *Folk-Lore*, 50 (1939), 45–57.

2. This, and the connection between the two of them, was first noted by Roy Judge, *The Jack-in-the-Green*: on pp. 42–4 of the 2nd, London, 2000, edition.

3. 'The Roof Bosses in Ely Cathedral', *Transactions of the Cambridge Antiquarian Society*, 32 (1932), 36; 'The Roof Bosses in Worcester Cathedral', *Transactions of the Worcestershire Archaeological Society* (November 1934), 75–86.

4. Margaret Murray, 'Female Fertility Figures', *Journal of the Royal Anthropological Institute*, 64 (1934), 93–100. Murray's interpretation of the figures as pagan divinities remained standard until the 1970s and 1980s, when it ran into the tide of revisionism. The work of Jörgen Andersen, *The Witch on the Wall*, Copenhagen, 1977, and Anthony Weir and James Jerman, *Images of Lust*, London, 1986, demonstrated that they were part of a package of motifs

developed in the Romanesque pilgrimage churches of France in the eleventh and twelfth centuries, and exported from there to Spain and Britain, and then to Ireland. As such, they appeared within an elite and pious Christian context, and the last two authors suggested plausibly that they were intended to warn of the evils of lust, rather than to provoke it. Despite this, they have been absorbed into the imagery of some parts of the recent Goddess movement, using the interpretation of them as female deities (or a female deity) spread by Murray. Accordingly, one of the readers of my proposal for this book to Yale University Press urged me to couple the sheelas with the Green Man in this present chapter or substitute them for him, as another example of a modern creation of a deity-form; the report suggested that this would also make a better fit with the female beings considered earlier in the book. It is an entirely understandable and intelligent recommendation, but I decided against it for the following reasons. First, the sheelas represent a single image and not a composite fusing of many figures and images as the Green Man does. Second, there may actually be some genuine ancient pagan input into the reception of the sheela motif in Ireland, where it appears at times on medieval secular buildings as well as churches, and in places where the human eye cannot reach. Nineteenth-century Irish folklore included the belief that the exposure of a woman's genitalia could ward off evil and misfortune, and this may perhaps be linked to local employment of the sheelas. For different recent considerations of the image, see Eamonn Kelly, 'Sheela-na-gigs in the National Museum of Ireland', in Michael Ryan, ed., *Irish Antiquities*, Bray, 1992, 173–84; and 'Irish Sheela-na-gigs and Related Figures', in Nicola McDonald, ed., *Medieval Obscenities*, York, 2006, 124–37; Joanne McMahon and Jack Roberts, *The Sheela-na-Gigs of Ireland and Britain*, Dublin, 2000; Catherine Karkov, 'Sheela-na-gigs and Other Unruly Women', in Collum Hourihane, *From Ireland Coming*, Princeton, 2001, 313–31; Barbara A. Freitag, *Sheela-na-Gigs*, London, 2004; Rosemary Power, 'Ionas's Sheela-na-Gig and its Visual Context', *Folklore*, 123 (2012), 330–54; Jack Roberts, *Sheela-na-Gig*, Port Townsend, 2019.

5. Margaret Murray, *The God of the Witches*, published 1933; the references in the 1970 Oxford reprint are on pp. 40–2, 48.

6. This contempt and loathing was associated with not just an evangelical rationalism but also an ingrained elitism. He believed that all advances in the human condition had been made by a few exceptional thinkers, with the masses playing no part in them at all. He regarded the great majority of humanity as stupid, weak, ignorant and superstitious, and so thought democracy an inferior form of government to dictatorship by a gifted ruler. Nor was he squeamish about the means that such a man might use to reach the top, declaring that those least scrupulous in acquiring power had often been best in using it. He despised non-European races, this feeling increasing with the darkening of their skin, but his contempt for, and fear of, the European working class, and especially that of the countryside, was almost as profound. He saw academics like himself as having the same role in regulating and indoctrinating the masses as justices of the peace had over domestic commoners and colonial officials over native peoples. Even for a person of his time, and especially among British intellectuals, these attitudes were unusually right-wing. They are examined, with much quotation, in Robert Ackerman's biography *J.G. Frazer*, Cambridge, 1987, but some are also in plain view in the most popular version of *The Golden Bough*, the abridged single-volume one of 1922, on pp. 12–13, 46–7 and 55.

7. This is apparent, for example, in the field of witchcraft beliefs, for which development see my own book *The Witch*, London, 2017, 3–43.

8. Frazer's relationship with the changing intellectual currents of his age is carefully explained in Ackerman's biography, preceded by R. Angus Downie, *Frazer and "The Golden Bough"*, London, 1970, and followed by Robert Fraser, *The Making of "The Golden Bough"*, New York, 1990. For later notable appraisals of his work and reputation, across the decades, see Edmund R. Leach, 'Golden Bough or Gilded Twig?', *Daedalus* (Spring 1961), 371–89; Joseph Fontenrose, *The Ritual Theory of Myth*, Berkeley, 1971; and Mary Beard, 'Frazer, Leach and Virgil', *Comparative Studies in Society and History*, 34 (1992), 203–24. I had to

reckon with Frazer's work in three books of mine from the 1990s: *The Pagan Religions of the Ancient British Isles*, Oxford, 1991, 325–8; *The Stations of the Sun: A History of the Ritual Year in Britain*, Oxford, 1996, passim; and *The Triumph of the Moon: A History of Modern Pagan Witchcraft*, Oxford, 1999, 114–24.Overall, my own relationship with Frazer's work falls into three different categories. The first consists of issues such as the interpretation of harvest customs, on which I have simply reported a debate, summarizing the theories of Frazer (and Mannhardt) and then the objections of their critics and concluding that at present the latter seem to be given more credit by specialists. I do not, however, state flatly that Frazer and Mannhardt were wrong, or indeed provide an opinion of my own. The second category consists of attitudes to the general methodology and arguments of *The Golden Bough*, where I concur with the dominant academic opinion that both are flawed, for reasons given here. However, as also stated here, I do not think that all of its ideas are wrong, or that it lacks any value. The third category consists of Frazer's conclusions (based partly on the work of Sir John Rhys) that Halloween was the pagan Celtic New Year and feast of the dead. This is the one point at which I have ventured opinions of my own: that in neither case is the evidence sufficient to sustain those conclusions. I have not claimed that either is disproved, but I do not find the deductions of Rhys and Frazer convincing. Since I published that verdict a quarter of a century ago, no experts in medieval Irish or Welsh literature, or Iron Age religion, or folklore, have challenged my suggestions (somewhat to my surprise).

9. For this, see John B. Vickery, *The Literary Impact of "The Golden Bough"*, Princeton, 1973; and Robert Fraser, ed., *Sir James Frazer and the Literary Imagination*, London, 1990. Unsurprisingly, one of the areas of culture on which the book made a significant impact was modern Paganism and witchcraft: as one example, the initiatory name of Alex Sanders, the 'King of the Witches' in Britain in the 1960s and 1970s, was taken from it, and Frazer's myth of the sacrificial king was an important one to him.

10. James George Frazer, *The Golden Bough*, London, abridged edn, 1922, 128–34, 297–300.

11. The key text here is Jacob's huge book, *Deutsche Mythologie*, first published in 1835.

12. Wilhelm Mannhardt, *Roggenwolf und Roggenhund*, Danzig, 1866; *Die Korndämonen*, Berlin, 1868; *Antike Wald- und Feldkulte*, Berlin 1877; and *Mythologische Forschungen*, Strassburg, 1884.

13. Frazer, *The Golden Bough*, 129, 322–3.

14. W.R.S. Ralston, 'Forests and Field Myths', *The Contemporary Review*, 31 (Feb. 1878), 526. Ralston was a retired functionary at the British Museum, and an expert on Russia.

15. This had been done long before. In 1903 the civil servant and writer on medieval and early modern theatre, Sir Edmund Chambers, applied the name to Frazer's vegetation god (in *The Medieval Stage*, published in London, vol. 1, 185–6). So did the classicist A.B. Cook in 1906, who was the first to give it capital letters, in 'The European Sky-God', *Folk-Lore*, 17, pp. 340–1). These early references were first hunted down by Roy Judge, for *The Jack-in-the-Green*, 2nd edn, 91. By the 1930s it was already circulating in popular culture in this context, and the occult novelist Dion Fortune employed it in this sense in *The Goat Foot God*, London, 1936, 165.

16. Mary Anderson, *Design for a Journey*, Cambridge, 1940, 112–15; Arthur Bernard Cook, *Zeus: Volume Three*, Cambridge, 1940, 1133.

17. *Medieval Roof Bosses*, Cambridge, 1948, 65–8 and plates 300–19.

18. By both Chambers and Cook, in the works listed in n. 15 above.

19. *Medieval English Poetry*, London, 1957, 219. Speirs had been proposing the same idea in articles since 1949.

20. In *Seasonal Feasts and Festivals*, London, 1961, 288–9.

21. Published in London in 1966.

22. Published in London in 1969.

23. *Down by the Greenwood Side*, first performed in 1969.

24. Ronald Sheridan and Anne Ross, *Grotesques and Gargoyles*, Newton Abbot, 1975: quotation on p. 8. Despite our different views on the evidence for surviving paganism, Anne and

I became friendly towards the end of her life, an alliance commenced when I defended her spectacular interpretation of the bog body called Lindow Man on the grounds that, as the find could be interpreted in various different ways, her reading of it was a quite legitimate, if speculative, reconstruction.

25. Exeter University Archive, MS 416/PRO/4. I owe this reference to Sara Hannant.

26. Shown on 16 November 1990.

27. This observation is based on my own knowledge of British Pagans in the 1990s, when I was writing my works on them and their history. Symbolically, one of the main shops of Pagan art in Britain's main New Age centre at Glastonbury took the name of 'the Goddess and the Green Man'.

28. The examples of which I am aware are Mike Harding, *A Little Book of the Green Man*, London, 1998; Clive Hicks, *The Green Man: A Field Guide*, Faversham, 2000; Fran and Geoff Doel, *The Green Man in Britain*, Stroud, 2000; John Matthews, *The Quest for the Green Man*, London, 2001; Peter Hill, *In Search of the Green Man*, Chieveley, 2004; Paul Broadhurst, *The Green Man and the Dragon*, Launceston, 2006; Gary R. Varner, *Mythic Forest, the Green Man and the Spirit of Nature*, New York, 2006; Mark Olly, *Revealing the Green Man*, Winchester, 2016; and Nina Lyon, *Uprooted: On the Trail of the Green Man*, London, 2016. The last of these shows how far the genre can be stretched, as it is a sophisticated and witty examination of the uses to which the figure can be put at the present day, and keeps its tongue in its cheek for most of the time. It, moreover, recognizes that there is no hard evidence for the associations of different figures and motifs made by Lady Raglan, so that the present Green Man is an interconnected series of myths. Nevertheless, the author still sees him as a symbol of the superior force of nature, with which our species needs to remake a relationship as part of a questioning of the fallacy of human progress; and she records her own instinctual belief that the medieval carvings were honoured by ordinary people as a fertility deity.

29. Fran and Geoff Doel were lecturers in Cultural Studies at the University of Kent. Conversely, the reviewer who treated their book critically in the journal of the Folklore Society, for being based too much on Frazer's methodology, was an independent scholar, a librarian: Elaine Bradtke, in *Folklore*, 114/1 (2003), 132–4.

30. Entitled simply *The Jack-in-the-Green* and first published in Cambridge by Brewer.

31. Like most of the key British revisionist writers, in history, archaeology and literary and folklore studies, Roy Judge was known to me personally. He contacted me in the 1990s, because he liked my books, and we became friendly.

32. The earliest records of it are drawings, published in London, which invariably show the Jack in an urban, and apparently metropolitan, backdrop.

33. This was my own in *The Rise and Fall of Merry England*, Oxford, 1994, where I considered the records for seasonal customs in the period between 1450 and 1700 and found them so rich that it seems hardly credible that one of them should have been carried on without a single mention. To declare that the first record for an activity is not the same as the actual time of appearance of it is only a tenable position if it can be shown that the evidence for the periods before that first record is patchy enough to allow a loss of information.

34. Roy emphasized that there is no solid evidence that the Jack evolved directly from the 'garland', though this had been suggested before and the two were sometimes confused at the time: on pp. 25–6. There seems to be no doubt, however – and this is much more important – that the *custom* of going round with the Jack developed out of that of going about with the 'garland', and that this originated with the milkmaids.

35. Judge, *The Jack-in-the-Green*, 76–7.

36. Roy Judge, 'The Green Man Revisited', in John Hutchings and Juliette Wood, eds., *Colour and Appearance in Folklore*, London, 1991, 51–5.

37. Judge, *The Jack-in-the-Green*, 2nd edn, London, 2000, 86–7.

38. As part of the general revival of traditional British folk customs in recent decades, the Jack-in-the-Green has reappeared as part of May festivities in different parts of England, especially at Deptford at the Kent end of Greater London and Hastings in Sussex. For an

excellent guide to the latter celebration, which completely understands and accepts Roy Judge's history while showing the power and historicity of the figure within Judge's context, see Keith Leech, *The Hastings Traditional Jack in the Green*, Hastings, 2008. I am very grateful to the author for the gift of this book.

39. Georgina Boyes, 'Dressing the Past', in Theresa Buckland and Juliette Wood, eds., *Aspects of British Calendar Customs*, Sheffield, 1993, 105–18. This essay was delivered at a conference on the former date, the proceedings of which needed nine years to reach publication.

40. For the records of this custom in Britain, see Hutton, *The Stations of the Sun*, 226–43.

41. Barbara Lowe, 'Robin Hood in the Light of History', *Journal of the English Folk Dance and Song Society*, 7/4 (1955), 228–39; Maurice Keen, *The Outlaws of Medieval England*, London, 1961; David Wiles, *The Early Plays of Robin Hood*, London, 1981; J.C. Holt, *Robin Hood*, London, 2nd edn, 1989; Colin Richmond, 'An Outlaw and Some Peasants', *Nottingham Medieval Studies*, 37 (1993), 90–101; Stephen Knight, *Robin Hood*, Oxford, 1994.

42. There is a stray early reference to a play about him at Exeter in 1427, but this seems an isolated occurrence which did not establish or observe a tradition.

43. Bella Millett, 'How Green is the Green Knight?', *Nottingham Medieval Studies*, 37 (1994), 137–51. In 2007 an American academic, Larissa Tracy, published 'A Knight of God or of the Goddess?', *Arthuriana*, 17.3, 31–55, in which she argued that the poem reflected a multi-faith society, part Christian and part pagan. I think that she makes some interesting points about the work itself but gets the cultural context wrong by misunderstanding Ludo Milis's edited collection and so confusing surviving paganism with pagan survivals (for all of which, see chapter 1 of this book). Not even she, however, suggests that the Green Knight is a vegetation spirit.

44. Brandon C. Centerwall, 'The Name of the Green Man', *Folklore*, 108 (1997), 25–32.

45. Bryant Lillywhite, *London Signs*, London, 1972, 246–50; Jacob Larwood and John Camden Hotten, *The History of Signboards*, London, 1866, 367 and Plate XV.

46. In the epilogue to *As You Like It*.

47. I saw a bough of foliage still being used as a sign that wine was sold at a house outside which it was displayed in the mountains of Viterbo, Italy, in 1981.

48. The two classic surveys are Richard Bernheimer, *Wild Men in the Middle Ages*, Cambridge, MA, 1952; and Timothy Husband, *The Wild Man*, New York, 1980.

49. Jeremy Harte, *The Green Man*, Andover, 2001, 16, thought they were mermen.

50. I. Weber-Kellerman, 'Laubkönig und Schässmeier Geschichte und Deutung pfingslichter Vegetationsgebräuche in Thuringen', *Deutches Jahrbuch für Volkskunde*, 4 (1958), 366–85.

51. Published at Ipswich by Brewer.

52. It was also returned to a religious one in Scotland in the eighteenth century by becoming a popular motif on Scottish gravestones, as a symbol of fleshly decay and/or resurrection: Betty Wilsher, 'Scottish Churchyard Memorials in the Eighteenth Century', *Local Historian*, 23/2 (May 1993), 70–1; and 'The Green Man as an Emblem on Scottish Tombstones', *Markers: The Proceedings of the Association for Gravestone Studies*, 11 (1992), 58–77.

53. Kathleen Basford, *The Green Man*, Ipswich, 1978, 8, 19–20.

54. Kathleen Basford, 'A New View of "Green Man" Sculptures', *Folklore*, 102/2 (1991), 237–9.

55. Rita Wood, 'Before the Green Man', *Medieval Life*, 14 (Autumn 2000), 8–13. Another independent scholar, Tina Negus, put a piece into another magazine, serving a combined readership of sympathetic archaeologists and earth mysteries researchers, which suggested that the Knights Templar played a significant part in spreading the motif, but this has not been taken up as the image does not seem to feature especially often or early in their churches: 'The Knights Templar and the Green Man', *3rd Stone*, 43 (2002), 45–8.

56. Later, Joana Filipa Fonseca Antunes, in 'Metamorphoses of the Green Man and the Wild Man in Portuguese Medieval Art', in Flocel Sabaté, ed., *Ideology in the Middle Ages*, Leeds, 2019, 333–58, noted that, in that nation, traces of colour survived on some of the heads and showed that they were painted gold as well as green, which makes a fit with Jeremy Harte's observation.

57. Jeremy Harte, *The Green Man*, Andover, 2001; quotations on pp. 8, 10, 18 and 19. I was unable during the epidemic to gain access to a library which had a copy of Jeremy's guide, and commented on the fact to him, whereupon, with typical generosity, he sent me a copy of his own.

58. This was also noted by Tina Negus, 'Medieval Foliate Heads', *Folklore*, 114/2 (2003), 247–61, who proposed the term 'green beasts' for the animal heads. Like Rita Wood, she found a range of Christian references which might have fitted the motif, whether human or animals.

59. Mercia MacDermott, *Explore Green Men*, Wymeswold, 2003: quotation from p. 163.

60. Richard Hayman, 'Green Men and the Way of All Flesh', *British Archaeology*, 100 (2008), 12–17; 'The Ballad of the Green Man', *History Today*, 60/4 (2010), 37–46; *The Green Man*, Oxford, 2010.

61. I do not want to give the impression that academic authors had neglected the subject completely: see, for example, Alex Woodcock, *Liminal Images*, Oxford, 2005, a study of medieval architectural sculpture in the south of England published in the British Archaeological Reports series, which deals with the foliate heads on pp. 47–63. I do feel, however, that they lagged behind the independent scholars in their treatment of it and that their conclusions tended simply to repeat those of the latter. Some have done valuable work by extending study of the topic geographically, such as Antunes's work on Portugal referenced in n. 56.

62. See, for example, the admirably impartial and objective summary of the state of knowledge by Luke Martin in his 'Enigma of the Green Man' website, accessed 8 December 2020.

63. Noted by various commentators on the subject: the most accessible reference is probably MacDermott, *Explore Green Men*, 2.

Conclusion

1. Published by Pennsylvania University Press.

2. On these, see especially Michael Ostling, ed., *Fairies, Demons and Nature Spirits: 'Small Gods' at the Margins of Christendom*, London, 2018. The editor makes his own interesting contribution to the debate over the terminology of 'pagan survivals' by pointing out that, although fairies and nature spirits may have had pagan origins, they 'are not just marginalized or diabolized pagan remnants, they are continually re-performed, recreated through Christian ritual and Christian discourse': p. 42.

3. One of the anonymous readers who provided reports on the proposal for this book to the press urged me to discuss female saints and the Virgin Mary in it as well, in the context of the medieval divine feminine. They are definitely related to that, and the proposal is an entirely understandable and meritorious one; but they are also very different in kind, as suggested here, and represent a very large subject in which I have little expertise.

INDEX

A' Chailleach 146
Abbots Bromley Horn Dance 4, 23
Aberdeen 93
Abundia, Lady (Abundance, Habonde, Habundia) 118, 120, 122, 123, 132
Adam 144, 184
'Adventure of Art, Son of Conn, The' *see Echtra Airt meic Cuinn*
Aecerbot (Field Blessing) 8, 46, 206 n17
Aelfric of Eynsham 8, 26, 200 n28
Aelfwine 76
'Aesir' 8
agnosticism 5, 15
agrestes feminae 78
Aislingemeic Con Glinne (anon.) 149
Alan of Lille 48, 49, 206 n19–20
Alberus, Erasmus 131
Alcamo 129
Alchemist, The (Ben Jonson) 104
alchemy 102
Alexander, Margaret 94, 101
al-Khidr 171 *see also* Green Man
Alps
    Lady of the Night 131, 134
    witch trials 123, 124, 125
Alsace 139
Althorp 99

America
    Afro-American religions 40
    Great Goddess theory 61, 69, 72, 73–4
    scholars 2, 10, 13, 39, 113, 157
    settlement 71
American Anthropologist 163
Amis, Sir Kingsley 169, 172
Ana Ní Áine 146
Anatomy of Melancholy (Robert Burton) 132
Anderson, Jonet 94
Anderson, William
    criticism 184–5, 186
    Great Goddess 171, 172
    Green Man 170, 172, 175
    Green Man 170
    influence 173, 175, 177, 184–5, 186, 187, 188
    medieval scholar 171
    psychology 170–2, 190
angels 77, 79, 82, 193, 194
Anglesey 154
Anglo-Saxons
    charms 7–8, 26, 38–9, 46–7, 199 n23, n24, n27
    elves 76–8, 211 n15–16
    gods 8, 26
    mythology 86

227

INDEX

animals
  Artemis 53
  Cailleach 144, 145, 154
  cults 3–4, 24, 203 n90–1
  Diana 112, 114, 122
  elves 76
  fairies 86, 129
  Lady of the Night 114, 117, 118, 122, 135, 136, 137, 142
  magic 31, 33, 124, 125
  Morgan 84
  Natura 48
  sacrifice 12
Anne of Denmark 99
Annwn (Annwfn) 89, 90
anthropology 61, 69–70, 161–3, 167
Apennines 127
Aphrodite 55
Apollo 34, 55
Apuleius of Madaura 43, 50
Aradia (Herodias) 11, 141
archaeology
  19th century 58
  early 20th century 18, 61–3
  feminist 72–4
  Great Goddess 61–7, 72–4
  later 20th century 64, 68–9, 71, 185
  Near East 58
Ardener, Shirley 70
Ardennes 113
Ardnamurchan 146
Argante, Queen 84, 85
Argyll 145, 154, 155
Aristotle 43, 44, 45, 46
Arles 113
Armagh 149–50
Art mac Cuinn 152
Artemis 41, 53, 156
Arthur, King
  Avalon 83, 84
  fairies 86
  Green Knight 178
  legend 83–5, 89, 97, 172, 201 n57
  literature 83–5, 86, 92, 97, 152
  Morgan 84, 211 n23
  Wales 89, 152
  witches 92, 204 n109
Arthur's Seat 92
Arthurian legend 83–5, 89, 97, 172, 201 n57
Artus de Bretagne (anon.) 86
Asia Minor 41–2, 58, 59, 186
astrology 83, 102

astronomy 32
atheism 5, 15
Athlone 145, 153
Auberon see Oberon
Auden, W.H. 70
Aue, Hartmann von see Hartmann von Aue
Augustine of Hippo 45, 46, 78
Augustus, Emperor 42
Auldearn 94
Aureola 98
Australia 61, 69
Austria 131, 139, 165
autumn
  Cailleach 146
  fruit 185
  Lammas 201 n55
  literature 207 n37
  Queen Mab 215
  thanksgiving 34
Avalon
  Arthur 83, 84
  fairies 86, 87, 91, 132
  Morgan 83–5
Avebury 71
Ayrshire 92

Babylon 90, 129
Babylonia 161
Bacchus 183, 187
Bachofen, Johann Jakob 59
Badb 150
Balkans 63, 67, 72
Barclodiad y Gawres 154
Barnsdale 178
Basford, Kathleen 182–4, 185, 186, 187, 188, 189
Bastille 51
Battle of Ventry, The see Cath Finntrágha
Bavaria 139
Bayeux tapestry 13
BBC 172
Beaker People 63, 64
Beara peninsula 144, 148, 149
Beaujeu, Renaud de 83
Befana 139–40
Bel Inconnu, Le (Renaud de Beaujeu) 83
Beltane 14
'Bensozia' 120, 121
Berchta (Berchte, Berthe) see Percht
Berdok 107
Bernard Silvester 47–8, 206 n18
Bernardino of Siena 123

INDEX

Berners, Lord *see*Bourchier, John
Bertold of Regensburg 119, 121
Bes 31
Bible
  Herodias 11, 114–15, 117, 140, 142
  Huldah 116–17
  nature 184, 185, 186
  paganism and 37, 163
  Wild Man 183, 184
Birtwistle, Sir Harrison 169, 172
Blackwood, Algernon 56
Blasket Islands 144, 146
boggins 4
BoghanaCaillich 145
Bohemia 182
Bonaparte, Napoleon 9
Botticelli, Sandro 34
Bourchier, John, Lord Berners 96, 102
Boyes, Georgina 175, 198 n6, 225 n39
Boyman, Jonet 92, 101
Bridget, Saint 62
Briffault, Robert 65–6, 71, 208 n71
Britain
  archaeology 61–3, 64
  architecture 170
  danger from the East 71
  elves and fairies 75–8, 87–8, 109, 158
  fertility rites 16–17
  Green Man 160–1, 168, 172–3
  Lady of the Night 132
  pagan survival in 1–4, 11–15
  religious tolerance 17–18
  scholars 11–13, 16–17, 36–7, 39, 59,
    60–3, 73, 162–4, 166, 182–5
  sheela-na-gigs 7, 161
  social changes 28–30, 109
  urbanisation 15–16, 19–21
British Association for the Advancement of
    Science 161
Brittany 64, 82, 84, 86
Brontë, Charlotte 53, 207 n34
Bronze Age 4, 156
Browning, Robert 53–4
Brueghel, Pieter 181
Bruidhean Chéise Corainn (anon.) 151, 153
Bryant, Sir Arthur 70
Buchan, John 5–6, 12, 14, 165, 199 n20
Buchedd Collen ('The Life of St Collen') 89
Buddhists 156
'Bull of Battle Was He, A' *see* 'Taru Trin
    Anuidin Blaut'
Burchard of Worms 78, 113–14, 117, 120,
    140, 215 n4

Burkert, Walter 42
Burton, Robert 132

Caesarius of Arles 112
Caillagh ny Groamach 147
Caillagh ny Gueshagh 147
Cailleach (Cailliach) **143–58**
  animals 144, 145–6, 154, 155–6
  goddess 148, 150, 153, 155–8
  humans and 194–5
  Ireland 143–6, 147, 148–53, 154,
    155–7
  Isle of Man 147
  literature 148–53, 154–5, 157–8
  name 149
  origins 143, 159, 196
  pronunciation 219 n1
  Scotland 143–4, 145, 146–8, 152–3,
    154–6, 157
  Wales 151–2, 154
  winter 146, 155, 195
Cailleach Bheara 148, 149–50, 153, 155,
    158, 219 n16, 221 n32, n46
Cailleach na h-Abhan 147
Cailleach Point 154
Cailleach uisge 147
'Caillech Bérri Bui' (anon.) 148–9, 157
Cain 141
Cairngorm Mountains 154
cairns 144, 145, 148, 154
Caitiarn, St 145, 146, 153
călus 140
Cambridge University 20, 39, 60, 162,
    167
Campbell, John Gregorson 155, 221 n40
Campbell, Joseph 73
Campion, Thomas 100
Canary Islands 83
'Carlin of Beinn Bhreac' 154
Carmichael, Alexander 154
Carmina Gadelica (Alexander Carmichael)
    154
carvings *see* sculptures
Castleton Garland 160, 175, 176
Catal Höyük 64, 66, 74, 208 n69–70, 210
    n102
Catalonia 130
Cath Finntrágha (The Battle of Ventry,
    anon.) 151
Catholic Church *see* Roman Catholic
    Church
Cave, C.J.P. 161, 167
Celticists 12

INDEX

Celts
    fairies 80, 81, 211 n15
    languages 158
    Mother Goddess 62
    paganism 201 n62
    see also Gaels
Centaur, The (Algernon Blackwood) 56
Centerwall, Brandon 179–81
Ceres 31, 42, 52
Cerne Abbas Giant 2, 18, 23, 202 n87
Cerus 42
Cevennes 120, 121
Chailleach, An 145
Champollion, Jean-François 73
Charles I 107, 204 n104
Charles II 105, 160
charms 7–8, 9, 26–7, 32, 38–9, 46, 94
    ancient 31
    Anglo-Saxon 7–8, 26, 38–9, 46–7, 199
        n23, n24, n27
    Christian 27, 46, 94, 205 n122
    fertility 8
    healing 7–8, 26, 39, 94
    literature 11
    magicians 9, 32, 100
    sale 105
Chartres 47
Chaucer, Geoffrey 48, 86–7, 206 n23
Chestre, Thomas 87
Childe, Gordon 64, 208 n67
China 40
Christ *see* Jesus Christ
Christianity
    criticism 162–3
    folk 2, 20, 26, 27, 31, 35–8, 39
    Islam and 187
    loss of power 5, 9, 12, 15–16, 28–9, 192,
        197
    Mother Earth 53–5, 62, 66, 74
    official faith 1, 15–17, 23, 44–5, 50, 157,
        161
    pagan influence 2, 7–8, 15, 17–19, 30,
        31–2, 34–8, 39, 45–7, 48–9, 161, 185,
        196
Christianization 1–2, 44, 157
Christmas 33, 123, 139
Christsonday 93
Church, Holy Lady 193
churches
    decorations 7–8, 15, 18, 25–6, 31, 160–2,
        167, 169, 180–1, 187, 188–9
    Middle Ages 2, 7–8, 15, 18, 25–6,
        160–1

    pagan elements 7–8, 15, 18, 25–6, 30, 31,
        36
Churchill, Sir Winston 70
Circe 83, 84
Claris et Laris (anon.) 84, 211–12 n23
Clark, Sir George 12
Claudian 45, 48, 60
Clontarf 151
Cohn, Norman 36–7, 39
Common Ground 170
confidence tricks 102–5
Connacht 144, 145
Connemara 144, 146
Conrad, Joseph 165
Constance, Lake 116
Corcu Duibne 149
Cork 144, 145, 157
corn dollies 64
Corn Mother 4
Cornwall 6
Corryvrechan 146, 150
cosmos 9, 32, 43, 45, 46
Cotswolds 18, 62
Counter-Reformation 15, 36
Couserans 120, 121
Coventry 3
Crawford, O.G.S. 64
Crete 59
'Cricket' 107
Cromarty 147
Cronk yn Irree 147
Crowcombe 180, 181
Culhwch ac Olwen (anon.) 89, 152
cults
    ancient 31, 43, 44, 64, 133, 135, 163
    animal 3
    fertility 164
    Cailleach 156
    Jesus Christ 30
    Lady Godiva 3
    Lady of the Night 112, 141
    literature 6, 12, 13
    nature 40, 41, 51
    saints 27
    sky god 65
    Virgin Mary 171
    witchcraft 9, 10, 12, 13, 37, 123–4, 141
cunning folk *see* wise folk
Cybele 41, 202 n66

Dafydd ap Gwilym 89
Dagda 150–1
'Dame Tryamour' (Thomas Chestre) 87

INDEX

Dames, Michael 72, 170
Dana 55
Daniel, Glyn 64
Day, John 108
Dekker, Thomas 98
Delumeau, Jean 36, 39
demons
  elves 76, 77, 78, 106
  fairies 84, 89, 95
  gods 26
  Lady of the Night 112, 115, 118, 119,
    121, 128
  literature 90
  Reformation 91
  sex 78, 79
  Wild Man 183
  witch religion 37, 79
Derbyshire 160
Devil
  Lady of the Night 114, 118, 127, 140
  literature 6
  Morgan 84
  sex 78
  witch trials 94
  see also devils, Satan
devils
  fairies 95, 97
  Lady of the Night 111
  magicians 12
  real 193, 194
  sex 78, 94
  witch trials 92, 94
  see also Devil, Satan
Devil's Own, The (Nora Lofts) 6
Diana
  Elizabeth I 98
  Lady of the Night 111–14, 120, 121–3,
    128, 132, 133, 138, 140–1, 196
  Mother Earth 60
  Roman goddess 96–7, 138, 162
  witch religion 11
Digde 149
Dindshenchas 150
Dionysus 179
Discourse on the Worship of Priapus, A
  (Richard Payne Knight) 16
Disir 137–8
Dives and Pauper (anon.) 132
Dolomites 124–5
Dorset 104
dragons 84, 181
Drayton, Michael 107, 214 n96
Druids 11, 204 n109

Dublin 94
'Dun Raven, white nun of Beare' (*cailleach
  Bérre bán*) 149–50
Dunbar, William 91
Dunfermline 90
Dunlop, Bessie 92, 101
Dusii 78

Earth, Mother **41–74**
  ancient 18, 41–4, 58, 59–60
  humans and 195, 210 n104
  late Roman Empire 44–6
  Middle Ages 8, 46–50, 110
  modern day 56–8, 65–7, 68–74, 75, 159,
    168–9, 170–2, 189–90, 191
  prehistoric 58–63, 64–5, 208 n58
  Romanticism 51–2, 58
  Victorian Age 53–6, 165
Easter 165
Ebendorfer, Thomas 122
Echtra Airt meic Cuinn (The Adventure of
  Art, son of Conn, anon.) 152
Eckhart, Meister 127
Eden, Garden of 56, 185
Edinburgh 92, 94, 152
Edwardians 20, 29, 60, 68, 176, 191
Egereon, King 96 *see also* Fairy King
Egypt 31–2, 43, 59, 73, 161
Ekhart *see* Eckhart, Meister
Elchyyell 102
Elfame (Elfhame) 92–3
Eliade, Mircea 13
Eliot, George 19
Eliot, T.S. 70, 165
Elizabeth I 97–8
Elphillock 93
Elspeth, Queen 92 *see also* Fairy Queen
elves
  Anglo-Saxons 8, 75–8
  Arthurian legend 84
  folk tales 35, 106
  goodness 141
  Green Knight 178
  humans and 194–5
  Lady of the Night 132
  literature 86–7, 91, 97
  magic 103
  Middle Ages 75–9
  sex 78
  see also fairies
Elvetham 98
Ember Days 125, 127, 128
Encyclopaedia Britannica 12

INDEX

England
  ancient monuments 2
  Anglo-Saxons 26, 76, 78
  architecture 161, 167–8, 183, 187–8
  countryside 21, 202 n78
  elves 76–9, 88
  fairies 87–8, 95–100, 102–6, 109
  Georgians 70
  Green Man 165–6, 167, 180
  Jack-in-the-Green 160, 161, 165, 166,
    173–6
  Lady of the Night 132
  literature 48, 51–7, 82, 95–100, 102,
    151, 177–8
  May Day 160, 165, 166, 173–6, 177
  Middle Ages 14, 70, 77, 79, 160
  mythology 86
  Scottish invasions 35
  traditions 3–4, 23–4, 34, 169
  Tudors 34, 96–8, 102
  urbanisation 19
  witch trials 12, 100–1, 102–3
Enlightenment 9, 58
Enna 31
environmentalism 170, 171, 173, 188
Epiphany 122, 123, 139
'Episcopi'
  canon law text 111, 138
  England 132
  Lady of the Night 111, 113, 115, 123, 128
  renewals 120, 122, 140
Epona 134–5, 138
erce 8, 46–7, 206 n17
Erceldoune, Thomas of 88–9, 93
Erec (Hartmann von Aue) 84
Erzgebirge 182
Esclaramonde 83
'Essay on the Worship of the Generative
    Powers during the Middle Ages in
    Western Europe' (Thomas Wright) 16
Essex 6, 88
Etienne de Bourbon 119–20, 121
Eurydice 85, 90
Eustace the Monk 178
Evans, Sir Arthur 59, 68, 207 n49–51
Evans, George Ewart 13, 22, 66, 201 n51,
    208 n73
Eve 144
executions *see also* trials 9, 10, 12, 101, 124
Exeter University 168
'Explore' series 186
Eyrbyggja Saga (anon.) 137
Ezekiel 183, 186

Faerie Queen, The (Edmund Spenser) 49–50,
    98
faierie 82, 85, 86, 90
fairies
  Cailleach 152, 154
  confidence tricks 102–5
  court 88–95, 96, 100, 105, 107, 195
  England 95–104
  female 83–5
  folk tales 17, 35, 75
  goodness 141
  Green Knight 178
  humans and 194–5
  Ireland 17, 80–1, 154
  Italy 124, 129
  Lady of the Night 132, 140
  literature 82–7, 88–91, 96–7, 98–100,
    106–8
  magic 87, 94, 101–5
  Middle Ages 75–9, 80
  Reformation 91–5
  Robin Hood 177
  romances 80–6
  Scotland 88–94, 154
  sex 81, 88, 93
  Wales 79, 81
  see also elves
Fairy King
  confidence tricks 104–5
  England 95–7, 99–104
  Ireland 94
  literature 85, 87, 88–9, 90–1, 96–7, 99–100
  Oberon 82–3, 96–7, 98, 99, 102
  Scotland 88, 90–1, 94
  sex 94
  Wales 89
fairy kingdom
  confidence tricksters 105
  early modern days 105–6
  England as 98
  literature 85–91, 99–100, 108, 109
  Middle Ages 77, 82
  Tudors 99–100, 103
  witch trials and 94–5
Fairy Queen **75–109**
  confidence tricks 102–5
  Elizabeth I as 98
  Elspeth 92
  England 95–8, 99–101, 109
  humans and 194–5
  impersonators 88
  Italy 129–30
  Lady of the Night and 132–3, 140

INDEX

literature 85, 86–7, 90–1, 96–7, 99–100, 104, 106–9, 153, 158
magic 91–3, 101–5
Middle Ages 75
Reformation 91–4
role 106
Scotland 88–94, 109, 132–3
sex 88, 93
Falkirk 94
Famous Historie of Chinon of England, The (Christopher Middleton) 97
fantasy novels 5–6
Fasciculus Morum 86, 132
Fassa, Val de 124–5
fatae 129
Fates 42, 60, 82
fauns 78
fays *see* fairies
felices dominae 119
feminists
  archaeology 72–4
  Green Man 190
  matriarchy 10, 65, 72, 157–8
  Mother Earth 65, 69, 72–4, 171
Ferrara 125
fertility
  goddesses 7, 61, 63, 135
  gods 7, 10, 41–2
  humans 2, 69
  images 168
  land 3–4, 8, 31, 41–2, 46
  nature 190
  religions 6, 16–17, 37
  rituals 25, 50, 140, 166
  veneration 16–17
festivals 6, 12
Field Blessing (Aecerbot) 8, 46
Fiemme, Val de 125, 127
Fife 92
figures *see* sculpture
figurines *see* sculpture
Finn mac Cumail 145, 147, 151, 152, 153
fires 2, 4, 33
Fitzwarren, Fulke 178
Fleming, Andrew 68
Flower Power 6–7
Folk-Lore Society (later Folklore Society)
  Baron Raglan 160
  early days 1, 3, 4
  Jeremy Harte 185
  Margaret Murray 14, 161, 168
  pagan survival 7, 18

renaming 25, 198 n1
Roy Judge 175
rural myth 22
witch religion 11, 14
Fool 4
Forman, Simon 102
Fortunate Island *see* Isle of Apples
Fortune, Dion 18
Fournier, Jacques 120
France
  architecture 25–6, 170, 183
  Christianisation 36
  Enlightenment 58
  Franks 111, 117, 128
  historians 10, 13, 36
  Lady of the Night 111–12, 119–20, 130
  literature 48–9, 80, 82, 120, 151
  Maid Marian 177
  mythology 86
  Revolution 51
  Roman 134–5
  sayings 179–80
  scholars 47–9, 58, 61, 67, 119–20
  traditions 24, 165
Franconia 112, 139
Franks 111–12, 116, 117, 128, 131, 134
Frazer, Sir James
  anthropology 162–4, 169, 222 n6, n8
  criticism 167, 175, 179
  Green Man 165, 168, 170, 172, 175, 176, 182, 187, 192
  influence 165, 168, 170, 172, 174, 179
  Mannhardt and 166
  pagan survival 20–1
  works 202 n76, 207 n55, 208 n68, 223 n10, n13
French Revolution 51
Freud, Sigmund 67

Gaels
  Cailleach 143–6, 148, 153–4, 155–6, 157–8, 195
  fairies 90
  gods 35
  poetry 220 n32
  see also Celts
Gage, Matilda Joslyn 10
Gaia 42, 205 n2, 210 n104
'Galadriel' (J.R.R. Tolkien) 108
Galway 145
gandr 137
Gardner, Gerald 14
Gaul 112–13

INDEX

Gawain, Sir 83
genii cuculati 136
Gentle Annie 147–8 *see also* Cailleach
Geoffrey of Monmouth 83–4, 211 n20
Georgians 24, 34, 70, 108
Gerald of Wales 77, 79, 210 n3
Gerhard, Eduard 58, 207 n46
Germanus, St 120–1, 128
Germany
  architecture 170, 180–1, 183
  folk tales 122–3, 139, 165–6
  Franks 111, 117, 128
  gods 8, 136
  Lady of the Night 111–12, 119, 130–1
  law texts 111, 113–14, 116
  literature 84, 126
  publications 50, 60
  scholars 3, 9–10, 58, 61, 67, 68, 166
  traditions 165, 182
  wars 71
  witch trials 131
Gervase of Tilbury 77, 107, 214 n95
Gimbutas, Marija 72–4, 157, 170, 209 n96,
    n99, n100, 210 n101
Ginzburg, Carlo
  Lady of the Night 113, 218 n57–9, n64
  Margaret Murray 13, 36–7
  pagan survival 39
  Richella 217 n38
  works 215 n1, n3, n5, 217 n31, n33. n35,
    n37, n40, 218 n57
Gloucester 79
goblins 35, 97, 100, 103
God (Christianity)
  arts 50
  Cailleach 154
  charms 8, 46
  creator 45, 47, 48–9, 53, 171
  daughters 193–4
  healing 8, 26
  Lady of the Night 142
  literature 17, 54, 56, 57, 163
  nature and 26, 45, 47, 48–9, 51, 53, 55,
    194
  stars and 32
God and the Goddesses (Barbara Newman) 193
goddesses
  allegorical 193–4, 196
  Asia Minor 41
  Cailleach 148, 154–8
  Celtic 150, 151
  Earth 18, 41–4, 44–7, 47–50, 50–8,
    58–68, 68–74, 165

Egyptian 31, 43, 50, 161
fairies and 81
fertility 7, 61, 63, 69
Greek 42, 53, 55, 56, 58, 128, 133–4,
    156
horse riding 3
Lady of the Night 111–14, 141
Mesopotamia 42
Middle Ages 193–4
nature 11, 14, 194
Neolithic 72, 74
pagan 35, 133, 193, 194, 195
Roman 11, 31, 34, 42, 48, 52, 55,
    111–14, 126, 134–6, 162
Scandinavian 136–7
Godiva, Lady 3, 198 n5
gods
  Celtic 35
  creator 44
  Egyptian 31
  fairies and 81
  fertility 7, 10
  Greek 55
  Green Man 161, 165, 166–7, 168, 169,
    171, 184, 186, 190
  healing 26
  Hindu 56
  horned 12, 14
  literature 17, 52
  Mesopotamian 42
  nature 11, 14, 43, 186
  pagan 195
  Roman 44, 55, 85, 87, 96–7, 179, 187
  Scandinavian 8
  sculptures 23
  sky 42, 53, 63, 64, 65
Gog Magog 153
Golden Ass, The (Apuleius of Madaura) 43
Golden Bough, The (Sir James Frazer) 162–4,
    166, 175
Golden Dawn, Hermetic Order of the
    17–18
Golden Isle 83
good ladies (good women) 120–1
Gossec, François-Joseph 51
Gothic period 187
Gowdie, Isobel 94–5, 101
Gower Peninsula 77
Gracia 130
Grahame, Kenneth 18
Grass King 165 *see also* Green Man
Graves, Robert 66, 70, 71, 165, 201 n51,
    208 n72

INDEX

Great Earth Mother *see* Earth, Mother
Great Goddess
  ancient world 58–61, 201 n51
  debate 68–70, 71–3, 156–8
  modern paganism 41, 172, 189, 193
  Neolithic 63–4
  worship 11
  see also Earth, Mother
Greeks
  goddesses 32, 42, 53, 55, 58, 59, 60, 64, 128, 133–4, 156
  literature 42, 83, 85, 134, 180
  medicine 26
  modern literature 96–7
  mythology 34, 35, 43, 44, 49, 78, 83, 86, 205–6 n2
  philosophy 43–4
  prehistory 72
green
  alcohol 179, 189
  ancient religions 183, 186
  Earth Mother 49, 54, 56
  elves and fairies 77, 85, 86, 87, 88, 89, 91, 100, 101
  Green Knight 168
  Green Man 160, 165–6, 179, 186
  Jack-in-the-Green 173
  al-Khidr 171, 186,
  May Day 160, 165, 176
  Middle Ages 178
  nature 17, 34, 165, 190
  religion 186
  Wild Man 181
Green George 165, 170, 172 *see also* Green Man
Green Knight 168, 170, 172, 177, 178–9, 190
Green Man
  demonic 183
  Earth Mother 168–9, 170, 171, 190
  environmentalism 170, 171, 172
  god 161, 165, 166–7, 168, 169, 171, 184, 186
  literature 168–9, 170, 171–2, 190, 224 n28
  Middle Ages 180–2
  modern day 168–73, 173–6, 177–9, 185–9, 192, 197
  name 161
  nature 190–1
  origins 159–61
  pub signs 161, 167, 169, 179–80, 182
  sculptures 160–1, 167, 169, 171, 180–1, 182–3, 187–8

sheela-na-gigs 169, 222 n4
  traditions 165, 166–7, 179–80
Green Man (William Anderson) 170–1
Green Man, The (Kathleen Basford) 182
Green Man, The (Henry Treece) 168
Greene, Robert 96, 213 n62
Gregory of Tours 112
Grimes Graves 62
Grimm, Brothers 166, 216 n9, n13, 217 n25, n27, 217 n48, 218 n58, n67, 219 n74–5, n77
Gui, Bernard 120, 216 n21
Guillaume d'Auvergne 118–19
Guy of Warwick (anon.) 82
gwrach 152 *see also* Cailleach
Gwyn ap Nudd 89
gypsies
'gyre carling' 152, 153, 212 n40, 220 n30 *see also* Cailleach

Habonde *see* Abundia, Lady
Habundia *see* Abundia, Lady
Hades 134
Haggard, Rider 17
hags 8, 143, 145, 151–2, 154–6, 158 *see also* Cailleach
Halloween 93, 94, 132
Hamlet (William Shakespeare) 97, 213 n64
Hammersmith 103
Hampshire 103
Hardy, Thomas 22–3
Harold Godwinson 13
Harrison, Jane Ellen 60, 66, 70, 207 n53
Harte, Jeremy 185–6, 187, 188, 189, 225 n49, n56, 226 n57
Hartmann von Aue 84
Hauteville, Jean de *see* Jean de Hauteville
Hawkes, Christopher 63, 71, 208 n65
Hawkes, Jacquetta
  early works 63, 71
  matriarchy 63–4, 66, 67, 71–2
  modernity and 69, 70
  works 208 n66, 209 n80, n84
Haxey Hood Game 3–4, 24
Hayman, Richard 187–8, 226 n60
healers
  Christian elements 205 n122
  folk 7–8, 26–7
  magical 92–3, 132
  Morgan 84
  women 157
Heart of Albion Press 186
Hebrides 90, 144, 146, 153, 154

235

INDEX

Hecate (Hekate) 41, 60, 133–4, 138
Heel of Ness 148
hell 53, 79, 88, 91, 92, 127
Henrietta Maria, Queen 107
Henry VIII 98
Henryson, Robert 90
Hera 53, 138, 215–16 n5
herbs
  Anglo-Saxons 8
  charms and 8, 46, 199 n24
  Earth 195
  Lady of the Night 124, 125
  Morgan 83
  Oberon 102
Hercules 135
Herder, Johann 58
Hereward the Wake 178
Herod 114, 115, 140
Herodias
  Aradia 11
  Bible 114–15, 117, 140, 142, 158
  goddess 114
  Herod 114–15, 140
  John the Baptist 114–15, 128
  Lady of the Night 114–15, 118, 120,
    121–2, 123, 127, 128, 140–2, 196
  villainess 117
Herodotus 180
Herolt, Johan 122
Herrick, Robert 107
Hertha 54
Hesiod 42
Hesse 139, 218 n49
Hicks, Clive 170
Highlands
  Cailleach 143, 145, 146, 154, 155
  fairies 93, 133
  mythology 35, 90, 155
Hill, Christopher 12
Hinduism 56, 205 n127
'Hobden' (Rudyard Kipling) 21
hobgoblins *see* goblins
hobs *see* goblins
'Hodge' (Richard Jeffries) 21
Holda (Holde, Holl, Hulda, Hulde, Hulle)
  114–17, 119, 131, 136, 138–9
Homer 83
Homeric hymns 42
Honnecourt, Villard de *see* Villard de
  Honnecourt
Horned One, the 12, 14
Hounslow Heath 105
Huldah (Olda) 116

hulden 119
Hull, Eleanor 155, 221 n41
Hungary 134
Huon de Bordeaux (anon.) 82–3, 96, 102,
  104

Iceland 136–7
incubi 78, 91
India 187
Indo-Europeans 61, 63–4, 72, 156, 157,
  209 n96, n98
industrialisation 16, 21, 51, 70, 171
Inguanta, Lady 129
Iona, Isle of 155
Ireland
  Cailleach 143–6, 147, 148–50, 151–2,
    155–8
  Fairy King 94
  folk tales 17, 80–1, 107, 154
  gods 34–5, 81
  high queen 62
  literature 55–6, 80, 148–9, 151–2,
    157–8, 211 n13–14
  medieval social structure 150–1
  mythology 86, 90
  sheela-na-gigs 7, 161
Irodeasa *see* Herodias
Iron Age 169
Isidore of Seville 83
Isis 31, 43, 50, 206 n6
Islam 31, 171, 186, 187, 195
Isle of Apples *see* Avalon
Isle of Man 90, 143, 147
Isle of Olyroun 87
Italy
  Christianity and paganism 31, 114
  folklore 10–11, 16, 113, 123, 125, 128–9,
    131–2, 139
  historians 13, 36–7, 61, 113
  literature 86, 120–1
  witch religion 140–1
  witch trials 123–6, 127, 141

Jack-in-the-Green
  England 160, 165, 166, 173–4
  god 161, 168, 170, 175, 190
  Green Man 170, 172, 175
  May Day 160, 165, 173–4
  modern day 176
  see also Green Man
James I (James VI) 91–2, 93, 99, 104, 132,
  204 n104
James, Edwin Oliver 168, 170

INDEX

Jane Eyre (Charlotte Brontë) 53
Jean de Hauteville 48, 206 n21
Jean de Meun 48–9, 120, 206 n22
Jeffries, Richard 21–2
Jesuits 50
Jesus Christ
  animals 124
  Cailleach 149
  charms 26
  Green Man 170
  Krishna 56
  sacred kings 162–3
  saviour 30
  vine 185
John of Salisbury 118, 216 n15
John the Baptist 114, 115, 128
Jones, Inigo 108, 214 n99
Jonson, Ben 99, 104, 213 n70–1
Judaism 30, 31
Judge, Roy 173–4, 175, 184, 224 n31,
  n34–8
Judith, Empress 116
Julius Caesar 82
Jung, Carl 67, 157, 170, 171–2, 190, 209
  n78
Justice, Lady 193

Keats, John 52–3, 207 n33
Kent 88
kerling 152 *see also* Cailleach
Kerry 144
Ketil's Saga (anon.) 137
al-Khidr 171, 186 *see also* Green Man
Killian, St 112
King (pagan cults) 3
'King Berdok' (Robert Henryson) 90
King of the May *see* May King
Kipling, Rudyard 21
Kircher, Athanasius 50, 206 n27
Knight, Richard Payne 16
Knight's Fee (Rosemary Sutcliff) 14
Kore *see* Persephone 133
Krishna 57

Labbacallee 145
'Lady Chatterley' (D.H. Lawrence) 57
Lady of the Night **110–42**
  Britain 132–3
  Epona 135
  goodness 141–2
  Hecate 133–4
  humans and 194–5
  Middle Ages 111–20, 121–6, 133–4

  modern day 138–42
  origins 110–11, 133–8
  Renaissance 126–31
  witch trials 123–8
'Lady of the Secret Isle' 82
'Lament of the Old Women of Beare, The'
  see 'Caillech Bérri Bui'
lamiae 118
Lanercost Chronicle 17
Lantern Bearers, The (Rosemary Sutcliff) 14
Lanval (Marie de France) 84–5, 87
Lapps *see* Sámi
Latha na Caillich 146
Lawrence, D.H. 18, 56–7, 165, 207 n45
Lay of the Nine Twigs 8
Layamon 84
Le Roy Ladurie, Emmanuel 13
Leaf King 165 *see also* Green Man
Legend of the Witches (Malcolm Leigh) 13
Leighton, Frederic Lord 34
Leland, Charles Godfrey
  Catholicism and 16, 202 n66
  influence 13
  Italian folklore 10–11, 16, 140–1
  pagan religion 10–11, 12, 140–1, 200
  n33–4
Levant 59, 63, 67
Lewis, Wyndham 165
Liège 114
Life of Merlin, The (Geoffrey of Monmouth)
  83
Lilly, William 102
Lincolnshire 4, 9
literature
  ancient 45–6, 47, 83, 85–6, 133–4
  documents 27
  early modern 96–8, 100–3, 106–8, 126,
  152–3
  England 48, 51–7, 82, 95–100, 102, 151,
  177–8
  folklore 153–6
  Ireland 55–6, 80, 148–9, 151–2, 157–8
  medieval 49, 55, 66, 80, 82–6, 88–90,
  106, 126, 136–8, 148–52, 157–8
  modern 5–6, 56, 66, 108–9, 165, 168–9,
  171–2
  Muslim 171
  pagan influence 30, 34
  Scotland 5–6, 88–9, 90–1, 152–3, 154–6
  Wales 66, 89, 152
  see also poetry
Little Leaf Man 165 *see also* Green Man
'Little-Little Prick' 107

INDEX

Little People 5 *see also* elves, fairies
Livingston 94
Lofts, Nora 6
Lombardy 114, 125
Lomond, Loch 153
London 6, 11, 65, 103–4, 105, 170, 173
Lord (pagan cults) 4
Lord of the Rings, The (J.R.R. Tolkien) 108
Lord's Prayer 46
Lothian 152
Loughcrew 145, 154
Louis the Pious 116
Love, Lady 193
Lowlands 90, 92, 93, 95, 132, 152
Lucifer 11, 140–1 *see also* Devil
Lucretius 44
Lugh 35
Luna 60
Luther, Martin 131
Lydia 41
Lyndsay, Sir David 90–1

mab 107
'Mab, Queen' (William Shakespeare) 106–7,
    109, 215 n104
mac Cuinn, Art *see* Art mac Cuinn
mac Cumail, Finn *see* Finn mac Cumail
Machen, Arthur 5
MacDermott, Mercia 186–7, 188, 189, 226
    n59
Mackay, J.G. 155, 156, 157, 221 n42
Mackenzie, Donald Alexander 156, 157, 219
    n4, n8, n12, n15
MacLellan, J.F. 59
Maeve 107, 109
magic
    astral 32
    condemnation 8, 28, 111–12
    Enlightenment and 9
    fairies 87, 94, 101–2, 196
    folk 8, 20, 32, 36
    healing 8, 92
    Hecate 133
    objects 8, 31
    powers 6
    rites 4, 8, 31–3, 101
    spells 141
    trials 100
magicians
    ancient 32
    ceremonial 32, 35
    devil worship 123
    folk 8, 9, 32, 37, 92, 100–1, 120

service 101–2, 103–5, 108, 110, 112,
    125, 127, 129–30, 140, 196, 203
    n101–2
    societies 17
'Maiden of the White Hands' (Renaud de
    Beaujeu) 83, 85
Malta 63, 68
Man, Andro 93–4, 101
Manchester University 182
Mannhardt, Wilhelm 166, 176, 223 n12
Mantua 125
Map, Walter 77, 78
maren 119
Marian, Maid 177
Marie de France 84, 87
Mary (Queen of Scots) 92
Mary (Virgin)
    magic 129–30
    Mother Earth 59, 171
    sculptures 31
    veneration 2, 171, 178, 226 n3
    see also saints
Massingham, Harold 18, 62, 70, 208 n63,
    209 n89
Master of the House Book 181
Master of the Nuremberg Passion 180–1
Matres (Matronae) 135–6, 138
matriarchy
    feminism and 10, 65, 74, 209 n99
    Great Goddess and 60, 63, 68–9, 71–2
    prehistory 10, 59–60, 61, 63, 65–6, 68–9,
        71–2, 156
May Day
    animal disguises 3, 24
    England 160, 165, 173, 174, 177
    Jack-in-the-Green 160, 165, 173
May King 160, 165 *see also* Green Man
Mayo 144
Medea 83
Mediterranean 59, 63, 113, 133, 186
Mee, Arthur 70
megaliths 63
Mellaart, James 64, 66, 72, 74, 208 n69–70,
    n74
Mercury 34, 90
Meredith, George 55, 56, 207 n37
Merry Wives of Windsor, The (William
    Shakespeare) 97, 213 n64
Mesopotamia 42, 58, 59
Meun, Jean de *see* Jean de Meun
Mhór Chlibhrich 154
Michelet, Jules 10–11, 16, 141
Micob 102

INDEX

Middle Ages
  Cailleach 148–53
  Christianity 16, 38–9, 46–7, 171, 178, 193, 196
  churches 2, 7–8, 15, 18, 25–6, 160–1, 169, 170, 171, 180–1, 183
  elves and fairies 75–9, 80–1
  Lady of the Night 111–23, 130, 133–4, 136–8
  literature 49, 55, 66, 80, 82–6, 88–90, 106, 126, 136–8, 148–52, 157
  paganism 1–3, 9, 10, 12, 15–16, 37, 38–9, 46–7, 164, 167
  Nature 49–50
  rural population 22
  Wild Man 180–1, 185, 189
  witch religion 140
Middle Earth 88
Middleton, Christopher 97
midsummer 33–4
Midsummer Night's Dream, A (William Shakespeare) 96–7, 108
midwinter 3, 33–4, 123
Milan 123–4
Mill on the Floss, The 19
Millett, Bella 178–9
Minerva 34, 47
Minoans 59, 68
Mirror of Souls, The (anon.) 122
Mohammed 152
Monmouth, Geoffrey of see Geoffrey of Monmouth
Monmouthshire 79
Montgomerie, Alexander 91, 132
moon
  astral magic 32
  Diana 96–7, 112, 141
  fairies 78, 100
  Great Goddess and 66
  Isis 43, 50
  literature 52–3, 56–7
  phases 66, 132, 134
  Roman mythology 43, 50, 60
Moray Firth 94
Morgan (Morgaine, Morgana, Morgen) Le Fay 83, 84, 85, 211–12 n23
Morrigan 150, 151
morris dance 3, 24, 25, 34, 203 n89
Morvern 145
Mother Earth see Earth, Mother
Mother Goddess see Earth, Mother
Mother Nature 41, 42, 45, 46, 55, 195 see also Earth, Mother

Mother's Day 4
Mothers see Matres
Muileartach (Muireartach) 147
Mull, Isle of 144, 145, 146, 154, 155
mummers' play 3, 23, 34, 169, 199 n13, 203 n88
Murray, Margaret
  criticism 36–7
  influence 13, 14, 15
  pagan survival 36, 161–2
  Sir James Frazer 163
  witch religion 11–13, 14, 162
  works 199 n22, 221–2 n4, 222 n5
mythology 34, 35, 37, 44, 58

nachtvrouwen 119
nachtwaren 119
Natura (Nature)
  Christianity and 196
  literature 53, 55
  Middle Ages 45, 47–9, 75
  modern day 58, 110, 194
  Mother Earth 41
  Roman goddess 43–4
  Romanticism 50–1
  see also Earth, Mother; nature
nature
  Cailleach 146, 147, 153, 154, 155
  celebrations 6, 23
  Christianity and 17, 26, 184
  Earth Goddess 41, 43, 52, 55, 58, 61, 68
  fertility 12, 190
  goddess 45, 46, 53, 57, 58, 62, 68, 97, 146, 147, 153, 154, 155
  gods 11, 14, 41, 53, 58, 61, 97, 162, 167, 168, 194
  Green Knight 178–9
  Green Man 162, 167, 168, 186, 190–1
  humans and 26, 33, 58, 190, 195
  literature 44–6, 52–3, 57
  powers 33, 44, 45
  scholars 58
  veneration 6, 12, 14, 23
  see also Natura
Nemain 150
Neolithic
  Great Goddess 61–3, 64, 68–9, 71–2, 73, 74, 157
  matriarchy 61, 63, 156
  monuments 144–5, 154
  paganism theories 28
  rituals 4
Ness, Loch 148

239

INDEX

Netherlands 114
Neumann, Erich 67, 70, 72, 157, 209 n79
New Testament 113, 114, 196
New Year 33
Newman, Barbara 193–4, 196
Night (goddess) 44
night riders 114, 116–19, 123, 137
night-walkers (night-roamers, night-
    wanderers) 78, 119, 121, 128, 132,
    141–2
Nine Hags of Gloucester, The 152
Ninhursaga 42
nocticula 118
Norfolk 62
Norse *see* Scandinavians
North Berwick Law 152
Northamptonshire 99
'Novel of the Black Seal, The' (Arthur
    Machen) 5
Nuremberg 180, 181
nymphs 78, 99, 100, 112

Ó Crualaoich, Gearóid 157–8, 219 n2–3,
    n5, n7, n9–11, 220 n18
Oberam 97 *see also* Oberon
Oberion 102 *see also* Oberon
Oberon
    Middle Ages 82–3
    poetry 108
    scholars 102
    Stuarts 107
    Tudors 96–100
    witch trials 104
    see also Fairy King
Oberycom 102 *see also* Oberon
Oberyon 102 *see also* Oberon
occultists 12
Odin 8, 137–8 *see also* Woden
offerings 8, 42
Okeanos 183, 187
'Old Religion, the' 10, 12, 14
Old Testament 116
Old Woman *see* Cailleach
Olda *see* Huldah
Order of the Golden Dawn *see* Golden
    Dawn, Hermetic Order of the
Order of Woodcraft Chivalry *see* Woodcraft
    Chivalry, Order of
Oriente, Lady 124
Orpheus 85–6, 90, 206 n11
Orphic hymns 42, 44, 134
Orrin 147
Ostling, Michael 226

Otranto, Terra d' 129
Ovid 44, 96–7, 206 n10
Oxford University 12, 60, 132, 162
Oxford University Press 12–13

Padua 123
Pagan Middle Ages, The 37
paganism
    Christianity and 2, 7–8, 15, 17–19, 30,
        31–2, 34–8, 39, 45–7, 48–9, 161, 185,
        196
    etymology 202 n72
    gods 7–8, 25–7, 32–5, 43, 46, 48, 55, 80,
        113–14, 136, 157, 161, 167, 169, 171,
        184, 190, 194
    Modern 12, 14–15, 32, 35, 40, 74, 172
    portrayal in popular culture 5–7, 13–14,
        20, 21–2
    religion 9–11, 13–15, 16–17, 27, 66,
        140–1, 162, 165
    rituals 4, 5, 25, 164, 175
    survival 1–5, 7, 10–11, 14–15, 23, 30–2,
        36–7, 46–7, 161, 167, 199 n14, n20
    Victorians and 8–9
    witch religion 10–11
Palaeolithic 61
Palermo 130
Pan 55, 78
parallel world 75, 77, 80
Paris 118
Parish, Mary 105
Parliament of Fowls, The (Geoffrey Chaucer)
    49
patriarchy 53, 60, 61, 65, 72, 73, 157
Patrick, St 144
Peirson, Alison 92–3, 101, 132
'Penny' 107
Pentecost *see* Whitsun
Percht (Perchta, Berchta, Berchte, Berthe)
    122, 123, 130, 131, 136, 139
Peredur fab Efrawg (Peredur son of Efrawg,
    anon.) 152
Persephone 133–4
Pevsner, Nikolaus 168
Phillips, Judith 103
Philosophy 193
Phrygia 41
Physis 43–4, 47, 48
Piggott, Stuart 64, 208 n64
'Pigwiggen' 107
pilwitzensee pixies
Pinner, David 6
Pitkin Guides 185

INDEX

pixies 35, 119
Plantagenets 84
Plato 44, 45, 46, 47, 50, 206 n8
Pliny 180
plough play 3, 23, 34
Plutarch 50
Pluto 85, 87, 91
Pócs, Éva 37, 205 n119
poetry
  Gaelic 220 n32
  Great Goddess 42, 45–6, 51–4, 55–6, 66,
    70
  Greek 116
  Middle Ages 48, 126, 150, 195
  modern 164–5, 170, 178–9
  nature and 43, 44–5, 48–9, 51–5
  Norse 137–8, 219 n73
  paganism and 17
  Renaissance 90–1, 106, 107, 131
  Roman 44–5, 60, 96, 206 n10, n15
  Romanticism 51–3
  Stuart 108, 132
  Victorian 53–6, 195
  see also literature
Poitiers 183
Pope, Doll *see* Phillips, Judith
Portugal 105
Portunes 107
Pound, Ezra 70
Poverty, Lady 193
Praecatio terrae matris (anon.) 45, 46
pre-Celtic races 5
Priestley, J.B. 63
priestesses 10, 11
Primitive Marriage (J.F. MacLellan) 59
prophecies 76, 79, 81
Proserpina (Proserpinc) 31, 51, 86, 87, 90,
  100
Provence 113
Prüm 111
Prussia 166
psychology 67, 70, 157, 170, 171–2
Puck 99
pucks 35
Pwyll Pendeuic Dyuet ('Pwll Prince of Dyfed',
  anon.) 89
Pyrenees 120, 121, 128, 130, 131

Rabanus Maurus 183, 185
Raglan, FitzRoy Somerset, Baron 160
Raglan, Lady Julia (Julia Somerset)
  criticism 174, 179, 182, 184, 185, 186–7,
    190

Folklore Society 160
Green Man 160–2, 165–6, 169, 170, 172,
  173, 175, 199 n22
  influence 167–9, 170, 172, 175
  Sir James Frazer 163, 164
Rainbow, The (D.H. Lawrence) 56–7
Ralph of Coggleshall 77
Randolph, Thomas 107, 214 n97
Ratherius of Verona 114–15
Reason, Lady 193
Reformation 15, 27, 91, 95, 131
Regino 111
Renaissance 95
'Return of the Green Man, The' (BBC)
  172–3
Return of the Native, The (Thomas Hardy)
  22–3
Rhine 128, 134
Rhineland 111, 113, 117, 134–5
Richella 125, 217 n38
Right, Lady 193
Ritual (David Pinner) 6
rituals
  Christian 30, 39
  disguise 4, 24
  fertility 3, 4, 25, 166
  Lady of the Night 131
  Little People 5
  magicians 17, 32, 33, 101, 102
  May Day 160, 174–5, 176
  popular culture 6
  prehistoric 169
  sex 12
  sites 71
  spring 4
Robin Goodfellow 99, 213 n72
Robin Hood
  god 162, 167, 168
  Green Man 160, 170, 172, 177, 180
  legend 177–8, 225 n41
  May Day 160, 190
Romagna 10–11
Roman Catholic church 16, 70, 91–2, 95,
  98, 105, 169
Roman de la Rose (Jean de Meun) 48–9, 120
romance (literature)
  Arthurian 84, 86, 97, 152
  English 85, 87, 96–8, 151
  fairies 80, 81, 82–3, 84–8, 89–90, 96–8,
    106
  France 49, 80, 82–3, 84–5, 86, 88, 151
  Germany 84
  Lady of the Night 126

INDEX

magic 177
Mother Earth 49
Scotland 88, 90
Tudors 96–7
Wales 89, 152
Romanesque period 187
Romania 140, 165
Romans
  Britain 2, 6
  Christianisation 44
  customs 162
  Egypt 32
  emperors 42, 44
  goddesses 31, 32, 42, 47, 51–2, 55, 96–7,
    111–12, 126, 134–6, 162
  gods 55, 85, 87
  literature 43–5, 50, 60, 85–6, 133, 180
  medicine 26
  mythology 34, 35, 43, 44, 49, 60, 78, 86,
    102
  sayings 179
  sculpture 182–3
Romanticists 51, 58
Romeo and Juliet (William Shakespeare) 97,
  106
Ross 145, 146, 147
Ross, Anne 169, 223–4 n24
Rousseau, Jean-Jacques 51
Runciman, Sir Stephen 13
rural population
  creativity 25, 164
  depiction in literature 5–7, 17, 20, 22–3
  folklore collections 3, 13, 66
  idealisation 21–2, 29–30, 202 n78
  mocked 20–1, 22, 164
  survival of paganism 3, 9, 19–20, 25–6
  urbanisation 16, 21
  witchcraft 13
Russell, Conrad 29
Russell, George 18, 55–6, 59, 207 n38
Russia 165
Rye 100

sabbath 37, 127
sacrifices
  ancient 42
  animal 12
  human 4, 5, 7, 12, 14, 36
  self 8
saints
  charms 26, 27
  female 64, 142
  literature 108

pagan deities and 169, 193, 194, 195
  Reformation 27
  veneration 14
  see also Mary, Virgin
Salisbury, John of *see* John of Salisbury
salves 78
Samhain 220 n24
Sámi 137
Sappho 116
Satan
  conspiracy 28, 123, 124
  Lady of the Night 111, 123, 124
  mythology 93
  rebellion 79
  witches 9, 27, 36, 123, 124
  see also Devil, devils
satanism 9, 27–8, 36
Satia 118, 122, 123
Satyre of the Thrie Estaits, Ane (Sir David
  Lyndsay) 90
satyrs 78, 180
Saxony 139, 182
Scandinavians 8, 26, 34–5, 136–8, 199 n27
Schlegel, Friedrich 58
Scotland
  Cailleach 143–4, 145, 146–8, 152–3,
    154–6, 157
  elves and fairies 75, 88–95, 100, 105–6,
    109
  Enlightenment 58
  folk tales 154–6
  Gaelic mythology 35, 90
  Lady of the Night 132–3
  literature 5–6, 88–9, 90–1, 152–3, 154–6
  witch trials 12, 92–5, 100–1
sculptures
  churches 7, 25–6, 31, 160–2, 167, 169,
    171, 180–1, 187, 188–9
  French Revolution 51
  giants 2, 23
  Great Goddess 59, 61, 62–3
  Greek 42
  Green Man 160–1, 167, 169, 171, 180–1,
    182–3, 185
  Lady of the Night 112
  Roman 182–3, 187
  sheela-na-gigs 7, 25–6, 161–2, 169, 171
'Second Battle of Moytura, The' (anon.) 150
Selga, Lady 127
Servius 60
sexuality
  depiction of pagan sex rites in the arts 6,
    12

INDEX

elves and fairies 78, 81, 93, 94
  fertility and 17
  goddesses 48
  Lady of the Night 141
  literature 6, 12, 49, 56–7, 82, 88, 150
  scholars on pagans and 36, 163, 202 n86
  sheela-na-gigs 161
  witch trials and 10
Shaffer, Anthony 6
Shakespeare, William
  admiration for 108
  fairies 96–7, 98, 100, 102, 103, 106–7, 109
  quotes 179
shamanism 37, 40
shapeshifters 82, 83
sheela-na-gigs 7, 25–6, 161–2, 169, 171, 203 n98, 222 n4
Shelley, Percy 51–2, 207 n31
Shinto 40
'Shire' series 187
Shiva 187
Shropshire 79
Shrove Tuesday 4
Sibilla (Sibyl) 124, 125, 127, 129
Sibyl of Cumae 124
Sicily 129, 187
Siena 140
Silesia 102
silvani 78
Sir Gawain and the Green Knight (anon.) 168
Sir Landeval see Lanval
Sir Launval (Thomas Chestre) 87
Sir Orfeo (anon.) 85–6
sky god 42, 53, 63, 64, 65, 170
Skye, Isle of 145
Sliabh na Caillighe 145
Slovenia 165
Solomon, King 129
Somerset 180
Somerset, Julia *see* Baroness Raglan
Sorcière, La (Jules Michelet) 10, 16
South America 169
Southampton University 178
Spain 130, 187
Speirs, John 168
Spenser, Edmund 49, 98, 206 n26
Spiritism 40
spring
  Cailleach 146, 147
  Ember Days 128
  green 146, 176, 184
  Green Man 176, 184, 185

  light 34
  Mother Earth 49
  renewal 34, 184
  Shrove Tuesday 4
St Andrews 93
St Caitiarn *see* Caitiarn, St
St Germanus *see* Germanus, St
St George's Day 165
St Killian *see* Killian, St
St Patrick *see* Patrick, St
St Swithun *see* Swithun, St
statues *see* sculptures
Steward, Sir Simon 108
Stewart, John 94, 101
Strasbourg 128
striga (strix) 115–16, 118
Struggle of Carnival and Lent, The (Pieter Brueghel) 181
Stuarts 24, 91–3, 99, 102, 108, 180, 204 n103–4
succubi 78
summer
  Beltane 14
  bonfires 33
  Cailleach 146
  dances 3, 34, 176
  May Day 160–1, 165, 166, 174, 190
  processions 175–6
  Whitsun 140
summer solstice *see* midsummer
superstitions
  fairies 95
  Lady of the Night 117
  paganism 21, 36, 58
  witch trials 9
Sussex 100
Sutcliff, Rosemary 14
Sutherland 146, 154
Swabia 139
Swapper, Susan 100–1
Swinburne, Algernon 54, 56, 207 n36
Swithun, St 79
Switzerland 139, 165
sword dance 3, 4, 23, 34
Sylvanus 135
Synge, John 165
Syria 59
Syria Dea 57

Tales of Thorstein (anon.) 137
Tannhäuser 126, 127
'Taru Trin Anuidin Blaut' ('A Bull of Battle Was He') 89

INDEX

Tellus 42
temples 31, 42
Terra Mater 42
Testament and Complaynt of our Soverane Lordis Papyngo, The (Sir David Lyndsay) 91
Thesaurus pauperum (Pope John XXI) 123
Thomas, Dylan 70
Thomas of Erceldoune (anon.) 88–9
Thuringia 139, 182
Tieck, Ludwig 58
Tiree, Isle of 144
'Titania' (William Shakespeare) 96, 98, 108
Titian 34
Tolkien, J.R.R. 108–9
Tom Thumb 100, 213 n73
Tonhauser *see* Tannhäuser
Transylvania 140
Tree of Life 171, 185
Treece, Henry 168–9
tregenda 128
trials
    accusations 10, 12, 13, 123
    early modern days 9, 200 n38, 204 n103
    England 100–3
    Germany 131, 200 n31
    Italy 123–6, 127, 141
    reviews 27–8, 37
    Scotland 92–5
    see also executions
Trier 111
Trinity 46, 48, 169
trolls 137
truten 119
Túatha dé Danann 81, 90
Tudors 34, 96–8, 102, 180, 204 n103
Turkey 64
Twelfth Day 4
Twelfth Night *see* Epiphany
Tydorel (anon.) 82
Tyrol 122, 127, 131

Ucko, Peter 68, 207 n48, 209 n83
Ulster 146, 153
underworld
    fairies 85–7, 89, 90
    Graeco-Roman 85–7, 90, 91, 134
    Lady of the Night 133–4
    literature 53, 85
    Scandinavia 137
UNESCO 63
Unholda (Unholde) 115, 119, 123, 128

unhulden 119
unicorns 181
University College Cork 157
University College London 11
University of California 72
Urania 47–8
urbanisation 16, 51, 70

Valiant Welshman, The (Robert Armin) 104
Valkyries 137–8, 219 n73
Velázquez, Diego 34
Venus 34, 48, 126–7
Venusberg 126, 128
Verona 114
Vertumnus 97
Victorians
    ancient Greece 60
    cities 29
    depictions 7
    folklore 153, 176
    Green Man 173, 191
    matriarchy 60, 165
    literature 53–5, 195
    love for the countryside 21
    paganism theories 15
    religion 9
    Robin Hood 177
Villard de Honnecourt 189
Vishnu 187
Vision of Mac Conglinne, The *see Aislinge meic Con Glinne*
Voltaire 9
Vulfolaic 112

Walahfrid Strabo 116
Waldensians 124
Wales
    ancient monuments 2, 154
    Cailleach 152, 154
    elves and fairies 77, 78–9, 81, 109
    literature 66, 89, 152, 211 n13–14
    mythology 90, 107
War of the Gaedhil with the Gaill, The (anon.) 151
Watson, E.C. 155
West, Alice 103–4
West, John 103–4
Whit Monday 165
White Goddess, The (Robert Graves) 66
Whitsun 140
Whitsuntide Lout 165 *see also* Green Man
Whore of Babylon, The (Thomas Dekker) 98

INDEX

Wicca 14–15, 66, 141, 201 n62
wiccan 8 *see also* witches
Wicker Man, The (Robin Hardy) 6–7, 199
    n21
'Wild Hunt' 165
Wild Man 165, 179, 180, 181–3, 189 *see
    also* Green Man
Wild Woman 180, 181
William of Newburgh 77
William of Normandy 13
Wiltshire 71, 72
Winchester 79, 181
winter
    Cailleach 143, 146, 155, 195
    customs 3, 4, 24, 33, 34
    Epiphany 122, 123
    Lady of the Night 122, 123, 127, 139
winter solstice *see* midwinter
Wisdom 193
wise folk 8–9, 26–7, 32, 100, 203 n101 *see
    also* magicians
witch-hunters 11
Witch Wood (John Buchan) 5–6, 12
witchcraft
    Diana 112, 141
    persecution 9, 10–11, 27, 100, 123
    religion 92, 165, 201 n62
    scholars on 12–13
witches
    accusations 8, 123
    Cailleach 151, 154, 156
    folk magicians 8
    Lady of the Night 139, 141
    positive depictions 10, 13
    religion 11–13, 14, 37, 140, 162, 200
        n37–8, n40–1, n48–50, 201 n58
    trials 9–13, 27, 36, 37, 92–5, 100–3,
        123–6, 127, 131, 141, 200 n31, n38,
        204 n103
    see also wiccan
'With Faerstice' 8, 38
Wodan 8 *see* Woden
Woden 8, 199 n27 *see also* Odin
Woman (pagan cults) 3

women
    Cailleach 149
    Christianity 2, 39
    demons and 79
    healers 39, 158
    Lady of the Night 110–12, 114, 117–19,
        120–5, 128–30, 137, 138
    matriarchy 59, 64–5, 156
    witch religion 10, 12, 125
Women in Love (D.H. Lawrence) 57
Wood, Rita 185, 225 n55
Wood Man 179 *see also* Green Man
Woodcock, Alex 226
Woodcraft Chivalry, Order of 18
Worcester 79
Worcestershire 84
working classes 10, 19
world soul (Plato) 44, 47, 50
Worms 113
worship
    ancient gods 28, 42–3, 60–1, 112, 134,
        202 n66
    devil 123, 124
    fairies 108
    fertility 16, 17, 61, 62, 63
    literature 141
    magic and 8–9
    Middle Ages 3
    Mother Goddess 61–3, 66, 67, 72, 156,
        201 n51, 210 n103
    nature 4, 14, 17, 40, 63, 162, 175
    pagan and Christian 30, 202 n86, 205
        n122
    satanic 27
    sky god 65
    solar 4
Wright, Thomas 16, 177, 202 n66

Yeats, W.B. 17, 55, 165
Yonec (Marie de France) 82
Yorkshire 178

Zabella, Lady 129
Zeus 42, 53, 60